The Joseph Communications:

From Here
To Infinity

Dedicated to David

The Joseph Communications:
From Here
To Infinity

Michael G. Reccia

Band of Light
MEDIA

First Paperback Printing May 2015
Fourth Paperback Printing March 2019

e-Book edition June 2015

Published by Band of Light Media Limited © 2019

Band of Light Media Limited,
Briercliffe,
Burnley,
Lancashire,
United Kingdom

www.thejosephcommunications.co.uk

ISBN: 978-1-906625-08-5

Printed in the United Kingdom by Pioneer Print Solutions Ltd.

Contents

'the Field' and 'the Fall' – a Brief Explanation

If you are new to *the Joseph Communications* and have not read *Revelation, Illumination, Your Life After Death, the Fall* and *Trance Mission* the first five books in this series, allow me to qualify the terms 'the Field' and 'the Fall', which Joseph refers to at points throughout this book.

The Field

When referring to 'the Field' Joseph is describing the conscious field of thought-energy we, as spirits on Earth, are surrounded by and live within. Every second of our lives we project our thoughts and beliefs as to the nature of reality into this energy field. The Field is actually created and maintained *by us*, but we have lost sight of this fact. As a result of us forgetting this, which is in itself as a result of 'the Fall' (see below), the Field is not operating as it was originally intended to. It was supposed to serve us, but at the moment we, in effect, serve it. It exhibits, and seeks to perpetuate in us, a negative charge and outlook, and, because of this and its disconnection with God-Light, is maintaining itself and us via a finite and dwindling amount of energy. The Field in its present state, and therefore also we as human beings existing within it, cannot last much longer. Joseph urges us to re-energise the Field with God-Light and, by doing so, to transform it and take control of it once again for the betterment and continuance of mankind and of the planet.

The Fall

...is a term that Joseph applies to a complex decision and action taken by human souls millions of years ago which resulted in a cataclysmic change in vibration that plunged the Earth into a darkness we and the planet are still suffering from and feeling the effects of. This change in vibration separated us in conscious thought from our God-heritage and resulted in the negative, violent, power-hungry world and society we currently live in.

Joseph and the two-way ladder of spiritual connection:
an introduction

...Consider for a moment, in opening this book, the ladder that features on its cover. A simple image, you might think, yet one that has been carefully chosen due to it seeming wholly appropriate in visually representing this title's contents and intentions. Indeed, that image of a ladder, of an ancient, tried and trusted piece of equipment that allows two way traffic – either descent from a higher level or elevation from a lower one – is hugely significant with regard to each of the six books that currently comprise the Joseph Communications.

At the time of writing this introduction, the highly evolved spirit communicator Joseph has to date descended the metaphorical 'ladder' that stretches down to physicality from his level of being some one hundred times – using me on each of those occasions as his means of impinging on the physical sphere of the Earth. In the early, formative days of our connection, distanced from me by some ten years as I write these words, it was a matter of me, as a medium, listening to his words clairvoyantly and of the information I then relayed from him being recorded so that it could subsequently be transcribed and formatted into book form. From a point during the delivery of his second book – *Illumination* – onwards, however, I would be taken into a trance state for the duration of each communication session so that he could 'occupy' and control my mind and body during those periods of spiritual 'interfacing', moving 'Michael, the personality' completely out of the picture to allow Joseph to more efficiently deliver his narratives without them needing to be filtered in any way by my conscious mind and thought processes in order to arrive safely in this physical realm.

To date the journey for myself, Jane, David and Tony (the four members of the 'Band Of Light' – Joseph's term for our little group) has been both a remarkable and a demanding one, with there having been little time over the past decade to consider anything other than the delivery, transcription, publication, promotion and distribution of Joseph's words. Not that we would have it any other way... the information that Joseph has made available is of vital importance to mankind and to the planet at this crucial time in our physical existence, and from day one there has always been a very real sense of the clock ticking in the background when bringing through and assembling the Communications books. Joseph has said this on many occasions and we believe it earnestly and completely: there isn't a second to waste in making this information available worldwide and in working to re-awaken the spiritual memories and capabilities of as many souls as we possibly can during our lifetimes.

When Joseph had delivered the seventeen chapters of **Revelation**, his first book, we had little idea that this initial collection of spiritual communications, that explained in contemporary language, in great detail, and in precise, no-nonsense, non-religious terms who we really are, why we are here and what we are truly capable of would not be a stand-alone title but, instead, would prove to be the first sturdy rung on a ladder of spiritual knowledge that was being constructed and lowered into this world from a higher sphere of consciousness, step by step. As we set about the task of promoting and distributing that first book, Joseph announced that there would be a second, and we immediately began to sit together regularly as a group to allow him to materialise the next vital rung in that ladder: **Illumination**.

Joseph had no intentions of stopping there, however, and third (**Your Life After Death**) and fourth (**The Fall**) books followed without any gap in the Communications on his part and with barely a chance to pause and collectively catch breath on ours, with the fifth book (*Trance Mission*) being transcribed as a complete record of the twelve public trance demonstrations Joseph held in various locations in the UK between 2009 and 2011.

When Joseph stated, following the successful completion of his fourth book – *The Fall* – that he would be delivering a further title in due course, I found it difficult to imagine what such a volume might contain ...after all, he had thus far examined our origins as angelic and physical beings, given practical and empowering exercises to enable spiritual seekers to improve their lives and to change this world for the better, had been our guide on a detailed tour of the afterlife and had spotlighted and explained the misstep that aeons ago had created and still maintains this world and our perceptions in a skewed, negatively-charged state... What more could there possibly be left to say?

As it turns out, and as you'll discover when reading the pages that follow, quite a lot of immense importance, actually. You see, each Joseph book, whilst intended and crafted by him to be read as a stand-alone title, also represents part of a deliberate sequencing on his part; one stage of a carefully calculated and measured unfolding of higher knowledge, with each book bringing into being a further step on that ladder of spiritual understanding, liberation and angelic capability, and with each set of Communications building on the presentations and many revelations of its predecessors.

The title *From Here To Infinity* sums up the following collection of addresses by Joseph perfectly, this book offering both an examination and an explanation of, from a spiritual perspective, some truly huge and hugely significant topics – amongst them Time, Space, the nature of God and the titular Infinity – and also presenting to the reader a collection of advanced methods to enable them, working individually and in connection with others, to at long last transform life, society and this planet for the better. For good. For ever.

There's a second image incorporated into the cover design that I am being urged to bring to your attention at this point – that of the 'trap door' or 'hatch' that the ladder is leading up to and down from, an image that represents a further, central and vital goal that runs through each of Joseph's books: the attainment of freedom and escape. Freedom and escape from what, exactly? From pain, sorrow and suffering; from restriction and lack; from heartbreak and despair, and from the seemingly unending, repeating and escalating merry-go-round of violence and ignorance that humankind continues to condone, to generate, and to ride on, and which has impacted to a lesser or greater extent on every human life that has been lived here since time immemorial. Having illuminated in previous titles what went wrong and what continues to be wrong, and having explained exactly why things are as they are in our lives at present, Joseph simply and effectively reveals in this new book precisely how we can play an advanced part in putting things right, and how vital and powerful each of us, when we acknowledge and draw on our spiritual origins regularly, can be in creating that new and better world we all long for and wish to see established as a reality.

As we conclude work on *From Here To Infinity* the titles of further themes have begun to gather in that holding area at the back of my mind with Joseph as their originator, whose wish is that further collections of his Communications be published at some time in the future. That prospect both frightens and delights me: it frightens me because the book you are holding took the best part of my life energies and thoughts for a full two years, with recovery from each session proving slow and gruelling, and with me yet to fully regain optimum levels of vitality ...it delights me because it is extremely fulfilling and a sheer joy to play a small part in bringing through information that is literally validated daily as being of immense value to the individual and to mankind and the planet via testimonials arriving from around the world. Our task for the foreseeable future, however, is to continue to expand awareness of the existing Communications worldwide, to alert spiritual seekers to the presence of that two-way ladder forged rung by rung by the release of the Joseph books – allowing a flow of advanced spiritual knowledge that elevates consciousness around the globe to reach us and for us to reach upwards to embrace it – and to introduce as many souls as possible to the world- and life-changing new information contained in *From Here To Infinity*.

Thank you for electing to be one of those seekers, and for caring enough about this world, about its many life forms and about the billions of souls on this planet to want to make a difference. In the following pages Joseph will step down that ladder via the 'hatch' that leads to the higher spheres of being and consciousness and meet with you as you, in turn, seek to climb it, allowing the two of you to connect in the middle so that he can introduce you to powerful new means by which you can transmute and elevate the quality of your own live and the lives of others on a daily basis.

May the Divine within you – the true you – guide each of your steps on that ever-ascending journey of self and global enlightenment and transformation.

Michael G. Reccia
April, 2015.

Chapter One
Concentric Circles and the Nature of God

Joseph: I want to begin this morning with a view of concentric circles and the nature of God.

What I mean by 'concentric circles' is the type of motion formed by a whirlpool or a galaxy, if you were to put the movement of a galaxy into reverse. There are two movements from God: one is a spreading *out* and one is a drawing *in*, and each of us is caught, at the moment, in a drawing in because God draws everything back to Himself. He draws those aspects of Himself – those sparks of Himself that are His children – back to Himself to embrace them, to debrief them and to send them out again.

Each soul brings back to the Godhead *experience*, and there is no fleeing from the Godhead. It amuses us to see various statements being made about there being no God ...that man is independent ...that it is up to man to explore his own destiny ... that he is completely free of Divine aspects when, in fact, the reverse is true because every soul is a 'sentinel' or point of experience that is *inevitably* drawn back to God. From the moment you are sent out into experience as part of the angelic host masked in physicality, you are moving back to that start-point. Your whole purpose in the *normal* course of things, excluding the effects of the Fall (in other words in other spheres of experience and in *this* sphere of experience once the effects of the Fall have been negated), **the whole course of your experience is to take you back to God.**

13

Always you are returning 'Home' – *always* from physicality, *always* from the point of view of being one of the angelic host – you are returning Home; you are reporting back; you are taking back *information*. So, the purpose of your life in the normal course of events (again excluding the effects of the Fall) is to bring back experience, is to share with the Godhead and with God's other children your particular findings, your particular route of creativity, your particular point of view which, when filtered away from the physical ...when concentrated on the *spiritual effects* of your journey... **enhance the Godhead.**

In other words, what you take back is not the pettiness of physical existence within this sphere – not the bickering, not the quest for power, not the antagonistic point of view. You take back the *effects* radiated on your spirit of all those things we have just mentioned but the *best aspects* of them – the growth, the learning, the expansion, the moving away from the pettiness of the surface. You take that sweetness and refinement of spirit back to the Godhead.

And, as a result of assimilating and viewing that information through millions and millions of viewpoints, the Godhead comes to conclusions about the future of the Godhead and the future of the Godhead's children.

So, life appears to be an expansion outwards; but, in effect, is an expansion *inwards*.

Do you see ...not the irony of that... but the beauty of that? What you consider to be an outward journey from childhood into adulthood, then a calming down, a decline and an end into nothing is actually a journey *back*. It is not an outward journey.

It is a journey outwards *only* to meet the fields of experience that allow you to become more, to understand more, to have unique viewpoints, and then to bring those unique viewpoints back to God so that God can make use of them to enhance you and to enhance Himself in order to make the whole business of creation and experience ...the outward journey and the concentric circles of your life that bring you back to the Godhead... richer, more fulfilling, more joyous, more *blissful*.

...Because let us remember that, outside of the effects of the Field, it is bliss that is your natural state. It is the bliss of experiencing, the bliss of being unique and also one – one with the Godhead, one with yourself – a unique bond between the two of You. There is bliss in your brothers and sisters and in experiencing and sharing their points of view because, don't forget, the points of view that you bring back can be shared and experienced by many. That is also the point – once those experiences are brought back to the Godhead they are *accessible*. They are, of course, accessible to the Godhead from the moment they are brought back and at other moments too, but they are also accessible *to His children* once they have been brought back. They can access those points of view in order to become *more* ... **always in order to become *more*.**

I would like to ask you to view your lives from this point onwards as a return ...not as a flame that is lit in the darkness and then is snuffed out... but *as a return*. Your progression through life is a return, and you are, at any point, within a concentric circle that, like a whirlpool, will draw you back to its centre. And all you have to do in order to be brought back to that centre is nothing ...**nothing at all except to *accept* that you are part of that process.**

You can slow down your return to that centre (as we have discussed in other books) by your refusal to accept that there is anything greater than you, that you are part of God's plan and that there is a plan for you, but *inevitably* (and if it takes a million years) you will discover that you are in a process of return – a return to glory, a return to higher things – so that you can set out again with another 'suitcase' and other furnishings that will take you into another arena of experience so that you can return again ...outwards ...inwards ... outwards ...inwards – as I described the movements of the universe in a previous book [*reference to chapter one of **Illumination**]*.

It applies to *everything*. Everything exists within the Godhead and, therefore, everything is a process of sending out in order to experience and to return. From the point of you becoming individualised as an angelic being; from the point of you deciding to undertake a particular journey; from the *very* point you set out, *you are returning*.

I wanted to open this book with something of joy, with something of upliftment as times seemingly get darker around you because they are not what they seem. **You cannot help but return!** When the day is dark, when the path is grey, when you cannot see ahead – remember you are returning and that those obstacles and challenges around you are simply illusions that you will pass through, and *inevitably* you will re-inhabit the creative heart of God and be sent out again in joy to experience again.

This might seem a strange way to introduce a book that you have no knowledge of rather than by just saying, 'Hello again!' But, from my point of view, it isn't *hello again* – it is simply that I have started speaking again at the point that I stopped last time at the end of the last book. There has been no gap for me, and I knew that you would *inevitably* return to this point where more information could be given out. So I warmly re-welcome you (from your point of view – not from mine) into the group. From my point of view, you have never been away and, from your point of view, I hope that reinforces what I have just said about concentric circles and about us returning to the centre.

Now, what is this book to be?

…This book is to be a further book of information on spiritual topics that need expanding upon – some topics we will have touched upon before as part of the examination of the state of humankind at this time, and there will also be new topics that we haven't had time thus far to examine. And so, with great joy, I invite a question.

Jane: Joseph, could I ask a question about 'stasis'? We are each an individual viewpoint of God, and that is the most precious thing we have. In the spirit realms people are consciously aware in most cases, and even in our sleep we have an awareness, but when souls want to reincarnate after the world has come to an end [*reference to the repeating cycle of cataclysm*] they have to be put into stasis. It seems a terrible thing that souls who want to come back to the Earth are not aware of anything for millions of years.

Joseph: There is never total lack of awareness, but we have been entrusted – as spirits who have gone some way in alleviating ourselves from the effects of the Fall – with the ability to make the path for those who are still steeped in the effects of the Fall and repeating the pattern as *painless* and as *easy* as it can be.

So, for those souls (once, of course, they have experienced the events that lead up to stasis) it is simply a matter of them leaving a point of consciousness and then waking up to another point of consciousness ...much as you would do in a dream. You go to sleep at night, leaving a certain set of circumstances behind, and you then awaken with no real concept of the passage of time. You are in a dream-state with a different sense of time within that dream-state, and from point 'A' to point 'B' it is as though the two actually meet. In a perfect sleep it is as though you close your eyes one second, you open them again, and you continue with your existence at the point you left off.

This, of course, doesn't happen with stasis because the point of consciousness that you re-awaken into is a *different* point of consciousness – it will be a different body; it can be a different *form* of body; it will be a different location. But, you have to remember that each person is still *at core* the spirit they were before they went into stasis, so there is a comfort with being who they are. If you consider yourself as you were when you were a child, you were not discomforted by the fact that you were in a new body. You were familiar with it, but it is not the body that you are familiar with – *it is yourself*. **You cannot take yourself away from yourself.** So, at the point at which a spirit goes into stasis, they are themselves as a spirit and recognise that. At the point that they awaken from stasis, they are *themselves* and still recognise that.

So, it is not the vehicle or the location that is a problem. It is the 'mountain' to face in, once again, *raising yourself* as a spirit out of the effects of the Fall, recognising that you should not and don't have to be tied to this set of circumstances, that you are not imprisoned in them and that you can *this time* – if you listen to your spiritual core and connection to the Godhead – alleviate the effects of the Fall and escape from them. Do you see?

Jane: Yes. Is there a group of souls who control the stasis? Like the groups who control the different environments in the spiritual spheres, is there a group that keeps them asleep and safeguards them somehow?

Joseph: It is an identical process to the one that is applied when a spirit decides to reincarnate. There is, with a spirit wishing to reincarnate *against all good advice*, a period when that spirit is prepared for reincarnation. There is a withdrawing from the spiritual world into a state of 'no-thing' (in other words – no physical molecules around that soul), preparing that soul for the time when it incarnates into physical matter. It is a similar process, and there is a... [*pause*] ...words again fail me here. I wanted to say 'a band of brothers' or 'a band of souls', but there is a *specific movement* that allows the process of going into stasis and being brought out of it to take place.

We are not involved in that. We are involved in the 'persuasive argument' (if that is the right term) to allow souls to escape from the effects of the Fall. But, there are angelic beings (as we are *all* angelic beings) that are tasked with surrounding the souls going into stasis with certain energies to cleanse from around them any physical entrapment from the life they have just been living and the lives they have lived thus far. The effects of those lives are stored with the soul. They are always there, but the actual *physical* molecules are cleared away from around them so that they can enter into a state of no-thing **...but still be a spirit.** Do you see that? They are still a point of God, but they are not surrounded by any 'thing'.

Then they are within a certain waveband of energy that is maintained by the love of those spirits that have put them into that state, but it is not a conscious thing on behalf of those spirits. They are not thinking all the time, 'I must keep these people in stasis.' They have put around them a certain wavelength of energy that maintains them in stasis, and that wavelength of energy is maintained by ...an analogy would be... 'something in the back of the mind' of those spirits who have put them into stasis.

And then (because we are talking about the Earth, stasis and the effects of the Fall) when the Earth has been rested and regenerated to the point where souls can once again inhabit it and *decide whether or not they want to move on from the bubble of illusion they placed themselves in at the time of the Fall*, they are pushed forward into another band of energy that draws around them physicality. This is a very simple way of putting it but they are, in effect, from the charge of one band of spirits given over into the charge of another band of spirits – the Lords of Karma – who then prepare them (as we have said in previous books) for incarnation again. Does that make sense?

Jane: Yes. Could I just ask one final thing? As each soul relating to the Earth is one of the two halves of an angelic being [*reference to the information given in the Fall book*], if one goes into stasis and the other is in the spirit realms waiting for millions of years, isn't that quite heart-breaking for them both?

Joseph: It is heart-breaking for us all. The most heart-breaking aspect of all of this is that you are not privy to (because of your encasement in matter) the boundless love that we are able to express and feel for each other.

Because of the effects of the Fall, you are aware through your physicality (unless you reach down into your core) only of conflict, only of love 'at a price', only of pale aspects of what love *really is*. It is our natural state to love each other ...not to just say the words but to express that love as a part of ourselves and our natural state. We are unable to show you what that love feels like …except in short bursts when you break through your physicality. And so it is heart-breaking for us all and not just those souls who have been separated by the effects of the Fall with one, as you say, in the higher realms and one, for example, in stasis or on the Earth.

But, you generally find that the link between such souls is so strong that they share the elevation *of the higher soul* on a subconscious level. It cannot be otherwise – they are one being, and so there is some consolation in that the two halves of the soul are rarely apart for too long. It is unusual for one half to incarnate …and incarnate …and incarnate when the other half has learnt to elevate itself.

There is also that allowance, because of the goodness and Love of God, for the soul in the higher realms to stay close to the lower realms or Earth plane, and attempt to donate learning and experience to its other half so that the other half becomes more aware of its spiritual self in a contracted amount of time.

As for the heartbreak and millions of years …'millions of years' is a concept that I hope we have explained fully in the books that have gone before this one. In other words, 'millions of years' is *your* concept; 'millions of years' is an effect of the Fall that embraces you and plunges you into what you consider to be linear time but is no such thing. And so, from the point of view of the soul on the other side, time passes at a *different* rate, and there is always the ability to unite with the other half of the soul during the dream-time or relaxing times of the soul still encased in matter. The separation is actually harder on the soul encased in matter than it is on the soul that is elevated away from that matter because the elevated soul can see the progress being made, knows that there is escape from the effects of the Fall, knows that the link with its other half can never be broken and knows that *eventually* that soul will come out into the Light. So, it is a different viewpoint.

Post Office Ltd.
CERTIFICATE OF POSTING

Netherton
315 Meltham Road
Netherton
Huddersfield
West Yorkshire
HD4 7EX

Posting date: 15/10/2021 16:05
Session ID: 2-599791
After last acceptance time?   N

Destination Country   UK (EU)
Address Validated?   N
Signed For 1st   £2.25
Letter
Weight   0.032 kg

Reference number
NV935667823GB
Building Name or Number   Postcode
AVIVA PO BOX 582   BS349FX

Delivery aim: next working day. Proof of
delivery and signature at royalmail.com.

PLEASE REFER TO SEPARATE TERMS AND
CONDITIONS

For information about Royal Mail services,
please visit www.royalmail.com

PLEASE RETAIN AS YOUR PROOF OF POSTING
This is not a financial receipt
Thank You

It is a good question because it illustrates the two viewpoints, and you can say to the people who are suffering on Earth at this time, thinking they are lonely or that life is stacked against them that, in effect, they have another half ...maybe that half is with them on Earth or maybe it is in the spiritual realms... but that other half is bathed in glory (as are they at core), and *inevitably* one day they will reunite. **Inevitably!** And so, in the darkest times of the souls on Earth who are suffering, there is something to look forward to because the suffering that is an illusion will eventually pass away, and they will *inevitably* be reunited with their other half. They will be reinvested with their spiritual values and abilities, and then they will move on *as one* back through those concentric circles to the point that is God ...and will be brought out again into more glorious realms of physicality and creativity *together*. Does that answer your question?

Jane: That's wonderful! Thank you.

Tony: My earlier experience on this Earth was in running and building businesses, and the process involved in making adjustments according to market information so that, if something wasn't working in a particular area, we could be flexible and move the business to more appropriate areas in which to succeed. I understand that we are here now working our way back to God and the experiences we have (which is the important part of us being here) are what we take back to God. From what you are saying, Joseph, the Godhead gains experience from millions and millions of us taking our experiences back to Him so that He can learn. What happens with all that information at the Godhead? If it's not working for people caught in the effects of the Fall, and if that is the experience of the majority of people coming back to the Godhead, is it feasible that the rules can be changed at a higher level to make the journey more successful and productive for us?

Joseph: There are things to consider here. You talk of the millions of souls going back to the Godhead, but what you have to remember is that there are billions and billions and billions of other souls *outside* the experience of the Fall that are returning to the Godhead in the normal course of events and according to God's law and God's will. So, to offset this tiny corner of creativity in the universe, there is a returning to God constantly of the experiences that those souls and the Godhead want.

I think this question illuminates the seriousness of the effects of the Fall – in that it illustrates how this *one small corner* has taken a step that has taken itself 'out of step' with the normal course of events. God's universe (as we have said previously) runs entirely through free will. The actions of His children are all free-will actions. **God cannot restrict part of Himself** (as we have also mentioned before). In the case of the Fall, through free will, those souls involved (albeit through thinking initially that their actions would result in a 'shining jewel' to bring back to God) divorced themselves from the normal course of events. It is free will that holds those souls on such an uneasy path …just as it will be free will that eventually brings them back onto the path that billions and billions of other souls travel.

God *is* free will. It is not a gift to His children – it is simply a part of Himself. So, it is not that He can change a rule; it is that He cannot change what He is. He is free will and, therefore, each of the souls within the Fall, are free will too. So, they are still operating within God's plan for His children …it is just that they have used that free will to put up 'a wall'.

You are correct in saying that, if something doesn't work in the business world, you revert to plan 'B' or plan 'C'. You look at it in a different way, and that, in effect, is what God is waiting for the souls entrapped in the effects of the Fall to do …to revert to plan 'B' …to look back and say: 'This isn't working! I'm going to leave it. I am not going to invest any more time, effort or creativity into it.'

And, at *that* point there *is* an option, but the option has to be created by the souls that are, at *this* point, trapped within the effects of the Fall. It is exactly the same process – as you would expect it to be – because, in business dealings or whatever a soul chooses to do in life, they are drawing on God-power. The way things come to them and stack up as a 'plan' for them is based on God-power. That God-power, in many, many cases, is then perverted by the wills and actions of the souls trapped within the Fall ...but the basic plan is God-power. So, if you look at *any* creative endeavour within the effects of the Fall, it is based on God-power. It cannot be based on anything else because *ultimately* there is nothing else. But, then it is coloured, built upon and distorted by the effects of the Fall and by the insistence of the spirit drawing on that original concept of being right: 'I am right. Therefore, this is still the way to go. This is still the *business plan* that needs to be adhered to!' ...even though, clearly, it isn't working. Do you see that?

Tony: I do. Thank you very much.

Joseph: This is where heartbreak comes in because, if you see your brother faltering and see a different way (which we have been able to see because the scales have fallen from our eyes through our own endeavours) then you wish to stand on a mountain, bang a drum and say,' There is another way!' And the fact that we can only do this *slowly* is heart-breaking. The fact that we can give this information out and yet have so many so immersed in the physical that they ignore it *is heart-breaking*. But, what *is* 'illuminating' (and I use that word carefully) is the effect of the people who *do* read the information, absorb it and remember it because they then become a point of Light. And a point of Light shines into other people's lives and illuminates what is right and what is wrong with those lives **and the need for change.**

[*Pause*]

At a low ebb, I am afraid, David. ...I *must* ask you for a question. We must start this new book with each of us asking something...

David: I was just going to follow on from what you said, and ask about people shedding Light on others and the amounts of Light they actually bring through compared with people who don't shed Light… i.e. you said in an earlier session that one person transmitting Light counters the darkness of a thousand who are not. Is that the case?

Joseph: It is entirely the case. I wish I could bring through an illustration of it, but maybe if I put it in these terms: **You are God**. Each soul is God …a portion of God, yes, but also God. When you talk to the Father and when you pray, in effect, you are praying to yourself. God's creativity is infinite. God's ability to love, to nurture and to guide is infinite. When you remember the Fall and remember who you are, you have access to Light within yourself but also *to all the Light within God* …**all the Light within God**. So, in the measure that you push away from you the beliefs of the rest of mankind, you are an infinitely powerful tool for illuminating the rest of the world.

How far does that Light go? Well, it always nourishes; it always ignites the spark within others. There is a 'pilot light' within each person, and that 'pilot light' is powered to the point where it bursts back into flame. Even if your Light falls within a soul so entrenched within the effects of the Fall that it can only see darkness, anger, perversion and violence, you are maintaining that 'pilot light'. You are preparing it for the time when it will burst into flame. And you channelling an infinite amount of Light from the Godhead …and another channelling an infinite amount of Light from the Godhead …and another …and another …and another *eventually* causes that 'pilot light' to burst forth into flame. It is an inevitability.

You are, as a consciously illuminated being, chasing away the 'shadows' within other people's souls because the violence …and the perversion …and the anger …and the greed …and the power-struggle are all nightmares. Each soul within the effects of the Fall, until they re-illuminate themselves (by their own efforts or with the help of others), is *dreaming* …dreaming a nightmare that they have invested in and believe in. What a terrible thing to believe in a nightmare and then to say, 'I am having bad dreams – my life is bad.'

...It is bad because you have invested in the nightmare, but the move into the Light is simply a matter of shining Light into the shadows to chase away the nightmare. If you put enough Light-energy into someone they cannot but remember who they are.

A good question to start with, and I would say to each person reading this: when you work for the Light you have infinite power because God is infinite, and you are part of God so you are drawing on that power. We gave the number before of one illuminated being combating a million souls who are encased within the Fall, but that was just a number. You are *infinitely powerful* when you reach inside and send out the Light of God – **INFINITELY POWERFUL.**

Each day that you send Light into the world, your confidence will grow: 'Now I am reaching more souls ...now I am reaching more countries ...now I am shining Light into the darkest corners of the world ...now I am healing the world. But not 'I' – the God within me is doing these things and I am a beacon for that Light.'

This is not an arrogance; it is simply a fact because, as an angelic being, that is your function – to create with Light as you create each day in heavy matter. ...You create what is ahead of you ...you create with your hands ...you create with your mind ...you create each second that unfolds before you. As an angelic being you do exactly the same thing except you create with brilliant God-Light that has not been polluted by the effects of that experiment that went wrong, and, as such, you are an infinitely creative being. Is that a sufficient answer?

David: Yes, thank you.

Joseph: At this point I would just like to say it is a joy to be connected again and to be transmitting information once more.

Chapter Two
Stasis ...The Space Between

Joseph: It is unusual this week in that I have been inspiring Michael with the title of what I wish to speak about and, as usual, he has been avoiding that title in the interests of keeping the message pure – which is a noble thing to do – but I did want to place in his mind the concept of today's chapter, and the title is ...'The Space Between'.

The Space Between – because I wish to speak about what happens to a soul once that soul has decided it is going to reincarnate on the Earth again. As we have said in the previous chapter and in previous books, the soul is taken into a quiet state, and its soul memories of being on the Earth are removed from it. Then it is placed into a 'queue' that will lead to the beginning of the process of incarnation again on Earth.

During this time we try to educate the soul so that, even though it has decided to go back to the Earth and relive some of the circumstances of past lives (hopefully this time to get things 'right' according to its own vision of things), we are able to influence it to a certain extent through *suggestion*. It is not the same 'suggestion' as you would find, for example, in brainwashing or hypnotism on Earth. It is a *gentle influence* to reinforce what we have been trying to say to the soul up to this point. In other words: 'Please make this your last incarnation so that you can move onwards once you come back to the spirit realms, and so that you can also be open to our suggestions when you come back to the spirit realms.'

There is a benefit of this (and I hope this will explain something that many people on Earth ask us): if we are successful in talking to that soul and in making it see that the earthly path is one that really shouldn't be trodden (until things have re-established themselves as they were before the Fall) then that soul is able to acquiesce to and embrace a *faster track* through the Earth plane – a track that will allow it to negate more of the karma it has accrued in past lives. In other words, the soul, at the mid-point between entering stasis and actually incarnating into another earthly life, **can see reason *even at that point.***

And, if it sees reason through volition and through saying, 'Yes, I agree to this,' it can then *more easily* be placed by the Lords of Karma into a life that will allow it to experience and overcome more of the challenges that have drawn it back into incarnation in the first place.

So, for example (and this will be contentious, but nevertheless it is so), the soul that finds itself in a condition where it is starving on Earth is actually fast-tracking its karma. It is not necessarily linking with situations from the past where it has starved before, but is linking with karmic situations where it has felt a sensation of lack ...*I did not have enough in this business situation ...I did not have enough in this marriage situation ...I did not have enough in this family situation in the way I regarded my siblings, my parents and the rest of my family.* And so the 'starvation' is not necessarily, for the most part (but can be on occasion), a reflection of a *physical* starvation with regard to food in past lives, but it is a reflection of starvation *in perception* by that soul in other areas of past lives which are now being brought to a culmination by this present experience.

It sounds terribly harsh, doesn't it? It is not a judgement – it is something that the soul has agreed to, having seen part-way through its period of stasis ...its dreaming between worlds as it were... that it would enable it to escape the pull of the Earth plane once that new incarnation is over. So, it is placed in a situation where the most good – *not harm* – **the most *good* can**

be done to that soul, with regard to releasing it from the effects of the Fall and successive incarnations, by the life it is about to live.

There are other examples, of course. Regarding severe handicap, for example, severe handicap is a *restriction* ...not necessarily the restriction that the soul inhabiting a restrictive body has gone through in past lives *physically*, but, rather a reflection of the restriction the soul has perceived as being around it in past lives and now seeks to liberate itself from. There are lives where, at a certain point in that life, restriction applies itself, or a sudden immobility is created ...from one day being fully mobile to being totally immobile the next.

I would ask you, with your hearts, to examine what I have just said, and you will view souls who are suffering, from your point of view (and from theirs on a conscious level), with a new perception and a new depth as to what is actually taking place.

What is hoped will happen is that the soul undergoing these trying and challenging circumstances **will weary of them,** and will come to the point when it passes over that it has *had enough of them*. It has got out of its system the need to challenge a perceived starvation or a perceived immobility in an area of its physical life. So, it comes back saying: 'Yes, I understand. I have sufficient soul memory from that *time between* to allow me to make an informed decision as to whether I will go on or not. I now decide to go on into the spirit realms, to leave physicality behind and to escape the effects of the Fall.'

Now, of course, this does not happen with each soul in the between state. If it did, then there would be no mobility on the Earth at all as everyone would be restricted because everyone would be facing those aspects of their past lives they came back to re-examine with a view to becoming tired of them ...growing beyond them ...escaping the effects of the Fall ...moving on to the spiritual realms ...and then on into Infinity.

So, we cannot influence *every* soul – although we do try. Once the soul is in the between-state, we surround it and infuse it with love. We try to hold back the pull of its past lives because, as it nears its new incarnation and the matter becomes denser around the soul, the pull begins ...*and begins to have more influence.* We try, as much as we can, to hold off that influence until the soul is actually born – in order to give it the best possible start in Light, so that it has time to re-evaluate its spiritual status before the effects of the physical world become so heavy on and around it as to pull it back into that cycle of thinking that draws it back to the Earth.

Where is the between-state?

...The between-state is 'no-where'.

It is not a sphere as such – it is a 'holding level of being', if that makes sense. The souls that are coming back have decided to come back, but they cannot *instantly* incarnate. They have to go through 'due process'. Neither can they move onwards into the spiritual spheres because they have elected, through free will, not to do so.

So, they exist *where*?

...They exist as a concept.

They exist as a concept of God (as do we all), but they are not in a space that takes up a specific role. They are *literally* 'between' – they are held by the love and thoughts of the angelic host, and by the love and thoughts of that part of the angelic host that is still escaping by travelling through the cleansing spheres towards Infinity. They are held as a concept, and so you have spirits on our side whose *sole purpose*, at this point in time, is to hold the concepts of those souls steady until the time when the process – placed around them by the Lords of Karma – begins, and they are drawn into physical incarnation.

From the point of view of the soul, the 'past' (as you would understand it) is wiped out. The past *spiritually* is wiped out. It is only when they incarnate that *for them* consciousness appears to spring from nowhere. They have no concept of having lived before or having been in spiritual realms. They start, conscious-wise, from that new pool of energy placed around them at the point of incarnation.

Because they are so 'hell-bent' (and I use the term deliberately) ...*hell-bent* on a new incarnation that that is their entire focus, it is only as they grow, and *hopefully* have been influenced to grow, into a situation that will give them pause for thought that they can at that point access their soul memories and their past-life memories. The point when they go into stasis is the point at which all logical and spiritual argument has failed, leaving that soul with only a forward motion to consider ...a 'forward motion' (from their point of view – not from ours) into a further physical incarnation.

The work to re-educate souls never ends.

The work to love souls never ends.

...And I hope you can see the juxtaposition of points of view here: in that you have souls who appear to be suffering on Earth but that is from their own volition, and yet, on the other hand, you have this great pool of love around each soul that maintains them, directs them and is trying always – even when they are not physically or spiritually conscious – to evolve and to enlighten them ...and by 'enlighten' I mean putting Light into them to infuse them with Light.

So, I would say to you – do not see the process as being harsh. You have to remember when you see someone suffering that they have agreed to that suffering ...either as part of a refining process they accepted before they incarnated again, or as a result of their thoughts, in their present life, reacting and interacting with the matrix of Field-energy that exists around the Earth at this time.

It is *never* a judgement.

It is *never* a punishment.

It is *always* a 'watering can' being applied to the 'seed' so that the seed-within might grow.

And that is the way I would ask readers of this chapter to regard suffering on Earth. You understand, of course, from the Fall that suffering is as a result of the speeding up of matter and the refusal to let go of the attitude that you were 'right' at the time of the Fall. You were 'right' ...*and you still believe you are right*. All the processes of suffering that come to a soul physically and mentally are there to shake that belief and to say: 'The 'right' that I thought was so right is only surface, only physical, only mental – **it is not me.** I need to blossom beyond this. I need to break out of it. I need to let it fall away from me.'

And at that point – whenever that point is (whether that soul is a few hours old or decades old) then the soul is returned to its original path. The suffering is imposed by the soul out of ignorance or a desire to re-establish itself as the spiritual being it really is.

We look forward to a time when there will be no between-states. We look forward to a time when, having evolved beyond the effects of the Fall, the angelic children of the Fall are able to visit planets in *full consciousness* of who they are to experience aspects of those spheres and then return to a greater spiritual reality, without pain or fear, **in full consciousness of who they are.**

That is the normal state of things outside the effects of the Fall. But, because of the effects of the Fall, you have drawn a 'curtain' around the way things are outside the physical sphere of the Earth ...and to a *certain extent* outside the spiritual realms, i.e. the cleansing realms that surround and interpenetrate the Earth. On the lower spheres of existence (but not the Lower Astral,

31

which is a turbulent area) the realisation of how things operate beyond the cleansing spheres is only understood by a few, and then only partially.

So, what I am suggesting is that there is a skewed view of 'Heaven' on the lower spheres because the souls there are, yes, moving away from the Earth, but still, in many, many cases, have yet to re-embrace the reality of how spiritual existence is beyond the Earth and beyond the cleansing spheres. It is a *gradual* awakening according to the soul potential and soul memories of each individual soul.

This may help you to understand, in turn, why many souls return to converse through mediums and exhibit a level of understanding only *slightly* removed and elevated from the level of understanding they had whilst they were encased in physical matter on Earth. They are still growing and still divesting themselves of the effects of the Fall.

There exists then a time when they have a *duality of nature* where they begin to appreciate their greater soul existence, soul potential and soul memory of who they were, and yet are hanging on to one aspect of their various incarnations or to one personality. In this case, mediums see those souls *at the same time* trying to communicate as a glowing, shining spirit and also as a personality in contemporary clothes wishing to talk to a family member about something banal or seemingly trivial.

So, the between-state I wished to speak about today relates to the between-state of souls in stasis before reincarnating on the Earth plane. It also relates, to some extent, to some of the lower spheres where people have not yet totally reinvested in their soul memories, have not yet totally reconnected with who they *truly* are, and are still seeing their surroundings and their path from the somewhat limited viewpoint of who they were in their last personality on Earth.

Can I invite questions at this point, please?

David: Joseph, in this between-state, where does God fit in ...the God-within? You say that the soul is 'managed' by the angelic host and that the angelic host converses with the soul's God-within to figure out what is best for that soul...

Joseph: The soul at that point is, strangely, in its almost *purest* God-form because, in order to get what it wants, it has relinquished most of its soul memories and most of its earthly-life memories. However, there is integrated with it – as a 'polluted' expression of God – the subconscious, almost sub-atomic structure of who it was, and that retains it as the sum of its memories without it *consciously* having those memories, if that makes sense. In other words, were that structure not there, the soul would be complete God-energy ...but God-energy without the individual imprint running through it. So, the individual imprint runs through it to maintain its individuality, but that imprint is at its most basic form because it is not influenced by the will or the memory of the soul with regard to earthly lives or spiritual lives *at that point*.

The God-within is at its strongest, but the God-within will not influence *even at that stage* – except through other manifestations of the God-within [*reference to the angel host*] who are attempting to reach that soul consciously and influence it ...by using their own free will. So, the soul is almost in its purest form, but it has activated a process, activated a desire and so must travel through that desire to get to the next desire or activation, which also has to be free will.

Does that make sense?

David: I think so, yes. In a sense it has been stripped back and its memories and so forth, up to that point, have been put to one side *by volition*, and, once that process has started, it has to be seen through to the end – the circle, in effect.

Joseph: Yes, and this is to do with the creative nature of ourselves as spiritual beings that there has to be 'due process' in everything that we do. It is the due process that was interrupted by the effects of the Fall. In normal due process you have an opening out to a desire ...you have a formation of that desire ...you have the experience that is brought to you by that desire ...and then you have a relinquishing of that desire so that a new desire can be opened up and formed.

Because of the Fall, the normal course of creative process, as applied to an angelic being, only goes three-quarters of the way – in that you cannot dispense totally with the creation you have expressed in order to experience your desire within. There is a minefield – almost a 'rubbish area' or an area of abused matter – that cannot return back into the creative matrix to be used again. So, that surrounds the soul, and the soul desires to go through that process. The problem is when it gets to Earth that process cannot be totally concluded on a physical level because of the effects of the Fall. Then you have, around that soul, the rubbish or the accumulation that is linked to that soul that religions describe as 'karma'.

Does that make sense?

David: Yes.

Jane: Can people reincarnate directly from the Lower Astral, or do they have to evolve to a certain state in order to have that spiritual dialogue as to where to go next?

Joseph: The Lower Astral is a sphere of intense desire – intense *self-desire*. It is an area of preservation. ...The soul wishes to continue ...wishes to stake its claim ...wishes to have its own personal territory ...wishes *more* ...wishes all aspects of creation for itself. That draws to itself a great deal of heavier molecules, and the soul has to first come out of that state of mind before it can be influenced again as to whether it returns to the Earth or not.

So, can it incarnate *directly* from the Lower Astral?

No, because it has to go through due process, and it is encased in a world of want ...and desire ...and need ...and anger ...and violence that will not allow, *at that stage*, the intercession of other angelic beings in order to create a new path, a new incarnation and a new physical body. The molecules are far too heavy, far too clustered, far too sharp and far too angular.

If you were to look at them, the molecules that surround the souls in the Lower Astral are dense, are jagged, are sharp and are a ...I don't want to say 'an aberration'... they are a further distortion of the way that things should be. The molecules around your earthly body are distorted to a *certain extent* by the effects of the Fall, but in the Lower Astral there is an amplification of all that is wrong on Earth taken into a spiritual (but not 'spiritual' in the sense of being 'blessed') level.

Therefore, the soul has to extricate itself by becoming tired of that process and then elevate itself so that souls can surround it, can minister to it and **can give it the choice**. Now, there is the choice at this point and, although those souls cannot incarnate directly from the Lower Astral, they can, having elevated themselves, be taken into the cleansing spheres *if they wish to continue their journey without reincarnating again*.

So, it is possible for a soul to come from the Lower Astral to learn, to grow, to be blessed with Light, and then to decide to move onwards – just as those spirits from the Earth Plane have decided to move onwards, having had enough of the experience that is bringing them suffering. In that sense they can be 'born again' into the spiritual realms, but they cannot go the route of Lower Astral to physical incarnation because they first have to come up into the sphere where they can be talked to and be given the choice through free will. Then they have to make that choice – as any other soul has that has come directly from the Earth plane.

Does that make sense?

Jane: Perfect, thank you.

Tony: Joseph, when you are in the 'queue' waiting for the Lords of Karma to place you, and you have already decided what aspects you want to address in the forthcoming physical lifetime, if in that queue advisory spirits persuade you that you can elevate yourself and bypass going through the same old things again – does that mean you have relinquished those ideas you joined the queue for hoping to work through on a physical plane?

Joseph: It means that you have come to the point where you are willing to *examine* them. For many souls in that nebulous queue, there is no question about it: 'I am going back to the Earth. I wish to examine certain areas of my life, and I wish to re-immerse myself in the aspects of the earthy life that I have found most challenging ...most pleasurable ...or which I did not feel I had brought to a successful conclusion during my last life.' So you have many, many souls who are blinkered in that respect.

What I have attempted to describe this morning is a process whereby enough spiritual logic and balanced argument can be delivered to the soul in stasis to allow it to *at least acknowledge* that it needs to examine its reasons for re-entering the challenges it is about to re-enter. This inflow of Light goes on at the most etheric level because, having relinquished their spiritual life as an ongoing process and having decided to reincarnate on Earth, they place themselves in a magnetic process. They are pulled into a process that will *inevitably* take them back to the Earth.

The change of attitude comes about by addressing the barest hint of structure around the soul ...by infusing that soul with an almost subliminal change of attitude ...by addressing the God-within still encased within that process of needing to reincarnate ...and by impressing on the very loose structure of the soul, at that point, enough argument to consider that, at the subliminal shell-level of the soul, **a change takes place.**

It is only when the incarnating soul is actually drawn into physical matter again that the reconsidering, which took place in that very fine 'shell of God-Light', *manifests* itself...

1) In the physical challenges that come to the soul – for example, the soul is born into an area where it is starving or physically or mentally restricted.

2) That volition is drawn into the physical consciousness of the soul so that it, at least, has the chance of examining its surroundings with a spiritual point of view with a view to escaping the effects of the Fall.

Joseph: Is that a sufficient answer?

Tony: Yes, it is. Thank you.

Joseph: We will at this point withdraw. I am holding the book that this series of addresses will eventually become, and you will find in relation to what we have discussed today (the in-between stage) we are putting in-between chapters to flesh out the concepts that had to be condensed into the four books you have thus far.

So, we are illuminating certain areas of how life works for you here and in the spirit realms, and the processes that take place, to expand the landscape of information that we have given the readers thus far. By the end of this particular book, you will see that each chapter should still be considered as part of one separate book, but will slot into place between the topics that we have covered thus far in order to 'fast-track' (again that term) *the entire message and need for change* that we need to get into the minds and hearts of people at this time.

Chapter Three
A Matter of Time

Joseph: The theme of the chapter this morning is: *A Matter of Time*. I want to speak about 'time' as you perceive it on Earth, and the reason you perceive it in a linear fashion.

Because of the effects of the Fall, you do not perceive existence or experience as we do. You perceive it as a journey from point 'A' ...to point 'B' ...to point 'C' ...to point 'D', and you observe (as you think) the passing of seconds ...and minutes ...and months ...and years ...and decades. But, in effect, what you are witnessing is not a passage of anything at all. **It is a layering of your existence**. I want you to consider what we have said in previous books regarding the nature of existence on the Earth plane and regarding your inability to let go of concepts, as you would do in the normal run of things *spiritually*.

In the normal course of events as an angelic being, you enter into a situation ...you extend your senses into that situation ... you donate to that situation everything you can offer to the circumstances around you at that particular time ...and you absorb from that situation everything it has to offer you in terms of your spiritual expansion and appreciating more of the God-essence outside of and within yourself. Having done that, you then move on to another situation.

And, you will say, 'Well, Joseph, surely that is a linear event?'

…Yes, it is but only on *one* level of perception and observation.

There is within you, as an angelic being, **a timeless point** – a point at which you observe *all*, and can radiate out a sensory 'beam' or width of vibration in order to experience aspects of what you have become thus far, and what *you may potentially become in the future,* according to your viewpoint. This is extremely difficult to explain because you will say that the future doesn't exist yet. But, if you take away the concept of the future and there is only the NOW and only the viewpoint then, of course, the future is there. **It is a matter of you being a *potential being* that circumstance will enhance.**

So you exist, of course, in the future from the fullness of the point of One because the future is part of what you are *now*. It is a projection. It is an enhancement of perception based on situations that you choose to move through as an angelic being to enhance yourself.

At any one time, from the point of the NOW, you can examine your potential, examine what you have accomplished thus far and examine your current level of involvement in a situation and current level of absorption of knowledge and perception. And, based on what you have accomplished thus far in the NOW, you can make adjustments in order to experience *specific* situations that will enhance you as you move on into other aspects of the NOW.

What a complex concept this must seem, but it is only complex because you have rooted yourself in the effects of the Fall. Before the Fall you visited the Earth to experience and to absorb into yourself those aspects of the experience you considered worthy and right to enhance you so that you could move on into another experience. And we have also explained in previous books the way that you can enter into a situation and then, having moved on from it, **let it go** and dissolve your involvement in it, leaving a clean 'chamber of experience' for the next angelic being who wishes to enter that level of being and creation.

Because of the effects of the Fall, you cannot do that. You enter into a situation on a daily basis – you wake in the morning, you stride out into the day and there are *consequences* of you having stridden out into that day. You leave traces of your involvement with others on a spiritual level, on a material level and on a psychic level. You leave actual *physical* traces of your involvement with the day upon the Earth. You leave the detritus of your having lived through that day: you leave your physical rubbish, you leave the remains of your meals and you leave your physical excretions. I make no apologies for mentioning this, but it is as a result of the solidified and heavier matter you find yourself in that you need to have excretion and to leave rubbish behind at all.

In the normal course of things as an angelic being, these heavier-matter occurrences would not happen. You would simply move on and extricate yourself from the situation, leaving a clean sphere of influence and appreciation for other beings to step into and experience within.

You cannot do that on Earth because you cannot dissolve the effects of your experience on a daily basis ...on an hourly basis ...from minute to minute ...from second to second. You leave behind the consequences of the Fall and the consequences of your thoughts and actions upon the Earth. And so, you produce a layer of experience that you leave behind, as individuals and as a species, across the globe. You leave behind your history in terms of layers of solidified matter that should *in spiritual reality* go back to the no-thing. You layer up one hundred years ago ... fifty years ago ...twenty-five years ago ...today ...yesterday ... and you cannot extricate yourself from the sphere of experience that you find yourself trapped in.

There is a danger to this in that you are psychic beings, you are spiritual beings, you are angelic beings, and so you are affected by the resonance or vibrations of the things you have left behind **...but in reality are *still* there.**

This effect on the things you have left behind, you describe as 'time'. You look at your bodies, and you say that the body is ageing and becoming wrinkled, stooped, and less efficient. And, yes, it is ...but that happens because you are layering onto the body experience that shouldn't be there. If you were to look, as it were, through a 'spiritual microscope' you would see that the atoms of the physical body in the new-born are bright, shining and full of energy. But, if you were to look through the same 'spiritual microscope' at someone in their fifties or sixties (in the normal course of things) you would see that the days of their experience have layered those atoms and molecules with a roughness and with a severe sandpaper-like quality that prevents them from functioning as they should do, as the perfect vehicle for the angelic being inhabiting them for a period. And so, your very physical existence is layered with the experiences of the days and years that you cannot dissolve. This, too, you perceive as 'time'.

From the viewpoint of the angelic being experiencing existence on a planet (other than the Earth affected by the Fall) it is a matter of going through every aspect of the experience *at the same time*. It is only *perception* that changes to allow you to experience the subtleness and sweetness of the various nuances of that experience. **But you cannot do that on Earth**. You cannot view the experiences of your life as being *one* experience. Because of the layering effect, it appears to be something that you move on from (again, using the analogy of time) ...second to second ...minute to minute ...hour to hour ...day to day. But you are, in effect, experiencing the NOW – the whole of the experience – but fragmented because of having to tramp through the amassed layers of 'used living' that normally you would simply dispense with and return to the no-thing.

My point in bringing you this information is to explain a little about the nature of time, and to set you free from the nature of time by saying that there is a simple plan to each day. At the end of each day, if you are weary, if you feel laden, if you feel the heaviness in your physical and mental vibrations, *enter the silence*, visualise the day you have just spent and take away the traces of your existence from that day.

In other words, having absorbed the conversations with people and the experience of the day **...let everything else go.** See the connections of that day that make you feel so heavy *dissolving* away into golden Light. Pour Light into the awkward experiences of the day – perhaps there has been an altercation with other spirits you are not happy about. Dissolve them! Take yourself away from them! You cannot destroy the experiences you have had, but you *can* take away the *links* to those experiences ...the links to today ...the links to yesterday.

You form so many hooks into the experiences you have built up around you that you age and become bereft of energy more quickly than you should. It is not that the energy is not there ... it is that the energy has to flow in so many different directions – to your 'todays' and to your 'yesterdays'.

You view the future as potential but, unfortunately, because of the effects of the Fall, you view the future as *negative potential* for the most part. How many of your brothers and sisters do you know who look at the future rosily, happily and with great expectation? Is it not true that, instead, you look at the ageing process and add to it ...you look at the ailing process and add to it ...you look at lack and add to it? Because of the effects of the Field and the Fall it is difficult to do otherwise, but you are *shaping* your future negatively because of the layers of experience you cannot get rid of from your past.

So, if you enter into a state (that can take perhaps only a couple of minutes) and negate those experiences of the day *not required on journey*, you will live longer, you will feel better, your spirits will literally 'rise' and you will go into the future without a preconception of doom and gloom and age and illness.

You wear wristwatches and that amuses me greatly. You have, of course, to have some measure of your passage through a daily ritual of constructing things (and then not being able to get rid of them), but the watches on your wrists and the clocks on your mantelpieces measure nothing. **They measure nothing** – they cannot measure something that *does not exist*.

We have talked in the past about the way we communicate with you and how it is all one communication. *It is all one communication* because, for us, it is not a matter of waiting weeks to connect with you again. It is a matter of us extricating from the connection that part of our consciousness relaying the information, and amusing ourselves with other aspects of creation until we dip again into the communication **at the same point at which we left it**. It is not that 'time' has passed, it is that *experience* has passed. Experience has taken place. Your perception of time is a perception of spiritual experience taking place, but it seems to move on and to be this *physical* attribute of the universe because you are living trapped in the effects of the Fall.

There is a saying 'no time *like* the present' and I would like to alter one word of that to say ...no time *but* the present.

There is no time *but* the present.

You exist to experience. Even though you are trapped in this sphere at the moment, you exist to experience and your experience is *now*. **It is always *now*.** The memories you have are always *now* because experience is an energy – not an energy that is segregated into days, and weeks, and months and years – **it is a constant**. It is an energy-field that you can press against and immerse yourself into, and (from your point of view) re-experience *totally* those aspects of the 'past'. They are not the past – they are simply points in the field of experience that you choose to visit by pointing your perception in that direction.

There is no time but the present!

There is no time but the present, and what you perceive as the ageing of your world, the ageing of edifices or the ageing of

43

bodies is simply the *weight* of solidified creative constructs that press on each other and then partially breakdown under their own weight.

What I am suggesting to you is that eventually your physical body breaks down under its own weight. Of course, there is a point when you must return to the spirit realms, but that is influenced *heavily* by the amount of weight you add to your physical body, to your mental concept of yourself and to the positivity that is your natural state as an angelic being. In other words, if you contra the positivity of your angelic-being outlook with the negativity of the Earth and the negativity of your 'past' experience – then you pull at the physical and mental vehicles, you add weight to them and they slow down. They are not as effective as they were ...which hastens your point of exit.

There is a tendency, particularly in the western world at the moment, for people to be more *weighty* than they were. This perception of themselves reflects the hastening of the end of society as you know it – if we are not careful. There is an increased investment in the detritus of the day, and a greater emphasis on accumulation and on those areas of being that link to skewed vibrations.

In the normal course of things as an angelic being, you would put away your 'toys' at the end of the day. You would dispense with them to bring them out of the 'toy box' tomorrow. But this is not happening at the moment and there is a deeper investment in materialism on Earth. You are investing in those things you cannot rid yourselves of ...I need the next shiny bauble – I need the next aspect of whatever this Earth can give me, in order to be happy... and that is being reflected back to the physical bodies as *weight*. **It is an actual *physical* representation of what is happening with the soul.**

The soul is investing more of its consciousness, not in the experiences of the Earth, but in experiencing the Earth through *the effects of the Fall*. 'Instead of the Earth – I love the bauble.

Instead of my fellow beings – I love the next piece of materiality I can surround myself with.' And the soul is expressing itself through the physical body and saying, 'This is what I lack. This is why I cannot lose weight because I am adding weight to myself by accumulating.' ...Not accumulating spiritual knowledge or experience, but the 'props' or 'film set' rather than the actual experience of living.

So, in addition to the meditations I have taught you in the past, I would recommend that, at some point *each day* (and the obvious time is before you sleep), you consider those aspects of the day that are no longer of any consequence to you whatsoever, and, through visualisation, sever those connections to you with a 'knife of Light' that separates you from them as you push those things away and let them go.

Let them go!

...Let them go for your *own sake* – for your own mental clarity, physical energies and ability to connect with higher realms. Let them go for the sake of the Earth that is being overwhelmed with the weight of the angelic beings who refuse to leave it. Let them go for the sake of your brothers and sisters who have enough weight of their own *on all levels* without you adding to them and buttressing their perception of how this world really works.

If I may add a pun at the end [*smiling*] – **the time to do this is now** ...and there is no 'time' at all... but time is running out.

In other words, the amount of experience or energy you have left is *dwindling*. It is not that 'time' is running out – *there is no time*. There is only a change in the way that you experience on the Earth plane, and that experience is becoming increasingly negative, increasingly weighty and increasingly an adoration of the 'experiment' that went wrong. Therefore, you are cutting off your connection to your own spiritual heritage and your ability to communicate with those of us in the soul groups who wish to help you. **Most importantly, you are cutting off your connection with God.**

I hope this illustrates (unless we can turn things round, and we are working extremely hard to do that) **the way in which things would end for society.** The point at which the souls trapped in the effects of the Fall have to return to stasis is the point at which the weight and detritus of the Fall – *created by you daily* – **becomes so overwhelming that the connection with God is impossible.**

At that point there is no choice but to return the angelic children to stasis, clear the Earth of the effects of you having lived on it for thousands of years and then return you here (for reasons we have illuminated in the other books) to once again experience from the *right point of view* and to finally let go of the effects of the Fall …to let go of your insistence that the experiment was the right thing to do and still is.

This is how civilisation has fallen on this planet in the past. It has fallen because you have reached the point – through your investment in the effects of the Fall and the skewed nature of creation on this level – where you cannot reach the God-within, where you cannot see the God-without and you effectively remove yourself from the cycle of existence that would bring you back through the escape spheres and out into Infinity. So, there is no choice but to return you here to live through similar circumstances, and this time (please, God) to make the right choices.

But, of course, we don't want that to happen, so take the 'time' to consider that there is no *time*. Take the time to consider what you need to remove from your daily existence in order to be a connection to the spirit worlds on behalf of others, a connection to the Divine on behalf of others, and a Light that invests this world with the ability to rid itself of the layers of existence that we place upon it on a daily basis.

I have – I think the term is – 'fried the connections' in Michael's brain this morning which might explain why he was removed from his full conscious approach to the Earth in order that I could move closer to bring these concepts through, but I will attempt to answer your questions.

David: We have a tendency to want to experience the same thing over, and over and over again, don't we?

Joseph: Yes.

David: If we made a conscious effort to experience *different* things daily would that help us break away?

Joseph: You need to look at *the core* of the experience you live time and again. You have to remember, in all things, to approach what happens to you from a *spiritual* rather than a physical point of view. As you are trapped in the effects of the Fall, your core belief traps you in a repeating pattern on a daily basis. So, yes, it is an excellent idea to move on to a 'new' experience (as you see it) but many people move on to a new experience and then find that, within the confines of that new experience, they are repeating the same pattern on a spiritual level ...the same things are happening but in a new 'disguise'.

Before moving on to a new experience, it is better to examine the experience you are repeating, and to ask for help in determining what the key factors making that experience repeat itself are. **Why is it, as an individual, you are trapped in a certain set of repeating circumstances?**

People will attribute it to the job ...or to a relationship ...or to being in a particular set of financial circumstances or a particular corner of the world, **but that is not true.** From an observer looking at the earthly experiences unfolding it appears to be true, but actually *at spiritual core* there is a reason why any being is connected to a set of repeating circumstances. Those repeating circumstances may be enlightening for that soul, but, for the most part, they are 'the record stuck in the groove'; they are a belief brought back into this life or set in childhood, and they are strangely a *comfort* because that is all that is known.

For so many people, if you were to suggest that they experience something different, they would retreat into a cupboard and not come out until you had gone away because change is frightening. To experience something new is frightening because, at core, we want to experience the same things we are familiar with ...and within that core there is another core that says *at the point of the Fall we were right.*

Layers... [*laughing*] ...there are so many layers to daily experience. Daily experience is not what it appears to be. I would welcome change in people, but, in order for *true change* to take place – it is not simply a change of job or simply a change of environment – it is a change of what the spirit wants from existence here ...otherwise the patterns repeat themselves and the matrix imprints itself in every change that comes around.

Do you see that?

David: Yes, thank you.

Joseph: Another question, please!

Tony: Joseph, I understand what you have been talking about today regarding the weight we bring upon ourselves by not letting go of experience. I assume that also takes place in communities like religions, for instance, and that they accumulate the weight of past debris and past constructs?

Joseph: This is why I mentioned within the talk this morning that you should let go *on behalf of others* because you consolidate (as you have said) in religions and in political circles. You invest in a set of beliefs and, if those beliefs are skewed because of the effects of the Fall (as they are for the most part), then you are crystallising, consolidating and making heavier those beliefs every day you live through them. And, you pat each other on the back and say: 'Yes, we've got the answer. Yes, we must move forward with this set of beliefs.' But, if you have a set of beliefs not based on Divine-law, *you are not moving forwards.* You are simply taking a 'shovel' and adding more rigidity, on a daily basis, to the mistaken beliefs you already have.

Again, in the earlier books, I have talked about the necessity of getting to the *spiritual core* of society in order to change things. You cannot change things with a layered, mistaken belief in religion. You cannot change things with a layered, mistaken belief in politics. You cannot change things with a layered, mistaken belief in a peacekeeping policy. You have to get to the spiritual core and say: 'We need to re-set things and sweep away these heavy constructs.'

We can see them. From our point of view, we see them as obelisks or monoliths surrounding and connecting huge numbers of people ...as a greyness ...as a rockiness ...as a blot or stain in the vibrational field. To see your thoughts on a spiritual level is an amazing thing – you are connected to so many things. And, of course, it is those connections and beliefs, and the weight of those connections, that brings you back.

I hope this explains a little more. I have quite fancifully said in the past that you come back because of the television set, or the glass of beer or to re-invest in your company status. And, yes, you do ...**but it is more serious than that.** It is because, over thousands of years, you have invested in these layered beliefs that connect to you, and when you come back to the spirit world they are still connected to you and are still pulling you. **They pull you back to the Earth.** Yes, you have to come back through free will, but you are *pulled back* because of your own beliefs and because of the connections you have made which in many, many cases you cannot let go of. And so we have panels that advise people and say: 'Can you not see the greyness connecting you to *this* aspect of what you wish to repeat? Can you not see the greyness of *that* aspect that you wish to go back into? Let go!'

LET GO!

And so letting go of the daily concepts around you is an excellent way of keeping your soul healthy enough to recognise when it passes from this state to the first of the spiritual areas that it should let go …that it needn't come back …and that what it has invested so much energy and time into is a waste and is an 'evil' – in that it is against spiritual growth, and is against the re-establishment of the spiritual perfection that existed here before the time of the Fall.

Is that sufficient?

Tony: Thank you so much.

Jane: Joseph, is the increasing population another example of the layering and the weight? Is it an effect of the Fall that people want to bring more children in because they think the 'experiment' is right, or is it because souls are all queuing up to come back here?

Joseph: From their point of view, it is an investment in the future, but it is also a further investment in materialism at this point in time. They look at the material aspect of having a child …it is a desirable thing …it is a 'doll' …it is something that 'everyone else has and, therefore, I must have too!' And once the creative act has put the shell in place, then there are many, many souls waiting to reincarnate and having to be placed by the Lords of Karma according to what will act out during their lifetimes.

It would be far better for the planet, and far better for the angelic children incarnated at this time, if there was an easing back on this perceived need to procreate, so that the concentration could then be placed on the souls who are in the arena at the moment …rather than the added complication of souls being brought into the same circumstances, having been pulled back by the effects of the Fall.

It has been thus at other times, but it is more difficult for the souls reincarnating at this time because they are reincarnating into that area of heaviness. **As the generations pass, the heaviness becomes greater.** So, the 'sins of the fathers' become greater and are piled onto the souls who are incarnating *before they even begin their journey*. In other words, they are already projecting themselves into a 'vehicle' that is disadvantaged and gives them a negative start in life. This is another point at which I can allude to the end of society and civilisation *if you don't make things right*.

You can see that there is an increased movement by the Field to have total dependence on it as it is – set to negative. And souls are pouring in – not to combat that need (for the most part) but to enhance it and to say: 'Yes, it is heavy. Yes, I need to be part of this weight. Yes, I exist within time. Yes, I need all these things around me.' And so it is *hastening* the point at which the majority of souls no longer embrace the God-within, the God within each other, or the ability, through their spiritual minds, to connect with greater souls around the Earth and the spheres that lead up from the Earth.

You can see the hastening of the end through so many means *...unless you change* **...unless you put Light into every aspect of your lives.**

Do you see?

Jane: Yes.

Joseph: I am about to depart. I have run out of the available energy. Thank you for your investment in a new way of approaching life on Earth.

Chapter Four
The Illusion of Space and Distance

Joseph: Having spoken about *time* last time we were together, it seems appropriate this session to talk about *space* ...or, rather, *distance* because man perceives himself as being *distanced* from his brother and sister, *distanced* from God and *distanced* from objects that appear to be far away and 'at a distance' from him.

I would like to suggest to you this morning that **all distance is an illusion.**

Let us begin with the illusion of distance from God. The distancing from God that man experiences on Earth is due (as we have said in previous books) to the effects of the Fall. The distancing is not there *except* in the mind, attitude and viewpoint of the individual spirit. If you remove that viewpoint – that perception of distance – the spirit is at heart, at soul and at core **one with God** *always*.

The distance comes from the difference in vibration caused at the time of the Fall and the resulting change of mind ...from an acceptance of being one with God to a perception of being individualised and at a distance from God. In reality the opposite is true – the spirit cannot be at a distance from God, and, because we are linked, cannot be at a distance from his brother and sister or from nature.

All is ONE and all is *here* NOW.

Here is a concept I would like you to consider ...that *everything exists here at the same point* because the only point that exists is the point of connection with God.

The only point that exists is the point of connection with God – everything else is an illusion.

And so, you project distance in order to experience. You project, in a linear existence, points at which you *perceive* your journey. You believe that you are travelling from point 'A' to point 'B' ...when, in effect, point 'A' and point 'B' are passing by you so that you can observe them. You expand the landscape from yourself *outwards* in order to experience different aspects of yourself along a journey which doesn't exist. (I am sorry that sounds like a cosmic joke ...*and it is*.)

...Let us get back to basics. You are angelic beings. As angelic beings individualised in *viewpoint only* from God, you travel outwards in vibration. You distance yourself from God in order to bring back to God more experience which you create by moving through the layers of illusion you place around yourselves in order to experience.

When you travel 'outwards' from God (and outwards is a relative term) you immerse yourselves in the creations of yourself and others. These creations are paper-thin and are not the material constructs they appear to be. They do not have width, height or distance ...except in their needing *to appear so* in order that you can travel through them at a level of vibration at a distance from God. In other words, the concepts around you and which you travel through are nothing more than 'dreams' that you have dreamed up in order to explore *possibility*, and to take the results of that possibility back to God to enhance the Whole.

This is known in other areas of spiritual reality. This is known in areas of spiritual reality that are not of the Fall. Yes, the traveller through a landscape experiences that landscape. Yes, the traveller through a landscape appears to be moving onwards in a *linear fashion* (to some extent) through that landscape. But, it is known *at core* that the landscape is, in fact, an illusion placed around a traveller in order that the traveller may learn and grow.

In your encapsulated existence, you have invested a greater belief in the landscape as being a *true* landscape. You, therefore, see your heavily linear existence as a journey through a set of landscapes that inevitably lead to the point of physical death, and then you are freed from that or enter a non-state (according to your religious beliefs). You have invested belief, to a greater extent, in the landscape.

Were you not in the effects of the Fall and were you, for example, living within another sphere of experience on another planet, you could more easily travel between point 'A' and point 'B'. You would not have to put on a rucksack and boots to walk across the landscape. You would simply *wish* to be in another part of the landscape ...and you would find yourself in another part of that landscape. You cannot do that on Earth because you are encapsulated in heavy physical bodies and are traversing heavy physical matter.

But my point today is that **the landscape is not actually there**. The potential for experience expressed through the landscape you have created is there ...but not the *actual landscape*.

Similarly, the 'landscape' that you place between yourself and others in terms of *personality* does not actually exist. The personality is a similar construct or 'landscape' for you to journey through, as part of God, in order to discover and grow by examining aspects of emotion, aspects of approach to certain challenges and aspects of how *you*, having created the landscape of one personality, inter-react with the landscape of *another personality*.

The personality around you and the personality around another are as ephemeral, transient and as paper-thin as the actual physical landscape you perceive around you every day. They are not really there, and if you view yourself and others from a God-point – *from the core* – you see that there is ...not only any *distance* between you, the person next to you and the person across the world from you ...but there is no *difference* between you, your brother and your sister and everyone else across the world.

This may make it easier for you to channel out Light to people, realising that the personalities you see and the traits you see in races and in certain areas across the world are actually a result of the Fall impinging on the original personalities that were around you as the angelic children at the time of the Fall.

As a result of the Fall everything has been brought into sharp relief ...the personality has been brought into sharp relief ...the sense of distance has been brought into sharp relief. You perceive things differently because of the effects of the Fall. You perceive your journey as stretching out ahead of you rather than passing in front of you – with you being the *observer*. You perceive yourself as entrenched within the landscape of the personality, and you carry that single landscape with you from birth to death *believing that it is you*. Yes, it exhibits aspects of you, but the personality is not you – it is a 'landscape' that has been created around you in order for you to experience.

If it follows (which it does) that the landscape or personality around everyone else is simply an illusion created around them in order that they may learn and experience, then it is easier to cut through your prejudices ...to cut through your hatreds ...to cut through your angers ...to cut through your fears and reservations ...and to see other people *as the identical aspects of God that they are*.

There is no difference!

This will shock you, but there is no difference *at core* between yourself and your neighbour ...between yourself and the person who is peaceful ...between yourself and the person who is violent.

At core you are identical.

You are a part of God and of each other.

Logically, therefore, if you love God and God loves you, and if you love yourself as part of God ...you have to love each spirit you meet (or don't meet) across the globe *equally* because they are an equal to you.

Let us look at the physical landscape. If the physical landscape is an illusion, and the distance between you and other points around the globe is an illusion, then the distance between you and *all other expressions of life* on this planet is also an illusion. Begin to look at the animal forms ...at the plant forms ...at the mountains ...at the rivers ...at the rocks ...at the grass ...as expressions of God that have been sent forth; expressions of deva-expression that are cloaked temporarily in a temporary landscape.

And, as I suggest you look at each other without that landscape and acknowledge that you are all equal, I suggest that you also look at the other aspects of the life that is abundant around your globe. And, in your meditations strip away the illusion of landscape and distance – whether that distance means that the forms you are looking at are at the other side of the globe, or whether that distance is simply an acknowledgment of you acknowledging yourself as a 'human' and seeing another form of life as a 'cow' or a 'tree' or a 'stream' or a 'mountain' or a 'rock'.

Strip away the illusion of that landscape and you will find *at core* that you are not only equal to those other expressions of life and they to you, **but you are identical to them** because, whether God manifests Himself as 'you' as an individualisation in angelic form, or manifests Himself as a deva form that then manifests out aspects of nature you are dealing with a single expression of God.

On other worlds there are other expressions of God, but they are cloaked in landscapes of illusion. They are equal to you. The planet is equal to you. The universe is equal to you – no more, no less important – but essentially, at core, *exactly* the same thing.

So 'space' in terms of space between 'you' – between aspects of you – doesn't exist. It is an illusion, and if you strip away that illusion you are viewing the same thing.

I hope that this helps in your combatting the effects of the Fall because, if you take to heart the meaning of this chapter, you can never look at any other form of life in any other way than as *a reflection of yourself*. You can never look at any other human being in any other way than *as a reflection of yourself*. And, in looking at a reflection of yourself, you have to acknowledge what you love about yourself in others. You have to acknowledge the God-Love at your core …you being worthy of it …but also everyone else and everything else being worthy of it too.

The reason I have given you this explanation *at this point* is to help you with your Light-meditations, because Light-meditations can be difficult because of the heavy aspects of the illusive landscape that you place around others: 'I would like to love that person but it is difficult because …they have this type of personality …they have this type of belief …they are in this part of the world …they have this physical aspect.'

All these things are illusion.

There is no space between you.

There is no distance between you.

There is no distance between you and God.

In addition to being able to view people differently, I hope that you can see, in what we are considering today, **the closeness of**

God-power to you. If there is no distance between you and God, if God flows through you constantly and with the same power that He did at the point when you were individualised (as you view it) then you have *that amount of power within you* to channel across the world in your endeavours to change the world and its people back to the way they were before the Fall.

In other words, it is not a matter of reaching out at a distance to God and receiving a percentage of Light (perhaps ten per cent or fifty per cent or seventy per cent). It is not that you endeavour and struggle to bring Light into yourself to send out to the world (except in your view of how you are connected with God). If you are connected with God *one hundred per cent*, if you are part of God *one hundred per cent*, then the effects of your meditations and your Light-bearing on behalf of others is *one hundred per cent*. **It *cannot* be otherwise!** It is only in the measure that you *perceive* that ability to bring Light to bear that you diminish the effects of yourself as an angelic being and channeller of God-energy.

This chapter is important because you need to understand these things in order to:

Love everything.

Be a channel for Light to the maximum effect.

Did the Christ not say, 'I and the Father are One' before he brought into being what people regard as miracles? ...He said, 'I and the Father are one' to focus his attention on the fact that there is no separation and no distance between ourselves and God.

I and the Father are One ...linked, connected, able to create as we have always created *since we were created* – since we were set apart as a fragment of God within the illusion – so that God can become more whole, more experienced and can evolve, due to our experiences travelling through the landscapes of illusion that we create in order to grow and to raise the One.

There is *only* the One.

What then happens when you set out on a journey? If one of you goes to your door ...and gets into a car ...and goes to an airport ...and flies across a continent ...and lands in another country ...and takes another car ...and finds oneself on a beach or in a hotel somewhere – what then happens?

...What happens is that you draw the journey to yourself. You place yourself within the illusion of the journey. You place a part of your God-consciousness within the illusion of you entering the car ...going to the airport ...flying across the continent ...getting out of the plane into another car ... and going to your final destination. You pull those experiences to yourself from your core, but you perceive them as being the other way round. You perceive them as being experiences that you enter into *physically* and that the state of experience around you changes – that you are entering different vehicles, that you are entering different countries, that you are arriving somewhere. What you are arriving at is a different experience that **you have already placed around yourself** *in advance.*

So, there is no travelling except as *perception*, except as involvement within a series of circumstances that you draw towards yourself.

Three men put themselves into a spaceship and the spaceship is fired off towards the moon. The spaceship lands on the moon and the men get out. They examine the moon and then get back into the spaceship to come back to Earth.

No.

They don't!

...Three *spirits* decide that that is the experience they wish to have, and so they draw towards themselves the changes in *their* landscape that allows them to experience the journey to the moon, the moon itself and coming back from the moon.

Does the moon not exist?

Well, yes, of course it exists, but it exists within a different *malleable* landscape than the one that you perceive to be true. It is not the solid matter that you perceive it to be. It feels solid, yes, because you have entered into an acceptance of it as being solid. It feels that it is a certain number of miles away because you have entered into the acceptance that it is a certain number of miles away.

But, in reality, it is a changing landscape that has been placed *temporarily* around you so that you can experience it, if you so wish, via the mechanics of illusion that you have as your tools at this time because of the effects of the Fall.

If you were existing on the Earth as a crystalline sphere with the moon as another sphere of influence within its atmosphere (both of those things having been created by the angelic children as areas of perception and adventure) then, in your purest form, you would go to the moon simply by *wishing* to be on the moon. You would experience the moon simply by *wishing* to have the moon play out its 'advantages' – with regard to your experience – around you. And, you would return to the sphere of the Earth simply by *wishing* yourself back in the sphere of the Earth.

I hope this explains the depths (and 'depths' is the right word) to which the illusion has encapsulated itself because of the effects of the Fall. Outside the effects of the Fall there are still *myriad* landscapes to enjoy. There are still landscapes to journey through, but with a different perception ...realising that those beautiful spheres, each one different to the last one, are coming to you and are as a result of your creation ...that you do not move through them – they move across your sphere of perception ...that they are temporary constructs ...that at any time, if you are moving through a landscape and wish to perceive a different aspect of that landscape, you can pass between what seems to be 'solid' into another landscape and then back again. There are multiple landscapes available to the 'spiritual traveller' in the true sense (i.e. the angelic child that is not trapped in the effects of the Fall).

...And *this* landscape is no different.

This landscape that you perceive as solid, hard and unable to be changed (except by the natural laws of weather and nature around the planet) is, in fact, as malleable and flexible as all the other spirit landscapes throughout the universes *were you to believe in it* and that, as a spirit, you could put your hand through a rock or a tree or through the illusion of another person. And what is the hand? You are only extending out a point of consciousness into another matrix of consciousness in order to experience. You do not believe, and so the landscape remains *what you do believe* ...unchanging, solid and unable to be influenced by thought, by Love, by Light.

This is a further point I want to make about your energies as you transmit the Light needed to transform this area back to the way it was before the effects of the Fall. Your energies – being God-energy, being God-Light – are *more than capable* of reshaping the world because the world as it is *remains as it is* because of the investment in the belief of the experiment that took place at the time of the Fall.

You, as part of God transmitting full God-power, know better.

So, you *can* help to transform the landscape through your Light-bearing, through your Light-focusing, through your thoughts. You *can* change the landscape back to what it was. You *can* heal the Earth. You *can* heal individuals. Because what you are doing is bringing, into the landscape of the Fall, a more *powerful* landscape – the landscape of God, the power of God – which overrides and transforms the landscape of the Fall ...*if* you believe it ...*if* you are willing to transmit it ...*if* you are willing to invest in it.

61

If you are not, then everything will remain the same.

Finally, I must talk about the distance that you perceive between yourselves and those who are no longer in a physical body – those who have removed themselves from this 'landscape of experience' and are experiencing the effects of the cleansing spheres in order to release themselves into Infinity.

When the physical presence has gone, because of your belief in a finite body and your belief in a finite personality *spiritually*, you suffer and you grieve. You feel that the person *might be* there, but you can no longer perceive them and you can no longer have access to them.

As a spirit you have constant access to those who are on a harmonious vibration with you – those that you love. When you are freed at night from the effects of the Fall *temporarily*, you are connected again to those you love; you discuss things with them; you examine your paths together in a glorious landscape and a glorious meeting place that is far more etheric and beautiful than the Earth that you perceive at this time because of the effects of the Fall. You are not separated, but it is unfortunate that the Fall separates you at the moment of consciousness again to this level. The overall belief in the landscape being as it is and in the state of the Earth being as it is cuts off all memory of communication that you have had with those people who have gone before you into the cleansing spheres.

Please believe me – this is not the normal course of events. As you become used to channelling God-Light (and, in the measure that you believe in the strength and ability of that Light to make change) then your feeling of being with those who have gone on ahead of you will increase. Your feeling of them being a constant presence with you will increase, because you are fighting and changing the effects of the Fall and remembering your spirit reality.

In spirit reality there is no – *and cannot ever be* – any separation from those people you are in harmony with ...except at times when *you wish* to experience the 'no-thing' and to experience isolated contemplation in order to grow. But, that is only a temporary thing, and you do not go into that isolation thinking, 'I'm going to separate myself forever from those that I love.'

It cannot be!

When you return from that contemplative sphere, you are instantly reunited by choice and forever with those 'aspects of yourself' ...(remember, the people you are in harmony with – be they here or in the cleansing spheres – are part of yourself)... you are reunited with them and can never be separated from them.

Questions, please!

Tony: Joseph, as a therapist, the one word that keeps springing up is 'emotions' ...so am I right in thinking that the biggest single thing that holds us back is our emotions?

Joseph: Emotions are a means of investigating the physical challenges that come to you. You have layered emotions. You have the bliss, and **the state of bliss and harmony that you have at core is the only true emotion.** That is your true emotional state, but putting the word 'emotions' onto that state is sort of trowelling on a thickness and a heaviness. That expression of bliss is something that, in the normal course of events in Creation, you express even when you are experiencing in matter and are travelling through a landscape of your own choosing in other worlds.

Because of the effects of the Fall, as you reach out in bliss that vibration cannot easily root itself in the surrounding vibration of the Earth at this time. Also, because of the belief that you put into the Fall experiment, your emotions become twisted and minimised. They cannot send out their experience of bliss to others and to the world as they should do. So, your emotions are a base reflection of the state of bliss, and giving, and harmony, and creation that you are at heart.

If you, in all circumstances, *attempt* with all your heart to infuse bliss into the way that you react to others emotionally, *your* part in those proceedings will then harmonise out and will become balanced …your anger will disappear …your frustration will disappear …the pressure you feel under will disappear …the stings of others against your small earthly ego will disappear.

So, in emotional circumstances – if you are the recipient of adverse emotions or if you are giving out emotions that you are not happy with – the secret in meditation and in quiet times is to infuse those emotions with a state of harmony, to love them, to enfold them, to nurture them with love and with bliss …and they will disappear. The state of bliss will overcome them, transform them and transform the situation. It will also lead to a greater degree of health within you, because the conflict will then not exist between your inner core and your physical and emotional shell that is a part of the Fall. Do you see that?

It is a healing exercise. It stabilises the emotions, and it minimises the effect of degradation – both on the physical and mental body – that otherwise exists and eats away at a person, because of those skewed emotions that are the end-expression of bliss, twisted and transmuted by the effects of the Fall.

Tony: So, skewed emotions or what I would call 'negative emotions' – like anger and fear-based emotions – can they accumulate over more than one lifetime?

Joseph: As we have discussed in previous books, you re-inherit the karmic implications of reincarnating again. But, as we have also said, you can transmute that karma by letting it go and by infusing it with God-energy, infusing it with Light and infusing it with harmony.

You *do* re-inherit karmic situations from past incarnations, and this is the danger of coming back to the Earth because the strongest of those tendencies comes back to haunt you, **but you can also transmute them *at any time* by letting go of them.**

They become 'precious' to people – emotional responses become precious and become repetitive. The faults of the past become precious because the spirit cannot see further than them, cannot see that it is a spirit, cannot see that it is part of God, and so clings on with a vengeance to all that it perceives it has and won't let go. But *at any time* it can let go. At any time it can transmute them, but first it has to examine the possibility that it is more than it appears to be and has to, through trial and error, discover that it is indeed a spirit. At that point when it begins to emanate Light, it can transmute its own karma and can also use that Light to 'lighten the load' *literally* of others and of the planet.

Does that make sense?

Tony: Thank you, very much so.

Jane: Joseph, could I ask a question about the illusion of personality which became skewed at the time of the Fall? What originally was the reason for the difference? Going back to the 'rope' analogy [*reference to chapter one of **the Fall***], was it because the strands were all different?

Joseph: The personality in its purest form is, if you like, a 'storehouse' of the *trends* that the spirit exhibiting that personality has invested more time in.

You are individual. You are identical, but you can have different paint on doors and windows, can't you? You can have different aspects to the brickwork and different aspects to the roof, but within the layout *is the same*.

So, as individualised aspects of God (*dreamed of* as individualised by God), you enjoy and specialise in different aspects of creation. One will love a certain aspect of creation – another will love a different aspect, and you choose, as you progress, to investigate and perhaps work with those aspects of creation. You then attract to the personality, a reflection of your

65

interest in those particular aspects of creation, and so your personality is different in that respect. It is like having a set of school books or a set of treasured belongings exhibited in the outer personality that determine you as being a specialist in this area or that area.

That is not to say that you will not eventually love *all* areas ... you do... but you choose, at different points in your eternal and infinite evolution, to focus on certain areas – as the group souls focus on certain areas. And so your personality, in its truest and purest form, reflects that ...you are a lover of nature ...you are a lover of creating planets ...you are a lover of understanding God ...and those are things that exist in the greater personality.

At the time of the Fall those things (as with all other aspects of the spiritual being) became trapped and distorted. You see there the beginnings of the fight for the ego – the fight for *what I have* ...the fight for *the ways that I am different from you* ...the fight to *keep me as 'me' and you out* – when originally those differences were not differences in terms of conflict, but differences in terms of *preference of creation* at that time. Do you see that?

Jane: Yes. Was the intention to give slightly different points of view to the individualisations so that God could, through them, experience different points of view?

Joseph: Each individualisation of God is a different point of view ...but the point of view is not the individualisation of God. The point of view is the accumulated *experience* of the individualisation of God. The individualisation of God is identical. Do you see?

If you collect certain things around you, if you frequent certain restaurants or go to see certain types of film, those are things that you accumulate around you as expressions of you ...but they are not the *core you*. And so, the original personality was an accumulation of preferences of creation and areas of interest that the individualisation of God had placed around itself *temporarily*, that would be added to, as the millennia and the experiences passed, and would be constantly changing, but it has coalesced into a physical personality.

I haven't much time left – do you see?

Jane: Yes, thank you.

Joseph: It is an area that I would love to talk upon at length, but we are running out of the connection at this time. David, is there something you would like to ask?

David: We have spoken today about the transmission of Light and how each individual is the same at core. If we were to transmit Light into another person or group of people, and those people consider themselves as separate, at a distance and as being apart from the One – can we accept that Light on their behalf, as we are all One? For example, if I was to transmit Light to somebody who needs healing but feels separated and doesn't believe and so forth, can I accept that Light on their behalf?

Joseph: What you are doing is not violating their wish to remain within the Fall; what you are doing is bringing in and transmitting God-Light (which is theirs by right and *is them* at core) to strengthen *their* core of God-Light so that, as time passes and enough Light is transmitted to their core, they begin to lift the lid on the illusion **...and that is when the change comes.** You are not forcing a change upon them. You are acknowledging them in transmission of Light to what they really are. You are strengthening their core to the point at which they can make a choice.

At the present time most people cannot make a choice because they do not have the available information and perspective from within. The only way to elevate someone is to 're-charge' them, is to irradiate them with enough God-Light so that they begin to remember and to make choices based on *angelic decision* rather than human decision from the point of view of the Fall. Do you see that?

David: Yes.

Joseph: We are never allowed to influence by force. We can't do that – all we can do is make available the information for viewing. But the information cannot be viewed by the *majority* of mankind because it has encapsulated itself so deeply in layers of matter, and in physical, mental and emotional illusion, that the Light-within is not given any opportunity to examine itself and its circumstances.

It is, in effect, like giving food to a starving child. You are sending the Light in order to reinforce and reinvigorate *that which we are* in the other person, so that that other person – at some point as it crosses its lifespan 'linearly' (from its point of view) – is given enough Light to begin to examine its circumstances from a *spiritual* perspective.

Then, from a spiritual perspective, it only has *one* choice.

That choice is not forced upon it, but is the *only* choice because it is the choice that it had before the time of the Fall. That choice is to look at its life and see it to be lacking ...and to look at the world and see it to be lacking ...and then to restore its life and the world through the further transmission of Light.

So, it is a network, with you being *one point* in that network lighting up the signals that are the *other points* of the network until the whole network has transformed itself and freed itself from the illusion that it has placed itself under.

Each point in that network will do so *voluntarily* by examining its point of view with regard to being within the matrix of the Earth and within the matrix of an individual earthly personality. It will examine that point of view from within, as a result of Light being transmitted, and will *inevitably* (if enough Light is transmitted) wish to restore itself to a state of bliss and the planet to a state of perfection ...because that is the *only* choice as a spirit it would wish to make. Is that sufficient?

David: Yes, thank you.

Chapter Five
Perspectives

Joseph: I want to talk this morning about *perspectives*.

I want you to imagine, if you will, perhaps, the perspective of a snail that is moving from point 'A' to point 'B'. From the perspective of the snail, all that is going on around the snail is being observed and analysed, and decisions are being made to enable that journey to take place.

If you then pull back from the snail, I would like you to investigate the perspective of the bird. The bird is also travelling from point 'A' to point 'B', and is looking down and perceives the snail in a *totally different* way than the snail perceives itself.

Then, if we pull away from the perspective of the bird back down to Earth to the person looking up at the bird – the perspective of the person is *totally different* to the perspective of the bird.

The person is looking at the bird that is observing the snail.

The person's perspective of the bird is a different perception *entirely* than the perspective of the bird ...which has a different perception *entirely* than the perspective of the snail ...which has a different perception *entirely* than the Earth that it is travelling across.

What I am attempting to explain in this way is that there are many different perspectives to life and to being. And, unfortunately, because of the effects of the Fall, the *true* perspective of the human being in our little analogy is not the perspective of a human being observing a bird at all, or the perspective of the bird observing the snail ...it is the perspective (from a *spiritual* point of view) **of the snail.**

The human being, having encapsulated itself in heavy matter because of the effects of the Fall, observes its journey across life as a journey from 'A' to 'B' and uses only its *physical* senses to perceive the world. It is looking for security. It is looking for power. It is looking for signs of danger. From the perspective of the physical mind, it sees itself as making a journey from point 'A' ...which is birth... across life, as safely and as securely as it can, to point 'B' ...which unfortunately, from that perspective, is death and *perhaps* oblivion.

Along that journey, because it is only using its physical senses, it assesses its being, its potential and its world based *only* on physical principles and physical parameters. Therefore, the science and understanding of the universe it perceives is based only on those physical parameters. Its emotional capability is based only on the physical parameters it has encapsulated itself within. Its spiritual potential is only *glimpsed darkly* and, again, is measured by the spiritual parameters of the 'shell' that it has placed itself in – the shell of perception, the shell of individual perspective ...that journey from 'A' to 'B' across a physical world.

What I would love to donate, to add to your physical perception, is a spiritual perspective ...the opening up of further dimensions. All along in communicating with you, I have had to condense and modify spiritual concepts and multi-dimensional concepts into a physical form or 'shell' so that you can glimpse them.

It is my intention today to say that there is so much more than you perceive.

There is so much more to life than the establishment of security, power and a comfortable passage from birth to death. There is so much more to existence than being encased within physical matter and regarding yourself as an individual. There is so much more in terms of potential than you can manifest when drawing purely on physical senses.

My reason for saying these things to you is to expand upon the idea of meditation and contact with your spiritual self. In incarnating again you have put barriers up – both *outside* of yourself and *within* yourself – with regard to what you can perceive and what you are capable of. And you can only remove those barriers and access those additional dimensions via meditation, via contemplation and via stillness and a divorcing of yourself from the physical world for some period *each day*.

I would like to suggest a meditation… it is some time since we have included meditational exercises in the books.

First of all, you must surround yourself with God's Love – both within and without. You must become quiet. You must turn off your television …and your phone …and your computer …and your thoughts …and your worries …and your pre-occupations …and your questing into the future and delving into the past mentally. Become STILL and move into the heart-centre as I have suggested in previous communications.

~ The Meditation ~

…Then, when you have become still, I want you to imagine that you are a snail, that you are surrounded by tall blades of grass, and that, in the midst of these tall blades of grass, there is a furrow that leads to a welcome puddle of water that you wish to reach. Imagine what it is like to carry your whole world on your back (in fact, of course, you *do* psychically-, spiritually- and materially-speaking).

Imagine that you are a snail. You cannot see anything apart from the path ahead and you are moving slowly – *oh, so slowly*

71

– towards that puddle of water that is your ultimate goal. Along the tiny furrow that opens up slowly in front of you there are obstacles. There are pieces of stone; there are dead leaves and twigs. And, with each obstacle, you have to adjust yourself to get round that particular challenge, and then move yourself back into the line that goes towards the puddle.

Feel how slow your progress is. You cannot look up because the grass is too high. You cannot look behind you because you cannot turn around. You can only move forwards slowly.

Now, withdraw your consciousness from that image of the snail and become the bird looking down at the snail. Now, you are soaring on the wind. Now, you are uplifted by the air currents. Now, you can see the curvature of the Earth in front of you and around you. And you can see the snail's slow progress below you. But still you cannot escape from the pull of gravity; still you have to look out for other birds and for your own protection. ...But soar lazily for a while enjoying the increased perspective... You can look down on the trees and houses below you. You can look further, towards the horizon.

I now want you to pull back from the image of the bird into the image of the human ...**into *your own* image**, but step into it with a new lightness. Imagine that you can now soar like the bird. Imagine that you can expand your senses beyond the senses of the bird, and draw back into the clouds themselves. Feel the clouds – as if you are part of the clouds – moving across the face of the Earth.

Then, pull back from being a cloud to being a particle in the upper atmosphere of the Earth, and look down on the planet. See the curvature of the planet, and the swirling clouds that you were a part of a few moments ago. Feel your connection with the other charged particles that surround the Earth.

Then, pull back from being a particle to being an observer in space looking at planets and stars and galaxies and gas-clouds, looking at light and dark. Look at the immensity of the *physical* universe, and feel yourself expanding into every part of the physical universe. Feel yourself experiencing the different planets that *you are*, the different vibrations of starlight that *you are*. Feel yourself travelling between the galaxies and becoming the galaxies. Feel the circular movement that revolves around God and that you are a part of.

And, having done that for some time, withdraw from that image and move into ...what?

What comes next?

What is *beyond* the physical universe?

Move into the 'no-thing' that we have spoken about in previous books and become the no-thing ...*nothing*.

...Nothing! No physical universe. No perception of being a cloud or a bird or a human or a snail. No perception of moving from 'A' to 'B' ...**just being in the no-thing**.

And dwell in the no-thing for a time, absorbing that wonderful feeling of peace which comes from not having to move and pull your 'house' with you on your back ...your concerns with you on your back ...your worries with you on your back.

And, having observed the no-thing ...drifting in no-thing ... suddenly observe the 'some-thing' – the *higher* vibration. See and observe colours moving into your vision – mauves and purples and blues. Feel the higher vibration of being where limitless souls await you.

You are now entering the cleansing spheres. You are entering those areas of rarefied vibration where you still have physical form, but that physical form is so much lighter, is devoid of the worries and illnesses and upsets of physical life.

Observe your connection (just as you were connected to and became galaxies) to the myriad souls in your soul group. See them around you, in front of you, behind you – millions of souls who share a colour-combination that is *identical* to the colour-combination you now exhibit in this enlightened state. Feel the love, connection, harmony and unification of purpose that you have with these millions of souls.

See the landscape that they live in and have chosen to create around themselves. What is it like? Is it a desert place? Is it a verdant place? Is it a spiritual city? Is it a collection of dwellings that you have never encountered before? Do the members of your group soul look outwards... across to other planets? Do they look upwards towards higher spiritual vibrations and towards other group souls? What is around you? What do they wear? Can you see the coloured robes that these people are wearing ... each of them a part of you ...each of them welcoming you into that dimension?

Now, look from the dimension of being connected to your group soul *outwards* to being connected to other group souls. See the filaments of power and energy expanding from your group soul to connect to other group souls – to millions of other souls united in purpose. And that purpose is to remember and recreate ...*to create again* as they did before the time of the Fall. And, see yourself lifted as you connect to other group souls – as electrons and molecules and atoms were connected together to form physical creation.

And then, look above you as part of millions, billions, trillions of souls and see *the Light* above you. See in the skies and the heavens above you a circle (because your way back to God will always be *through a circle*), and glimpse into that circle of infinite, everlasting Love and power. Know that one day you will pass through into that dimension ...*those* 'dimensions', *plural*. And stare for a moment into the faces of your brothers and sisters – the angelic host who were connected to you at the time of the Fall, and have been waiting for you to reconnect to them since that time.

You cannot go through that hole yet. You cannot become a part of the Whole again yet – not mentally, not physically, not spiritually – because you have to move through the cleansing process of those spheres that contain the group souls that are moving upwards towards that escape.

But, escape exists for you. And, beyond that escape exists a whole new set of dimensions (from your point of view) that enable you to think …and to be …and to create …and to move with so much more power, with so much more perception, with so much more joy, with so much more freedom **as the angel that you once were and *still* are** within that shell that, unfortunately, we have to now bring you back to.

And so, with one last look at that circle above you – at the Light above you, at the potential, at the joy, at the destination above you that you must surely reach one day – pull yourself back *slowly*. Reverse the journey…

You come back to the connection with hundreds and millions of group souls.

You come back from that connection into your single group soul.

You pull back from that connection with your single group soul into the no-thing.

You pull back from the no-thing into the physical universe.

You pull back from your perception of galaxies and stars and planets into the upper atmosphere of this planet.

You pull back from that perception into the clouds surrounding this planet in the atmosphere.

You pull back from those clouds into the mind of the bird… and from the bird into the snail …and from the snail into *yourself*.

But, as you come back from that last image, remember what you have seen and felt and sensed. These are not illusions – this is *reality*. **This is your passage out from the effects of the Fall.**

And, asking God to protect you, at this point you come out of your meditation.

...I hope that when you do so your perception of the physical level is unsettling, is lacking, is restricting for you and that you miss the images and sensations that you felt during your meditative journey.

I hope to unsettle you because I want to *challenge* your view of reality ...challenge what you may perceive to be an open, full and all-knowing life ...challenge your perception of what you feel is 'intelligence' from your point of view ...challenge your perceived isolation ...challenge your individuality ...and to plant a seed of unrest, because you need unrest to work out of the rut that that 'snail' finds itself in.

So that you can return in your meditation, repeat the meditation at regular intervals and be given, during that meditation, inspiration from higher levels of consciousness.

Now I want to address how you perceive others. Remember that that journey you have been on as a visualisation **applies to every other soul around the Earth,** and that, when you perceive someone as not meeting your standards or as being a lesser being, you are only addressing *the surface.*

When you perceive someone as being a criminal or a murderer or an instigator of terror or a controlling force ...remember *what is within* that being (and by 'being' I mean that separation from God momentarily). Realise that if you address the potential of the being within – if you elevate other souls during your meditation (see yourself as gathering up the other souls around the Earth and taking them with you on this journey of changed perception and infusing them with Light) – you will begin to change them. And they will begin to change their perception of who they are and what they are capable of.

We view ourselves on Earth through a very limited lens, and put *ourselves* into categories: 'I am a good person' …'I am a bad person' …'I am a diseased person'. All these things apply to the *outermost* surface, and we invest in them because we are struggling to find our being, our individuality, our perception of ourselves.

And the perception of ourselves that we need in order to change this world is our perception of ourselves **as the angelic beings that we really are.** Now, that is difficult on a daily basis because of the cloaking effect of the Earth (that is *itself* cloaked because of the effects of the Fall) and the cloaking effect of the physical body, which in actuality *doesn't exist*, but is simply a consolidation of will and purpose projected by those souls that fell. Your physical body is a projection of *where* you think you should be and *what* you think you should be.

What I am asking you to do is to look beyond that perception, to realise you are not the physical and to realise that you are not any label that you give yourself …except the label that says *I am God*. That is the only label that sticks. That is the only label that is truth. **I am God – I am angelic.** Anything else is a lie. Anything else is a misconception. Anything else is a constriction.

I can suggest, through visual imagery, how you can expand your view of who you are, but I cannot do it for you. If I were to sit with you in your house – day in, day out – for your whole life I could not do it for you. **You have to do it for yourself, and you have to take action.**

Part of your spiritual growth and your re-emergence into the angelic form that you really are is to question; is to shake yourself free of restrictions; is to expand your consciousness; is to expand your view of yourself, of others and of the Earth.

Unless you take that journey, then your journey across the Earth will just be the snail's journey from point 'A' to point 'B'. It will be a journey out of perceived danger towards perceived security and a point where you feel you have 'arrived'.

...And then you die.

...And then you come back to repeat the *same* small journey.

There are other journeys ahead for you – far more spectacular, far more meaningful, filled with potential and filled with the ability to create ...*to create anything*. But, in order to embark upon those journeys, you have to question. You have to question who you are. Even with the most perfect life, you have to question what that life is about and whether there is *more*. And no one can come up to you and give you a 'box' that contains 'more' and you say, 'Thank you very much – now I have more.'

You have to dig for more, you have to work for more, you have to *want* more. And in wanting more, working for more, perceiving more ...*then* you begin to escape the effects of the Fall, and you give yourself the ability to help others escape the effects of the Fall.

Yes, of course, I have just mentioned that I cannot do it for you. Therefore, you cannot do it for others, but you *can* create the *atmosphere* in which they begin to do it for themselves. This is what people will ask, saying, 'Joseph, I'm not allowed to interfere – they have their own free will.'

Yes, they do. But, if you raise yourself, you raise the vibrations of the Earth – perhaps infinitesimally – but you raise the vibrations of the Earth. If, through advising and teaching others to do the same thing, you raise *their* vibrations, then you create a different Earth than you had. You create a different Earth in the evening than you had in the morning, and the souls that now exist on that different Earth have to – because of the vibrations that surround them – view things in a different way.

Isn't it true that you view things in a certain way because of the vibrations that are around you now – the effects of the Fall? If you raise yourself and others up mutually through the effects of the Fall then you raise up others because they find themselves in a different landscape with a different perspective. So, see yourselves as on a journey of discovery, a journey of escape and expansion, and a journey which will enable others to begin *their* journey.

You are not the snail …you are not the bird …you are not the human being …you are not the clouds …you are not the galaxies …you are not the no-thing …you are not the landscape of the group soul. You are the potential, the driver, the expander of all these things. You exist within all these things, but you are not all these things. **You are GOD. You are ALL.** You are the created centre of ALL, and that is a far more magnificent thing than gathering around the coffee machine at ten o'clock and saying that *the office is not going so well today.*

Forgive my forceful words, but, if I am not forceful, I cannot make you see. And (as we have said in all the books) the time is coming when you *have to* see – **you simply *have to* see.** You cannot say: 'I can't address the additional perspectives of my being because I'm going out tonight. I can't address the additional perspectives of my being because I have work to do that will not wait …I have something to sign …I have something to take somewhere …I have somebody to meet.'

You are running out of time.

Which do you want to be …the snail moving along the path that can see so little …or the being that is All-Being?

ALL-BEING… because that is your potential and that is your *ultimate* perspective. If I am able at a future date, I will examine with you some of the delights beyond that 'opening' that leads to Infinity which I talked about in the meditation. But *you* are that Infinity. You have always been. You will always be. Why do you spend so much time *here*? Why do you spend so much time believing that you are right and this is all that life is?

This is not life! This is a repeating pattern that you have immersed yourselves in, enclosed yourselves within, and locked yourselves in.

Are there questions, please?

Jane: Joseph, at night when we are in dream-state, do we partly escape here and go to higher dimensions?

Joseph: As you have quite rightly said, it is a *partial* escape because the effects of your waking consciousness on your sub-consciousness are great. So, your experience of freedom at night is limited to the degree that you have changed your perspective, and to the degree that you are willing to accept a spiritual world, willing to accept your part in it and willing to accept your ability to travel to and from it at night.

The reason that your dreams sometimes feel threatening and make you feel uneasy is that you invest your sleep time, on a conscious level as a physical being, with the effects of the Field. So, there is only partial escape at night. It would be better and a happier time for you if you remembered each night to talk to God and to ask for that escape. Ask for that time to visit spiritual realms with your spiritual relatives and with your spiritual teachers and to absorb something of their vibration to bring back with you in the morning ...to give your sleep a purpose, and not to make your sleep simply a means of ending one day and beginning another day with enough energy to get through it... That is back to the snail's perspective.

You have to say to yourself at night and to God: 'Father, I am willing to learn tonight.' (And, you will say at this point, 'Well, Joseph, I don't want to do any more work at night.' ...It is not work – it is *bliss*. It is spiritual understanding. It is spiritual exploration. It is spiritual learning.) And so, you ask God and say: 'Father, *with Your protection*, may I go to – and come back from – the place where I am best suited to go to learn and understand what I need to learn and understand?'

And, you can apply this to different aspects of your life. You can say to God: 'Father, my snail's journey is ill at ease. I am suffering in certain parts of my *perceived* physical body. I wish to relieve myself of those ailments, and I wish to go tonight to an area where I can heal myself or others can apply, with my permission, healing vibrations to me so that when I come back in the morning I am repaired.'

You can take into your sleep (with God's permission and your permission) the challenges that you have in life – not so that they will drag you down, but addressing God before you go to sleep and saying: 'Father, in a 'box' I have this particular challenge. It will not affect me during the night, but I need to know what to do during the day. I realise this might take some time, but I am going to give this challenge to You. I ask that I journey with it to You this night so that I can be given the perspective I need in order to solve this challenge, and so that I can be given the energy and power I need to bring the solution back into my consciousness and waking life on the Earth.'

So, your sleep time (this is a good question and a good area that I can expand on) is not simply there to release you from the effects of the day so that you can repair yourself on a physical and mental level, it is a time of great potential. It is a time when you can return 'home' for comfort. It is a time when you can return 'home' for advice. It is a time when you can return 'home' to connect with those members of your family that have gone on ahead. It is a time when you can return 'home' to learn – to sit in the great arenas of the cleansing spheres and listen to the bright and wonderful spirits who come to talk to us. It is a time when you can repair yourself *spiritually*.

It is a time when you can prepare yourself for what is ahead in your life. It is a time when you can examine the paths of your life and see where they are taking you. You are not allowed to see the entire unfolding of your physical life, but you have earned the right (because you have already created it) to see a little further ahead and think: 'Ah …well, I can meet *this point* if I continue along my current path, or if I make other decisions *then these points* will make themselves available to me.'

So, the sleep time is a time of great constructive power and of great advancement, and should be built into your life as such. You should look forward to it, not just for the relief of being away from the Earth plane, but because of the potential and because of your ability to do what you *want to do* ...but are restricted from doing because of the confines of the physical body and physical mind.

Does that make sense?

Jane: That is fantastic! Thank you.

Joseph: Another question, please!

David: Joseph, speaking from personal experience, when we come back from sleep and awaken to the new day much of it is forgotten. Is that then taking up the position of the snail again? In other words, there is kind of a barrier between the potential of what we really are and what we are in our daily lives.

Joseph: Perception is also a matter of *recognition*. In order to perceive something, you have to be able to recognise it. For example, during your daily lives (as you have just said) you are unable to see the spiritual realms, for the most part, because you do not recognise them. You are unable to see the influence of your spiritual mind on your physical body, and the spiritual intervention and inspiration that comes to you daily, **because you do not recognise it**. The purpose of today's chapter is to allow you to recognise your greater potential because, in recognising it, you then perceive it more and bring it into your consciousness more.

What happens with the majority of people is that, as they return to their physical bodies in the morning (or whenever it is that they awaken), such is the weight of the things that they *do* recognise ...their disease ...their discomfort ...the challenges in their life ... the fact that they are unhappy ...the fact that they have placed themselves under financial or emotional stress ...that all these things crowd in instantly because the physical mind clicks back into being. It switches on – rather like a computer switching back on from sleep mode. As it does so, it accesses all the files available to it – which, for the most part, are the physical, mental and emotional files from the previous day.

What you have to do is to add more of the 'spiritual files', and also to ask and to say: 'Into this file that I have marked *Awareness of the Night Before*, I wish You, Father, and I wish me, Father, to place understanding and acknowledgement of what has happened to me in a way that I can recognise.'

So, until you recognise it instantly on awakening, you should understand that – *because you have asked* – where you have been and the essence of what you have learned at night will be revealed to you by the things that happen to you during the day. You will be given …'clues' is the wrong word… you will be given a *picture* that repeats itself. You will be given patterns that make themselves available more than once during the day that your physical mind can access and make sense of, by mixing that pattern with the information that you have in your 'spiritual files'. It is not fanciful – you will recognise what has happened to you the night before because of what is brought to you during the day.

Do you see that?

David: Yes, it is a matter of practice, practice, practice.

Joseph: It is practice, and it is discipline in addressing the spiritual side of you in saying, 'My life is in two halves.' You have the day and the night for a reason. You have the light and the dark – each to remind you of the other – not to divide yourselves into two halves, but to say: 'This is the day. Having prayed and brought spiritual principles into it, I will now traverse the day. But the night – my time away from this sphere – is specifically for X, Y and Z …is specifically for these spiritual reasons …is specifically for me connecting to God, saying: "Father, teach me! Remind me! Show me! Allow me access".'

It is not God who denies you access – it is yourself to the extent that you are weighed down by the cares of the day and the potential cares of the future. You, therefore, restrict yourself from being free, from soaring like the bird …like the clouds …like the galaxies, and moving into that advanced state of consciousness that will bring you answers to your questions and infuse your physical life with a new vitality and a new *perspective* – which is the word that we have been looking at today.

Is there another question, please?

Tony: I don't have a question, Joseph. Mine has been answered by the previous two questions.

Joseph: You probably wonder whether I am aware of the book [*reference to the then-newly-published Joseph Communications book – **Trance Mission** – which had been delivered from the printer earlier that week*]. I have always been aware of the book. [*Smiling*] I was aware of the book before you were born. I am aware of the other books. I am aware of the need to change perspectives. And the need to change perspectives (from the group soul's point of view) is manifest in the book, but it will also be manifest in other books and in other addresses.

I do apologise, but the work is not over – the work is just *beginning*, and there will be many more demands on your time, your focus, your perspectives and your energies as your lives progress. You agreed to all this; you know it is about to happen.

And so, yes, I am aware of the book. I am proud that you have produced it. I am happy that you have stayed the course …but what else could you do? You were picked to stay the course. You were picked to be at this point. You were picked to hear this. You were picked to experience and to open up that which *to you* is still in the future, but *to us* is on the 'giant chart' that we have in front of ourselves as points of Light. And, because the book is now in form, another point 'A' is connecting to a point 'B' in the *right* direction that leads through that 'hole' and into Infinity.

I wish you peace at this time of year [*reference to Christmas*] – and I wish you peace at 'this time of year' because it is more dangerous than other times of the year. There is more concentration of the journey of the 'snail' at this time because (and, please include this in this forthcoming book) **you have at Christmas a concentration on *solidifying the effects of the Fall.***

Solidifying the effects of the Fall!

And, the core of the Christmas message (from this point of view and in this part of the world) is totally forgotten. Imagine our bemusement at watching a celebration to celebrate a message that has not been heard, that is not acknowledged and that is not put into practice.

The core message, of course, is identical to the message that we are *redelivering*. It is a 'redelivery system'! The core message has been sent back: 'Return to sender!' ...Return to God! We are *redelivering* that message through the books, through your involvement in trying to address what is wrong on Earth and in trying to make people see and look up from that 'snail's perspective'. We are redelivering that message, but at Christmas that message is totally, totally, totally, totally LOST.

And so I would ask, at the Christmas time and the turn of the year, that you double your efforts – and encourage people to double their efforts – to put Light into the world to deliver the *true* Christmas message.

...The true Christmas message is: you are lost and you don't need to be. You can find yourself instantly by going within, by loving, by sending out the Light, by doing what you were asked to do **two thousand years ago** ...and, beyond that, thousands of years earlier ...*and you are not doing it.*

Please, *please* change your perspective!

Chapter Six
Lack and the 'GOD IS' Perspective

Michael's observations: In this chapter Joseph addresses for the first time one of his key intentions in dictating this book: that of providing those of us who wish to spend time bringing Light into this world in order to change it for the better and to elevate consciousness on this planet with advanced spiritual methods of doing so. The 'GOD IS' Perspective referred to in the title of this chapter and throughout Joseph's address, is an affirmation, a conviction and a re-connection to God-power which, when understood and correctly applied, is a powerful tool for personal and world illumination, as Joseph will now explain...

Joseph: I am urging Michael to speak, and there is a reticence with him because he doesn't know what I am going to say, but that is the way it should be, as that makes for the best communication that we can possibly have.

I want to talk today initially about *lack* and about people's perception of lack. It is a question that many people have: 'Why is there a lack in one area? Why is there a lack in my life? Why do I need so many things that I can't find?'

...And the answer is: you don't. The answer is: '*GOD IS*'.

GOD IS!

In *every* situation, the perspective '*GOD IS*' should be applied.

Lack is an echo from the Fall. The feeling of lack that each human being has, to a greater or lesser extent in their present incarnation, is an echo from the Fall. It is an echo from that moment of conscious disconnection from the God-within, which manifests itself as:

'My relationship is fine, but there is a lack – it doesn't seem as fulfilling and as blossoming as it could be.'

'My job is OK – it brings me the finances I need, but not enough. It should be expanding into something more.'

'The house I am in is fine, but a bigger one would be better.'

'Always the position I am in leaves me wanting more – leaves me feeling that I am unfulfilled.'

It is the separation from God at conscious level that has caused this feeling.

...And it is re-connection with God that brings fulfilment in *all* areas.

If there is a perceived lack in any area, the mantra that should be used is: *GOD IS*.

GOD IS restores the balance. *GOD IS* re-makes the connection between yourself and your potential, your inheritance, your origins and your ability to create. And *GOD IS* shifts you in perspective. By affirming *GOD IS*, you move yourself away from those situations that bring you a greater perception of lack into those situations that bring you a greater perception of *fulfilment*.

When you perceive yourself as lacking something, you resonate and link with other souls who similarly perceive a lack within themselves, and so you pull yourself into a vibrational link and a 'magnetic lock' with souls *with a similar perceived level of lack*, and, therefore, you enforce, enhance and strengthen *your* position of lack and your feeling that there is lack in certain areas. In other words, **you bring to yourself *more* of what you perceive to be true …in this case – lack.**

And so, the souls who have trouble with relationships find that they step out of one relationship because they feel it brings them a sense of lack, and then step into another relationship *which has the same level of lack attached to it* because they are sending out a signal that says: 'I perceive lack at this particular level …do you? If you do, let us link together.' All this goes on on a subconscious level, but that is what is happening.

The job that does not bring fulfilment can be moved away from, and then another job comes along which brings the same level of discomfort because the signal from the soul is still, 'I lack …I lack in my job …I lack in what I wish to achieve.'

When you affirm that *GOD IS* (not 'I am', but *GOD IS*, which signifies that you are God, that YOU ARE and that there is no lack) you then move away from those parameters of lack, and place yourself in different vibrations that bring you fulfilment.

However, no externalised earthly experience can ever bring you the sense of fulfilment that you can discover *within yourself* by stating and experiencing *GOD IS*.

GOD IS!

And *GOD IS* changes situations.

In a situation of illness, stating *GOD IS* …**and *believing that*** on behalf of yourself or the person who is suffering, shifts the vibrational magnetism and vibrational pull away from a sense of lack on a subconscious and conscious level to a sense of fulfilment, and prompts them towards a re-establishment of health in either yourself or the person you are praying for.

In personal relationships – not just marriage but relationships where there is antagonism, a quest for power and a quest for dominance of one person over another – by stating *GOD IS* within such circumstances, you move the relationship away from antagonism and back towards harmony.

In situations in your life where you cannot see any escape, change or graduation into a better situation, hold the situation to you, and permeate and infuse it with *GOD IS*. That situation then cannot resonate with similar vibrations and pull them in, so the sense of lack and of things being wrong has to change, and the situation itself has to change and resolve itself.

There will *never* be on this level, during your present physical incarnation, a complete sense of fulfilment.

That is not a negative thing to say. I am simply stating that you cannot be totally *whole* in a situation that promotes, adores and perceives *only lack*. In other words, you can never feel totally whole while incarnated on Earth at present because of the effects of the Fall.

Once the effects of the Fall have been negated, transposed and transmuted, then there will be the sense of wholeness on Earth for the spirits visiting this sphere and, after the effects of the Fall have been removed, there will be the sense of wholeness that is experienced by angelic beings within physical bodies that exist outside of this sphere of disturbance.

So, *the sense of wholeness* that you can, even in meditation, only *partially* experience is something that you should, nevertheless, attempt to escalate and build into your meditations daily. Push aside all those thoughts that come in to say: 'I need to deal with *this* situation. I am not happy with *that* situation. What do I do in *these* circumstances? How do I sort out *those* circumstances?' Push all those things away for a few moments and state …live …*believe GOD IS*.

What do I mean by *GOD IS*?

...GOD IS is the state of God.

God knows nothing about lack. God knows nothing less than the quest for expression, the quest for fulfilling potential in different ways and the quest for *perfecting* perfection ...building perfection upon perfection. God does this in joy. God does this in complete comfort. God does this (and this is difficult to translate into earthly terms) with a sense of complete fulfilment and with a sense of complete patterning, expansion and planning into new areas. And God does this with no sense of failure being a possibility. **The concept of failure and lack is something that exists only on Earth ...*only on Earth, because of the Fall.***

So, within your meditations, I am asking you to examine and consider ...a state of perfect balance ...a state of perfect expansion at the right rate through harmony ...a state of linking into, and being a part of, all other things *everywhere* ...a state of love for all things ...a state of love for purpose ...a state of love for self (but not the *physical* self) ...a state of love for expressing being part of God – **which is how you feel and how you operate as an angelic being.** And this *can* be experienced in meditation over time and with practice – not to the extent that you would feel it once you are outside of the effects of the Fall – but certainly to the extent that your life changes *radically*.

Isn't it wonderful to think that you can condense everything that you feel is so complex, so irreversible, so inaccessible, and so unchangeable into *GOD IS* and liberate yourself from all these things?

GOD IS superimposes itself over illness, over conflict, over violence, over fear, over power struggles and resets things as they were. It is the *GOD IS* that you are attempting to bring into your life and the lives of others.

And the *GOD IS* is contained within the White Light.

White Light is an expression – a bringing forth of the term 'GOD IS'.

I bring through this information today to add into your examination of self in meditation, and your encapsulation of others in the Light in meditation, **but it is a step** *beyond* **the White Light**. It is a state of being that is *within* and *permeating* the White Light.

The White Light is a visualisation of God-power.

The *GOD IS* **is the acceptance, understanding, expression and living of God-power.**

So, the White Light sent into situations and coupled with those moments when you can appreciate the *GOD IS* within you, within the world and within situations, **is a very powerful weapon for change.**

I would ask you to try it in situations: to direct it to souls who are suffering to the extent that they may be aggressive towards you or others, or may seem to be 'lost causes' with regard to mental or physical health. As and when you can, permeate them with the *GOD IS* and see the remarkable change that will take place because you will have shifted their vibrational charge away from that of the Fall and more towards the Heart of God where all things are not only possible, but ARE.

Does what I have said thus far make sense?

David, Jane and Tony: Yes.

Joseph: Can we then open up the arena of questions on this subject?

David: Joseph, should we then be using this 'GOD IS' not just in creative things like taking on a new job or a new house but also in the closing down of things as well? For example, you may be moving away from a house and want to leave it in the right condition for the next person to move into, and so forth ...in other words, should we be using it in *every* walk of life?

Joseph: That is an interesting topic. The *GOD IS* is a step beyond the Light-meditations I have given you so far, because the *GOD IS* gives a completely different *perspective* to the situations you have just mentioned, for example. There is, of course, a blessing that you can bring into physical objects, **but the *GOD IS* is a different way of *seeing*.**

Very often souls focus on a certain set of circumstances and say: 'This is what needs to happen in my life. This is what needs to happen in the lives of others.' And these things, although they seem to be quite spiritual in intent to the person examining and originating them, can be, nevertheless, close to the surface. So, the human being measures itself in terms of placing itself within a timeframe and relating to certain circumstances around it: ...it needs the house to change ...it needs to live in a certain area ... it is getting older ...it is on a road to knowledge. And, yes, all these things *are* taking place close to the physical plane – very often *on* the physical plane – but just *behind* the physical plane, as well, in terms of thought and intention.

The *GOD IS* is a different and more complete expression that, because it is not of the physical, has a greater intent at heart, and has the greater intent of the soul that is thinking thoughts about its physical life in mind. **Therefore, the *GOD IS* addresses the *greater purpose* of that soul and addresses the *greater purpose* of the situation.**

How can I put this? Imagine you are looking at a point of colour ...and then your perspective changes as you pull back from it, and you see that the dot of colour is not, as you first thought, on a wall or straight surface, but is on a curved surface, and then you pull back further, and you see that the curved surface is part of a huge sphere ...and then you pull back further, and you see that the sphere is a sphere of light within another sphere of light ...and then you pull back further, and you see that those spheres are spiritual atoms within a huge sphere of light that is a planet ...and then you pull back from there, and you see that that planet is a *thought in a purpose* that is being brought forth by angelic hosts.

That might sound quite complex, but what I am trying to explain is that what you feel is your perspective on an earthly level is the equivalent of looking at that dot ...whereas the *GOD IS* is the equivalent of looking at the whole picture. And the whole picture puts the earthly perspective *into perspective*. Do you see?

David: Yes.

Joseph: It is a complex thing to try to 'shoehorn' into words. What I am suggesting (and I hope this brings the nature of this book to light) is that there are perspective-shifts that are available to the evolving spirit on Earth, *if* the evolving spirit on Earth knows how to access them, and that part of negating the effects of the Fall is to bring to mankind (and initially this must be done through those points of Light that are working to bring White Light to mankind) an ability to *shift perspective*, to look at the things that the person thought were important and to put them into context and into scale.

I am attempting to give you the ability to escalate the value of the White Light that you put out. The way to do that is to infuse yourself with the '*GOD IS perspective*', which is not something that should make you sweat or feel inferior. It may be that you only connect with the *GOD IS perspective* for a tiny moment during a number of meditations, but I have to make you aware that it is there, that it exists and that it shifts your perspective.

In order to relate to God, *you* have to relate to God *as God*.

If you are bringing to God problems with a house, or a relationship, or a work condition, then you are bringing to God something that is of the Fall, when you moved *away from* God by volition. So, you are attempting to relate to God via aspects of your Fall-experiment that are not coming from the God-centre of God. (They are 'God' in the sense that they have come from the angelic children who made the mistake, but they are not from God *at heart*.) So, in order to bring God into your situations, you have to link through the *GOD IS*, which then changes your perspective on the situations.

You can regard this *GOD IS* connection as a *different way* to pray – as a *more effective way* to pray, and I hope it answers for some of the readers the question: 'Why does God not inform me about my house or the car or the relationship? Why has nothing been done?'

Well, there is always something being done, but it requires a shift in your perception in order to infuse the situation with God-Light, because the situation you are addressing and talking to God about in terms such as, 'This is terrible! I need to change it and I need *Your* help,' **...is of the Fall** (which in itself divorces it from God-intention) and is *often* only the tip and the surface of what you truly need.

So, the *GOD IS* brings you what you truly need and fulfils those parts of you that need fulfilling. More often than not, those are *not* aspects of the situation that you perceive as being wrong ...which brings us round in a circle to that **perceiving of lack.** The lack is not what you see outside of yourself – it is not the house, it is not the relationship, it is not the work upset – it is lack of *GOD IS*.

So, in restoring the *GOD IS*, you restore your equilibrium as a spiritual child, and you restore your ability to create and make a difference, and also to see things as they really are. What a gift that is – not to see this world in terms of the hard matter of a street of houses, or a work place, or the 'black and white' of a relationship or power struggle – but to see it *as it really is*, to see what lies beneath, to see the God-energy and the God-intention.

And, seeing with those eyes – with God's-eyes – is *true praying* on behalf of yourself and of others. It changes that surface view for yourself and those others that have bought into that surface view because it transmutes. In prayer, what you are saying to God *in all situations* is: 'Change the situation, Father! I need! … I lack! …Change the situation!' *GOD IS* gives you the power to change the situation because it is a more powerful tool than anyone else's prayer in that situation …unless they, too, are linking into *GOD IS*. Do you see that?

David: Yes.

Tony: As a therapist working with patients on a one-to-one basis, I find that the issues they have are nearly always some form of 'lack' …but should those surface issues be addressed at a far deeper level – i.e. not the patient's perceived life but actually all the way back to their original parting with God?

Joseph: The *original* parting or individualisation from God (which we know is not truly an individualisation, but just a viewpoint sent out to bring back experience) is not a lack of *GOD IS*.

The lack of *GOD IS* came at the point of the Fall when the experiment speeded up matter, locked the souls within this area of belief and took them away from God.

With regard to your patients, it is a different way of healing in that – no matter who comes to you – you are healing a *single* aspect of belief. That single aspect is *lack* and can be healed by enveloping the person within the *GOD IS*.

Now, that will not sit well with many healers because it appears to be too simple. We have discussed simplicity thus far in the books, and you may not have noticed, but throughout the books there has been more seeming complexity of information, but a greater simplicity in *addressing* and assimilating that information and in changing what is wrong.

...And, broken down to its essence, what is wrong is that there is a lack of the *GOD IS* perspective in the perception of this world – both *globally* and at *individual level.*

The souls you are dealing with will very probably not share your view (nor would they understand it if you explained it to them) so you have to pay 'homage' to the *perceived* wrongs within that person ...be they oppression from people ... oppression from past experiences ...oppression from jobs ... oppression from past relationships ...oppression from self. You have to acknowledge those things **without giving them any power.**

But then, having paid homage to those situations in a person's life by examining them in conversation, when you have quietened the patient (and at times when the patient isn't even there) **...you acknowledge that GOD IS.** You see not the perceived wrongs and disharmonies that the person has been describing to you (perhaps in depth and perhaps for weeks) but you simply see that *GOD IS.*

GOD IS!

...And *GOD IS* chases away the darkness. *GOD IS* reinstates perfection and harmony, and *GOD IS* heals that person. You have to be strong and you have to realise that your strength comes from *GOD IS*, and that **GOD IS is stronger than 'God is not'.**

GOD IS is stronger than 'my life is lack'.

GOD IS is stronger than 'I am ill'.

GOD IS is stronger than 'I cannot get by'.

GOD IS is stronger than 'my thoughts are wrong'.

GOD IS is stronger than 'I am violent'.

...because all those things are surface clusterings of belief on behalf of the soul that has presented itself to you. At the core of each soul is *GOD IS*, and re-establishing that *GOD IS* in another re-establishes harmony.

The measure in which you believe in and can wield the *GOD IS* determines how the patient then responds because *ironically* the patient uses the *GOD IS* (i.e. that creative ability and establishment of all power) to re-enforce their feelings of lack. You are both using the *GOD IS*, but one is using the *GOD IS* to re-establish harmony, and the other is using the *GOD IS* to shore up beliefs in things being wrong and in need of attention. Do you see that?

Tony: I do, indeed.

Joseph: So, we are talking today about a great *simplicity* that re-establishes a great power and a great harmony. I hope I have also been able to illustrate that what the reader may feel is wrong with them in their perception of their personal life is, in most cases, a *surface* situation only.

That is not to belittle those situations or to push them aside as though they are not important, but it is, nevertheless, the true perspective. And, the person who masters *GOD IS* (i.e. masters that connecting to God) can then brush aside those situations and see them for what they are. Having established *GOD IS* they will not see them as 'situations' any longer – they will be 'surface irritations' only because that, in truth, is what they are.

Even the most deadly physical illness is a surface irritation because, if you think about that, *if* you a spirit (which you are) ...*if* you are an angelic being (which you are) ...*if* you are part of the *GOD IS* then the physical life is surface. The physical life is a 'membrane of belief' that you have invested yourself into to the extent that you believe it is all there is and you give it dominance over your true inheritance.

Is there a further question, please?

Jane: Joseph, can I ask something about the *GOD IS* with regard to creativity and effort? On this level, if we want to express beautiful creativity – through art, music or dance, for example – we have to put a lot of effort in to do so, which is probably because we are in a physical plane. In the spirit worlds and the angelic realms, is it more effortless to express God's creativity?

Joseph: What you experience in attempting to create here is the drag, the pull, the counter-balance, the slowing down that the effects of the Fall put around the manifestation of your creativity. Your creativity seems to be wrought in angst and in great effort because you are immersing that creativity into the Field. If you produce a beautiful goblet, that goblet has to exist against the perception of the Field *that the goblet isn't beautiful.* If you are attempting to produce a lasting ornament in that goblet that will go on forever, the Field says that it cannot be so, and the Field instantly attacks it and attempts to attach a belief to it.

So, your efforts to create something permanent, beautiful and wonderful are diluted by other people's perceptions of that creative act, and by the effects of the Field on that creative act. The Field does not wish there to be harmony, but wants turmoil, which feeds its desires from its negative perspective.

The act of creation as an angelic being is one of ultimate bliss and joy – *bliss and joy* that cannot be easily translated into something that will appear in a book and leap off the pages, transmitting that bliss and joy to the person reading it ...because the book is within the effects of the Field ...a physical person is within the effects of the Field ...and the person's physical mind is within the effects of the Field.

Everything requires effort. For me to communicate with you requires effort. For me to turn my attention to something requires effort, but effort needn't be *strenuous.* Effort – *at its purest* – can be an examination of potentials and alternatives through which then decision is made and creation brought forth. Effort is involved, but it is the effort of discovery. It is the effort of solidifying and giving form to one option from many options.

Creation on a spiritual level can be a matter of quite calmly and quite slowly examining options. Imagine bringing forth an option and saying: 'I *may* choose that …I'll hold it there whilst I bring through another option, and compare the two.' And, looking at the two options, you may feel that there are aspects of 'Option One' and aspects of 'Option Two' that are wonderful, and you will bring forth a third option that is better, as a combination of the two, than the two are separately. Through *the joy of effort* you slowly examine different possibilities until you create the ultimate potential that you wish to at that time. You can then deconstruct that potential.

Each potential that you bring through in its highest creative form is of honour to God. It is something that you 'bring home after school' to your Father and say, 'Look what I have made!' Then it adds to your Father's perspectives because of the effort you have put into it and the joy of bringing together something that may have been formed before or, perhaps, hasn't.

So, it is easier and certainly more productive creating *outside* of the effects of the Fall, but it still involves a volition, an examination of potentials and a desire to create the best and to create something *new*.

All these aspects I have been talking about with regard to creation happened in the Fall, and we go back then to the Fall having taken place with the best possible intentions but with the worst possible outcome.

And, within the creative matrix there is the knowledge of *other* souls – souls that have created before and older souls that are expressions of God that have been individualised for a longer time. So, when you create something, you observe it multi-dimensionally from a spiritual point of view. You look into your creation, and within it is the potential of what it could be ...but also the knowledge of *similar creations from the past*, because, as you create, you touch on the creative abilities of every other soul around you.

What happened in the Fall was that those tendencies and warnings within that creative matrix were not heeded. Within the potential to speed up matter there was a warning that it would be a long course rather than a shortcut back to God ... and that was ignored.

Creation is a multi-dimensional pursuit on a spiritual level. Again, very difficult to put into earthly words, but infinitely more rewarding and with infinitely more potential and possibilities than it has here.

Does that in some way answer?

Jane: Yes, absolutely. Thank you.

Joseph: Is there a final question as the energy dips, please?

Jane: Can I ask something else relating to that? On Earth when making decisions, if you have the time, you can tap into your intuition and it gives you the feeling of which is the right way to go. During the Fall-experiment why didn't we tap into our intuition, because we didn't even have a head-mind then so we should have just been able to *know* from our heart-mind?

Joseph: This links into what I have just said about the potential for creation holding within it the 'advice', as it were, of other souls who have attempted similar things. There was a thrill that went through the angelic children at that time – in that they believed that they were bringing back to the Father 'at the end the day after school' something of great, great worth. That thrill and excitement *blinded* them to the negative possibilities of proceeding with the experiment that went wrong.

Also, understand that there was a *partial* physicality (I believe I have spoken at length about the way that souls inhabit heavier matter in order to experience) and they infused the heavier matter of the area they were inhabiting with that thrill and desire, which took away their 'common sense', if you like. This is why the debate went on for so long. This is why the souls sank further and further into their own belief that they were right over a great deal of 'time' (as you would measure it on Earth). During that time they infused their belief more and more into their limited physicality to the extent that that became their viewpoint rather than their heart viewpoint. Do you see?

Jane: Yes …I just wondered why their intuition didn't warn them that there was a *bad feeling* about this. You know how we have a 'gut feeling' – so why didn't they have it?

Joseph: You have a gut feeling *now*, but you didn't have a gut feeling *then* because it was all play. Your gut feeling is, in effect, your shift from the physical mind to the heart-mind. Those moments of intuition are the GOD IS moments …the moments when you are closer to *what you actually are.*

You moved away from that and made the decision to invest in the potential of your creation at the time of the Fall, but not as you do now, from a very solid head-mind that dominates all you do. It was from a skewed perspective through your *excitement* at what you could create, what you believed you were bringing to the table and what you were bringing back to God.

The shift was gradual and was like a 'thief in the night'. It was a gradual shift that reinforced itself …and reinforced itself …and reinforced itself …and reinforced itself to the point where the angelic children involved were saying: 'No, we can do this! This is right – you will see!'

But that was still done out of love. It was done out of a wish (which then became an arrogance) to say: 'We have a different way, Father. It's Your way because You are operating through us, but we have seen a loophole. We have seen something that You haven't seen, and, by showing You what it is, we can show You a better way to evolve and to perfect Yourself further.'

That volition moved them away from the original intent, and then it became a matter of reinforcing their viewpoint and saying to the other souls involved in trying to *dissuade* them from what they were about to do, 'No, we *do* know what we are doing and we will show you.' ...And at that point things went wrong.

Does that make any further sense?

Jane: Yes, thank you.

Joseph: My blessing to you before I leave, and my viewpoint on your various physical problems at the moment is ...*GOD IS.*

Chapter Seven
Loss

Joseph: I wish to talk about *loss* this morning – *loss* as an 'enemy' and *loss* as a 'friend'. Let us first consider loss as an 'enemy', and the way in which loss plays such a huge part in our lives.

Life on Earth is centred on loss at this time.

From the moment you are born, you find yourself in situations of loss ...the toy cannot be found ...the friend disappears and is never encountered again, and, as you grow older, there is the loss of the people around you ...souls that are here and then, inexplicably, are gone from your life. As people grow on this level, their existence becomes attuned to and *almost looking for* loss.

Loss is the enemy:

'I have to acquire because loss is the enemy. Therefore, I have to have everything that I need *and more* so that I can bring in more of what I have, to compensate for things that become lost.'

'I have to steel myself as I go through life because the people around me that I love will not be there forever. I have to appreciate them whilst I can because one day they won't be there and will be gone from me forever. The love-link that connected me to them will be gone forever ...all their intelligence ...all their humour ...all their warmth ...all their love ...all their contributions to my life ...*gone forever.*'

You, therefore, base your life on loss. Loss is the enemy and loss is to be safeguarded *against.*

Let us examine loss as a 'friend'. From birth to death you accumulate experiences. Those experiences are right for your soul, but you drag along with you the continuing vibrations of those experiences into your present life and your *now* point of view. And so, as you read this, you are experiencing the words from the book ...but you are also experiencing the situations that have occurred in your life that you haven't let go of. Because you are conditioned to deal with loss and are expecting loss, you hoard to yourself every aspect of what happens to you – not just the experience itself but the *structure* of the experience.

And, the structure of the experience can only be let go of when *you choose* to let go of it.

Because of the vibrational qualities of the Fall on Earth, anything you set up exists until you dissolve it, until you let go of it, until you choose to lose it. And so, loss can be a friend ... in that it can rid you of the vibrations that hold you back ...in that it can rid you of the situations that you no longer need ...in that it can rid you of perspectives that are no longer of use to you, which prevent you from evolving as the spiritual being and angel that you really are.

So I invite you, as you read this, to consider those areas mentally that are still *alive* with you and that need to be discarded. Those experiences from the past ...pain from the loss of the people around you ...pain that you hoard as a 'friend' (perversely) in case you lose it. I invite you to look at those areas and decide to let go of those vibrations that hurt you and hurt *others* because you are holding on to them. And I invite you, on a weekly basis, to go into the 'meditation chamber of your heart' to view those areas that are still sore points with you that you are keeping alive ...and to let go of them ...to lose them.

~ The Meditation ~

See yourself walking though a field of high corn. As you begin the journey from this point in the field to a point on the other side of the field, you sense with you – as 'travelling companions' – all those negative situations that are still very much alive with you: ...the pain ...the hurt ...the anger ...the need for revenge ... the inability to forgive. See them as 'creatures', if you will – as manifestations of negative vibration that are travelling through the cornfield with you ...but only *you* know the path through the field.

As you walk through the very tight, high stalks of corn, see and sense those negative 'travelling companions' becoming lost and being held back by the corn as you walk the one true path through to the other side of the field where the sun is shining.

As you traverse the field, see your companions becoming fewer and fewer, and the stalks of corn becoming lower and lower until you emerge from the cornfield into a beautiful meadow ...alone ...peaceful ...able to commune with yourself and with those who have gone ahead of you into the spiritual cleansing realms – your relatives and your friends. See them in this beautiful meadow, there to meet you.

And realise in that moment that, having lost the negative trappings of your life in the cornfield, you have left yourself open to the vibrations and promptings of your relatives *who are not lost at all,* and who are constantly trying to communicate with you and inspire you, but have found it difficult to do so under previous circumstances because of the amount of worry and 'baggage' that you needed to let go of, but haven't done until now.

In this meditative state, here in this beautiful, bright meadow, under a perfect blue sky and wonderful golden sun ...you can meet with ...and be inspired by ...and be comforted by ...and be directed by your relatives and friends who have passed through the veil into the cleansing spheres of the spiritual realms.

You can now, at this point in your meditation, *commune* with those people. Greet them ...see yourself hugging them ...see yourself talking to them ...see yourself discussing your earthly conditions with them. Become quiet and *listen* – and you will get true advice, inspiration, comfort and love from these souls that you are *eternally and infinitely connected to*.

And then, when you feel that you have been filled with their Light, and their wisdom, and their health, and their happiness, and their love, turn in your meditation and come back through the cornfield.

You go back through the area of moderately high corn, through to the denser regions of the cornfield, but this time (remember that you know the way through *instinctively*) you do not pick up those vibrations that you have now lost. You do not pick up those 'travelling companions', and you find yourself returning to yourself (to wherever it is you are doing this meditation) *free from those vibrations*, and inspired and comforted by the knowledge that the people you thought you had lost ...**you have not lost at all.**

A word more about the loss of companions and relatives, because this is a factor that concerns every soul on Earth as, throughout your life, you *one moment* have the physical representation of somebody and the *next moment* lose
that physical representation. Consider that that soul, in passing to the spiritual cleansing realms, has *lost* a burden ...has *lost* a body that had become wearisome and heavy for them ...has *lost* situations that were pulling at that soul and darkening its vision of reality. And, consider that **that soul, in losing, has *gained*** ... in losing that physical representation has gained... because it has, for a time (and we pray for a *great deal* of time) escaped from the effects of the Fall and has returned 'home'. But, in order to return home, it has first had to lose.

Also, consider that the soul you think you have lost is an infinite angel, is an infinite representation of God. That soul continues, that soul expands, that soul is linked to you forever. Consider that you, similarly, are also an infinite being, an infinite angel, an infinite part of God and are infinitely linked with that soul.

So, you cannot *in reality* ever lose anyone. You cannot lose them – it is simply that the darkness of the Earth plane has clouded your vision of where they now are.

There was a time when all this was plain, when leaving a denser representation of yourself was a matter of choice and clarity, when communing with those that were not travelling in the sphere you were travelling in was simple, was taken for granted, was never questioned because those souls were at hand whenever you considered them. Those souls were visible whenever you wanted to see them. Those souls were in communication whenever you wanted to talk to them. It is the effects of the Fall that have clouded your spiritual judgement. It is the effects of the Fall that impose a *seeming* separation between yourself and the people you love who have gone on ahead of you.

But remember, *in reality* that connection to them is the same as it always was. It has not altered; it is only your temporary perception that has been altered. And so, in order to receive comfort in times of loss, you again need to go *within*. You need to let go of the cloying, pulling qualities of your life and, in your 'chamber of meditation' within your heart, there acknowledge and accept that you are in communication with the souls that are part of your spiritual family. Of course, we are *all* family, but I am referring to those specific connections that you have made whilst in an earthly body and regard as close family ...as mothers and fathers and brothers and sisters and so on.

Loss is also something that you should consider not as an 'enemy' or as a 'friend' but as a 'nonsense', because loss is something that motivates millions and millions of lives on Earth because the souls living those lives *expect* loss. When they rise in the morning they expect loss of income ...they expect loss of

energy as they grow older ...they expect loss of companions ...
they expect loss of the objects around them. Always, as their
creative expression of life day-to-day, they are striving to avert loss.

What a terrible waste of creative time to spend so much of it
trying to avert something that does not exist in the first place.
[*Laughing*] You cannot lose what you do not have, and the
objects around you that you consider you 'own' are not only *not
there* ...they are *not yours*.

Consider that!

'Ownership' is an earthly concept. The angel that you are does
not need to own. The angel that you are simply *is*. Therefore, all
aspects of the angel that you are, are available to you whenever
you desire to immerse yourself in them. You do not seek to own
anything as an angel. The concept is completely alien.

**You only seek to own because you perceive there to be limited
power on Earth because of the effects of the Fall.**

It is difficult because, due to the effects of the Fall, the objects
you create around yourself cannot be completely or easily
disassociated from you and 'dissolved', as it were. They are
around you even when you have lost them. They rot down slowly
and flaunt themselves in front of you as things that once were
beautiful but are now decaying and are now *less* than they were.
This contributes cleverly, via the Field, to your perception of loss.
You look out on a landscape that suggests loss, suggests decay
and suggests that things are escaping your control.

Whereas, in your spiritual reality, any sphere that you have
created in association with the devas or are visiting in association
with the backdrop that the devas have created *for you* in order
to experience that landscape, you simply immerse yourself in it.
Then, when you have fully experienced all that that landscape
has to offer you, you either dissolve the landscape completely or
extract yourself from it (dependent on whether you are an

architect of that particular sphere or a visitor to that particular sphere). It is as simple as that!

And, there is a greater ownership involved on a spiritual level because you own – not the objects that have allowed you to interact with the spheres you are constructing or visiting – *but you own the experience*. **You don't own the artefacts …you own the experience of having interacted with the artefacts.**

And, as above – so below.

That is your reality *spiritually* on Earth, even though you will not perceive it as such. You exist *here* in this physical sphere to interact with others and to interact with the artefacts around you – not to own those people (because we consider people to be our 'possessions' too, do we not?) or those artefacts – but to own the experience of having interacted with them. That is true ownership. That is spiritual ownership. That is angelic ownership. And, you can see it is not 'ownership' as you understand it at all [*laughing*] because (if you will forgive the pun) in entering into these various spheres as an angelic being *you have nothing to lose* …and everything to gain. But, here you cling on to the scenery rather than the experience.

You watch the stage and the theatre rather than absorbing the *meaning* of the play.

You are so tied up with loss …and I suggest to you that you should examine loss regularly in your meditations. You should consider the meaning of the objects around you. That is not to say that you should not enjoy them or make full use of them, but you should not invest all your time in the objects, as society at the moment is doing. You should invest your time in the result of having interacted with the objects, of having played the 'game' and of having moved the 'chess pieces'. Similarly, you should not regard the people who go on ahead of you as being lost. In fact the opposite is true – the people who have gone on ahead of you are 'found', and it is *you* who are 'lost' in the mire of the Fall in this sphere.

And consider that, if you think people always to be lost and out of reach beyond the veil, you are creating an image of the afterlife that is composed of loss and lack. Those vibrations that cluster around you will create problems in your perception of the *actual* afterlife that you will be immersed in when you leave this world. Also consider that when you leave this world, if you leave it with a sense of loss for the people that have gone on ahead of you …you will also have built into yourself a sense of loss of the people who are still on Earth who are part of your remaining family. And so, you will put obstacles in your way with regard to communing with them through their intuition and through love.

Loss is self-perpetuating, like any other concept.

You need to rid yourself of it, and I promise that if you do so miraculous things will happen to you. It will be as though the people you feel you have lost are still around you. You will perceive them almost in physical form. You will be able to listen to them quite naturally, peacefully and easily, and to discuss the challenges in your life with them as though they were still here (which they are because 'here' is a relative term). You will know that they are active in your life, influencing you and offering advice as they are able to do so.

Finally, on the subject of loss, there is a key to happiness on Earth …**and what is the key to happiness on Earth?**

…To lose yourself in the spiritual service of others.

If you do this, you will notice for the periods when you are working to bring the Light to others …the disability doesn't affect you …the perceived lack of funds doesn't affect you …the health issues don't affect you …the relationship issues don't affect you …the worries of life don't affect you because your point of perception is moving from self …self …self …SELF within the heavy matter of a physical body to God-Love sent out on behalf of everyone else …*Light* sent out on behalf of everyone else.

You lose yourself and you find yourself. Lose yourself – lose your sense of loss and you will find greater happiness on a daily basis, and will also be an increasingly strong agent for the Light so that you can help other souls across this globe to lose themselves too.

And, ultimately, there is a positive sense of loss that we all need (and we have spoken in detail about it in this and the other books) – you have to lose *eventually* (sooner, rather than later, please God) the effects of the Fall. You have to lose this core *sense* of having been right *and still being right* that goes back to the point of the Fall. You have to lose it. And, in letting go of this way of life that you feel is so precious, so right and needs to be 'pulled to your bosom' constantly, in losing that you gain your original spiritual perspective.

Don't misunderstand me – I am not for a moment suggesting opting out of life. I am talking about opting out of *this way of life*: resetting the Earth to what it was, resetting your perception to what it was and losing the 'scales' from your eyes. And that is what you should be working towards.

That is the *ultimate loss*, the most triumphant loss because, in losing that attitude and that belief in being right that causes the negative world you see around you, you *regain everything*. You regain your connection with God ...you regain your ability to create and un-create purely and perfectly ...you regain knowledge of your spiritual family ...you regain knowledge of your place in this universe and others ...you regain your connection with billions and billions of angelic beings who are your family ...you regain your total peace of mind because you know that there is no death and no loss.

And that has to be something *worth* a corner of your week, a corner of your day, a corner of your meditation on a regular basis.

Is there a question, please?

David: People often see themselves as losing out when they look at their neighbours, covet what they have and then try to catch up with them, and so it spreads. Does this increase the effect of the Field and drag them further into the Fall?

Joseph: The Field *increasingly* manifests itself as heavy matter and as skewed creation within this sphere. And, yes, the perception of 'not having' and of competition is a distraction and reinforces the vision of material objects as the universal panacea and comforter that brings total happiness to all. So, you have millions of souls investing that skewed ideal into chunks of metal, into pieces of wood, into bricks and mortar. And, because of your need to compete and your belief that you 'have not' you are perceiving an ever *more solid* representation of the Field.

So, yes, that material competition with others solidifies the effects of the Fall and encases the spirit-within in increasing layers of the 'fog' of the illusion. As time goes by and people become more and more materialistic, because of that belief in material things bringing happiness, there is less chance for the angels encased in physical matter to realise who they are.

You have to *literally* 'see through' physical matter. We can actually see through it, and physical matter, *if we choose it to be*, is not there. Physical matter is transparent like water or air. And *you* have to be able to see through physical matter – not in that way – but to see through *its purpose*. And its purpose as it originally was (and still is under layers of masking) is to provide you with a landscape through which to travel – as you travelled in the meditation I gave you earlier [*reference to chapter four*]. It is a landscape through which to travel so that something can be accomplished by you *spiritually*. **That is all physical matter is.**

And you might say: 'The spirits that come to visit us from your sphere – they have physical objects.' And yes, we do, but in a similar way they are a part of the landscape that we choose to travel through, and they are also expressions of ourselves. The objects of art and the style of our houses that we choose (or do not choose) to put around us at any particular time reflect where we are and what we are. There is no 'real estate' in the spiritual realms. There are no estate agents. There is no 'value' (apart from the infinite value of creation) placed upon the objects that we have except that they are externalisations of ourselves.

At any time we can collapse all the constructs around us and exist (as we have said previously) in the no-thing because we know that all those objects, that are very solid when we externalise them, are really, *in reality*, an expression of ourselves ...and nothing more. We do not have to go outside to find the vase or the picture or the house. The vase or the picture or the house – whatever expressions of ourselves we feel we need or simply wish to create – are here inside us.

And it is the same with you.

That will be so difficult for the readers of this book to perhaps understand, but I ask them to meditate on the fact that what they consider to be so real and outside of themselves originates *inside of themselves*. And, if they create the right atmosphere of growth within themselves, then what they wish to have outside of themselves will manifest itself.

They have to be careful, of course, that when they do manifest things outside of themselves (perhaps the wealth or the objects they feel they seek) that they then treat them in the right way. That they appreciate, love and care for them because they are precious, but realise that they *do not own* them and that they are not, as externalised on Earth, a part of themselves.

They are a representation of the vibrations they are putting out, but they are not a part of themselves. You cannot take your car, crush it down and push it into your heart-centre, can you? But that is what people, in effect, are trying to do at this time. They are trying to hold on to and to control everything, when it is the *essence* of the car they have – that has emanated from them in the first place that allows them to have the car. But they worship it. They want the physical manifestation and seek to bring it inwards rather than to bring 'lack of loss' – or creation – outwards into the world.

Do you see that?

David: Yes.

Jane: Could I just add something about the manifestation of abundance because there is a lot of talk about *drawing abundance to oneself*. Although that is OK in the spirit realms and beyond where it doesn't cause a problem, on Earth I don't think you can have mass abundance without damaging the planet because everything that is manufactured is to the detriment of the planet in terms of pollution. So, we can't all have abundance here until we have changed the world by bringing Light into it.

Joseph: There is an inherent flaw in that argument. That argument assumes that you do not have abundance and it is something you have to seek. You are part of all abundance. You are part of God, and God knows nothing about lack. Lack is a creation on Earth.

You must not mistake abundance with manifestation of abundance in the wrong way. The more you celebrate your abundance – the more you have everything that you need without taking anything from anyone or anything else. Do you see that? The abundance is with you now – it is part of what you are.

I understand your argument about pollution, and that is because you regard abundance as being part of the matrix of objects that society has created. You are looking out at present society and seeing the car, the house, the picture, the furniture, the holiday – these things represent abundance to you. So, you have first skewed what you consider to be 'abundance', placed it outside of yourself and then seek it to bring into yourself. That is not abundance.

Abundance is not having to seek for anything because you know that it is already there within you.

The spheres that are not the Earth are abundant. Angelic life is abundant and brings forth further angelic life, but it does not bring forth angelic life through factories that spew out pollution. It does not bring forth angelic life that drives around in cars. You have skewed creation here. It is because you seek (and *have to*, to a certain extent, until you put Light into the world) to externalise all that is really inside of you that you create and take these objects from the Earth. We are back to the sense of loss and back to, 'I have to create this or I will lose out.' It is ultimately the Earth that is losing out.

But, in your meditations *eventually* you find that you are without lack, that you have everything you need and that it is not a 'sin' to regard abundance as something that is part of you. If you concentrate on and affirm your spiritual abundance, then the objects that you manufacture and create on this physical level *as it changes* will not be objects of pollution because you will not need them.

Abundance is also finding the solution to the problems of pollution and mismanagement of the Earth, and you feel at the moment that you do not have them. Those are not secrets. They are not things waiting to be discovered – they are already within you. It is not discovery that they are waiting for …it is being brought out of you that they are waiting for.

And so, the abundant society *spiritually* does not seek to mismanage, does not seek to destroy, does not seek to rape the Earth. The abundant *needs not* because it is abundant. Do you see?

Jane: Yes, I do.

Joseph: In conclusion (and something I didn't touch upon) I want you to consider how you look at situations and feel that you either win or lose in them. If you are playing a game you either win or lose. If you are buying a lottery ticket you either win or lose. If you are going for a job interview you either win or lose. You become used to looking at all aspects of your life in this way **...you either succeed or you fail.**

NO!

...Let me save you a great deal of misery from this point onwards. In any situation you do not win, but neither do you lose. You do not succeed, but neither do you fail. **You simply** *experience.*

It is your approach to every situation ...and the way that you immerse yourself in the situation ...and react to the situation ... and move through the situation ...and out of the situation that is the important thing. It is what you as an angelic being take on board *from* that situation that is important. Not the winning – not the losing.

That does not mean that you should not give wholeheartedly to every situation that you enter into – you should! You should give of your creative best, your mental best, your spiritual best and your moral best in order to affect the situation and allow it to affect you. But neither should you accumulate years of past knowledge of situations by saying: 'I lost here. I failed here. I tried here but wasn't up to it.'

By approaching each situation in this way, thinking that you failed, lost or didn't do what you should have done, you pull yourself deeper into physical matter. You pull yourself deeper into the effects of the Field because you are reinforcing those lower vibrations that are around you all the time.

Not only that, but in creating a sense of having failed or having lost all the time, you open your physical body (which is permeable) to the effects of lower physical vibrations. Is it not true that in an illness situation you feel that your body has failed

116

you, and that you are in a fight that you may win, and continue to be healthy, or may lose and lose your life?

And so, in building into yourself a sense of always losing and of always failing, you pull yourself more into the lower, heavier and skewed vibrations of the Fall, where what is created cannot be completely destroyed – nor can it be created *purely*. So, you immerse yourself in a level of consciousness and materialism in which you are open to attack and to the belief in 'dis-ease', illness and failing health.

So it is important that, on a daily basis, you view your challenges of life as *experience*. Not as something that you approach to succeed or fail in, but experience – a positive thing, and something that enriches your soul, something that prepares you for that time when you take that leap of consciousness away from the Fall and say: 'Enough of this – I will not return. Enough of this – it is illusion. Enough of this – I have to put it right by sending Light into the world.'

Be in love with your life. Be in love with the challenges and situations that come to you. Do not seek to dominate those challenges. Do not seek to have a conclusion to them that you can write up on a score sheet as a 'win' or a 'lose'. Seek to pass through them being the Love that you are, exuding the Love that you can exude and giving out the Light that you are able to give out. And, you will find that life is healthier, you will find that you gravitate towards others of a more angelic disposition and you will find that you are a far greater help to us and to God in changing this world and its citizens back to *what it once was* and *what they once were*.

Does that make sense?

David and Jane: Yes.

Chapter Eight
Your Life is a Projection

Joseph: In the *life review* that follows physical death you are presented with a projection of your life. The analogy I have used in the past is of a theatre, where what has happened during your incarnation is presented as an 'adventure film', as it were, that you view and, in conjunction with your advisors, comment on and assimilate with regard to how you have progressed as a spirit.

The life that you have just lived is a projection, but what I want you to understand today is that **the life you are living** *at this moment* **is also a projection.** It is a 'film' that exists in front of you, behind you, to either side of you, around you and through you ...but it is a *film*, nevertheless.

And where is this projection coming from?

The projection comes from the point within you that is your individual expression of God.

At that point all action and reaction takes place but, in order for you to appreciate it within the confines of the effects of the Fall, it has to be projected *outwards* – as it is on an angelic level but in a less dense state. As an angelic being you know *absolutely* that everything takes place within you. As an angelic being you know *absolutely* that you create and bring forth a series of landscapes and opportunities so that you can interact with those

118

landscapes and opportunities to bring to yourself experience and knowledge. But, the interaction between yourself and the projection actually takes place *within you*.

What I want to explain today is:

That your life is a projection and is not as it seems. It is not taking place outside of yourself *at all* in reality.

I also want to explain that everything comes back to your centre. Everything comes back to finding God, and God is at your centre. God is *within*. That might sound a simple statement with regard to what we have discussed in this book and in other books, but consider how many souls around the Earth expect God to be outside of themselves, expect God to be found through religion, and expect their daily experience and growth to take place outside of themselves.

If you consider that everything, in effect, takes place *within yourself* then you have more power over what you do.

Isn't it true that many, many people around the world feel that they are at the mercy of the forces around them? They are at the mercy of what happens to them during their working day. They are at the mercy of the people they interact with. They are at the mercy of political systems, of so-called spiritual systems and societal systems. They are at the mercy of the elements. They are at the mercy of their level of income. **None of this *ultimately* is true** because the societal system, the political system, the amount of income and the interaction with other people all begin and end *within*.

If I were to strip away your societal system, your political system, your income system, your interaction with others and the fabric of your world – you would still exist, and you would still have within you all the complexities that you think are outside of yourself in your life at this moment. They do not go away when you take away the heavy matter and the trappings of *apparent* creation around you on this level of consciousness.

All the interactions with other people, all the currents and eddies of life that you experience, all the pain and the joy (and everything in-between) are created within you by your attitude towards things and towards others, **and ultimately you are expressing *outside* of yourself what you believe to be going on *inside* of yourself.**

...If that is so, why, then, is life so difficult for so many people ...for *all* people around the Earth?

Well, of course, we have to go back to the Fall and examine the roots of what went wrong. But, we also have to examine why – *if life is a projection* – is it a discordant, skewed and difficult projection for so many souls.

The answer lies at the centre. ...At the centre of your being there is the *true you*, and at the centre of your being there is also *God* ...**and the two are the same thing.**

You are a part of God individualised by illusion in order that you can bring back *experience* to God. Originally, before the Fall, your intent was to bring back experience, coloured and motivated by the colours and motives of your God, but because of the Fall the two volitions have become separated to a greater or lesser extent, depending on the individual in question.

The way to bring harmony and accord into every aspect of your *seemingly exterior* life is to first centre yourself in God. Remembering that you are a spirit and an angelic being, centre that knowledge of being angelic within the centre that is God.

Because of the masking vibration you have placed around yourselves because of the Fall, you have to **constantly realign your angelic intent with your God-intent.** This, as the angel you really are, would not be a problem. This, were you living in another area of the illusion that you have brought forth as angelic beings, would not be a problem as the two are constantly in harmony ...the two are nested within each other and complement each other.

But, because of the effects of the Fall, you have placed a barrier of heavy vibration between your angelic centre and the God-centre. That vibration manifests itself most readily in your exterior life and in the effects on your physical body, your energies and your mental processes, **but it also manifests itself within you**. It has wrapped around your essence *the original intent of the Fall*, which acts as a filter ...as a mask ...as a mesh ...as a veil between yourself and your connection with God.

The point of today's communication is to remind you that your God is *within*. You will not find your God inside a church, but you *will* find your God within the people who are sitting in that church. You will not find your God in the prosperity or power you seek on a physical level, but you *will* find the power within yourself that you need in order to change things. You have a constant companion throughout this projection, this 'film' that is your life ...and that companion is your God ...is what *you are*.

So, in order to seek change in the projection that is your world, you have to first seek change within yourself. You have to, each day and at every twist and turn in your exterior life, refer to the God-within. And you refer to the God-within (as I have said so often) by referring to the heart-centre and emitting an earnest plea and connection between your spirit-centre and your God-centre for guidance, for companionship, for harmony in all your choices and in all your perceptions between yourself as an individualisation of God and God Himself / Itself / Herself – which is also within you.

It is like using a muscle. The muscle is weak at the beginning of training, but during the training sessions it becomes stronger and more resilient. That connecting with God is an exercise you need to undertake daily. It is not a matter of simply going into meditation saying,' I connect with God.' That is an excellent, wonderful and powerful start-point to each day, but there are many, many points in a day. There are thousands of vibrational demands and pulls in various directions on you as an individualisation of God throughout a day. There are many decisions that need to be made throughout each day, and many, many individuals feel alone and powerless in making those decisions, when in truth they are *all-powerful* if they will connect to the God-within.

The God-within is a powerhouse for your life. The God-within is a directional compass for your life. The God-within is a changing force in your life ...a force that enables you to see that life outside of yourself is a projection, that enables you to see through the illusion and enables you, via that connection, to constantly change the illusion.

You are the director of the 'adventure film' that is your life but you do not realise it. You are allowing the film to dictate to you the way in which the adventure unfolds. You have to turn that on its head and begin to direct the 'film' by channelling the God-intent within you out, first into yourself and then out into the illusion.

Life then begins to change, and I know many who read this book will ask: 'If I project Light-energy from the God-centre into the illusion, how can I then change the 'film' because I am only one of a number of actors and actresses within that film?'

First, you have to change your own personal adventure, your own aspect of the 'film'. Then, as you send out Light into the projection, you give others the opportunity to examine from within whether they are at the mercy of their lives or whether, in fact, the life that they are living is alterable, is malleable, is able to be controlled and expanded upon in a positive way from within.

So, you change your projection first by sending Light out into the 'film'. But, in doing so you are also changing the projections of the people around you – the souls, the angels around you – so that they look at their 'film' and find it wanting: 'I thought I could count on this adventure, but now I can't so much. Why does it not fit into my world-view any more? I must do some soul-searching.' *Literally* some soul-searching!

And in searching you find the soul.

And in finding the soul you find that life is a projection.

And in finding that life is a projection you find that you have the power to alter it ...to change it ...to illuminate it ...to regenerate it ...to dispel what went wrong so long ago ...and to dispel *in this current incarnation* your 'demons' – those things that seemingly prey on you.

They prey on you because you think that they are outside of yourself, and the moment you think they are outside of yourself they are drawing on power from the Field. And, the Field wants you to feel that you have demons, wants you to feel that things are wrong so that it can prey on your energies and maintain the status quo and maintain things as they have been since the time of the Fall.

Many people say: 'I'm not looking forward to that life-film – that story of my life projected on to the 'screen' in front of me once I have left the Earth.' The essence of today's communication is that that life-film **is *still* a 'film'**. It is not something ahead of you to be frightened of – to dread. You are projecting that 'film' NOW. All that happens, when you move to the spirit side of life, is that you *review* that 'film'. You see what you have already created and, if you are ready to move on, you realise that you have created it.

You have not just taken part in it but *you have created it* – it is a projection.

All experience is a projection outwards from the centre. As we have said in previous books, the wonderful landscapes that group souls surround themselves with are projections. The wonderful houses and places they choose to live in are projections. The physical universe (as you perceive it from your point of view) is a projection.

Everything is a projection that comes from a volition. The volition initially was from God to experience Himself in greater ways. The volition became *you* – the angelic beings. You, as angelic beings, bring through angelic children and other angelic projections of reality ...of illusion, in actual fact. And then, here you are, trapped in the effects of the Fall – in a projection that is a horror story, a tale of terror and a story with an unhappy ending (or so it seems) ...but it is only a projection.

You are the director and you are also the projectionist. The projection is malleable. It is at its *most* malleable when you go to the point within you that is God – the centre ...when you are God-centred. The world will change when everyone is God-centred again. God-centring on a daily basis brings to you God's perspective. God's perspective is not a wish. God's perspective is not a command. God's perspective simply *IS*. It is a state of harmony. It is a state of perfection in creation. It is a state of safe seeking and safe examination of what experience is.

So, in linking with the God-centre you are not (as many religions would have you believe) coming under the command of a self-righteous God. **You are coming under the influence of what you really are.** And, *what you really are* perceives areas that work harmoniously and areas that don't, and, by examining those areas that don't, gradually leaves those aside to place harmony in their stead.

There, in microcosm, is the process that actually happened in the Fall but became arrested. There was an examination through the angelic children of what they felt would be a harmonious situation but proved too late not to be harmonious. 'Disharmony' really means 'disconnection from God', and such was the extent of the disharmony that they on a conscious level (and to a certain extent on a sub-conscious level) disconnected themselves from God.

God is always seeking harmony. Harmony means communication. Harmony means examination of matter, of purpose, of spirituality in a creative group. Disharmony is the aspect of the universe that is examined but no longer required. If you require harmony in your life and are tired of *dis*-harmony in the interaction of the objects and people around you and in the interaction of yourself with all aspects of this life, then you have to project harmony ...the harmony that you already own as part of God. That harmony exists within you. Change exists within you. Progress exists within you. Ultimately *everything* you see exists within you.

When you move from this life to the spiritual cleansing spheres, it is not that you are leaving this life behind. You are just leaving the projection behind – the mass-projection or beliefs of millions of souls. That is all! The physical body, too, is a projection. It is a heavier construct than you express as an angelic being, but it is a projection. At the end of a film you have been watching, you do not say, 'There is nothing more!' You have enjoyed the film and you then put it away. **And that is all physical death is ...a putting away of this current projection.**

Whilst you are here, there is an opportunity to enhance that projection, to realise that you are in control of the illusion, and to enhance that 'film' so that every other soul around this world will eventually come back to the spiritual realms and realise that they, too, are watching a projection.

It is easier to leave a projection than to leave what you consider to be 'absolute reality', isn't it? And so, if you view this as an illusion and as something that can be taken with you (as you might carry around a film on a disc) then it loses its power over you because you can put it away ready for the *next* projection, and know that when you start the next projection *you* are in charge of it. The landscape will have been placed around you by millions of souls (just as this one has) but you will enter that new 'film' knowing that you are in charge of what happens to you and that you can project what you want to project.

My particular 'film' today is coming to an end and my particular projection into your atmosphere is coming to an end, but I seek earnestly today to get across two things:

The first is that **your reality *is not reality*.** It is not reality and your life that appears to be so complex, so demanding, so time-absorbing and so energy-less is not that at all, and you can go within and change that illusion.

The second thing is that within you and central to you is your connection with God. Not just a *connection* with God – BUT GOD. **Everything that God is exists at your centre *now*.** Not *apart* from you ...not *outside* of you ...AT YOUR CENTRE... accessible, available for communication, available for reconnection and contemplation of the God-perspective NOW!

So, not only are you changing your life and changing society by what you project outwards, you are also already connected with the God that so many religions tell you is waiting in judgement outside of yourself when you leave this life behind.

Recognise your power in very real ways. We have talked about projection of Light and about changing the world. **Recognise how powerful each of you is.** *True power* – not the distortion of power, not the seeking of power, not the manipulation of others, not the disharmony caused to others by your seeking material gain ...but *true* God-power, which is *not* yours and yet *is* yours. [*Laughing*] It is not yours at the level you see yourself as a physical being wielding power believing: 'I have the power of God – I can rule the world.' No! At that level it is not yours.

At the God-level it *is* yours – the level of harmony, of love, of selflessness, of bringing back into the fold those souls who at the moment are seemingly lost. That is the power – that silent, wonderful Light that changes every single situation that needs to be brought back into a state of harmony, and that releases the world from this 'film' that keeps replaying itself through the projector time ...after time ...after time ...after time.

And, once you have changed this 'film' there are other 'films' to be enjoyed around the universe, other experiences and wonderful journeys that you will traverse in the way that you are meant to – harmoniously, with full knowledge of the God at your centre and of you as an angelic being passing through a landscape that only exists in order to bring experience to you and for you to bring experience to God.

Are there questions, please?

Jane: Joseph, could I ask a question about individual projection and the mass events of the illusion? For example, in the First World War how did all those individuals end up in the horror of the trenches? How did their individual projections join together as such a terrible mass projection?

Joseph: The effect of the Fall is the repeating pattern that I have just talked about with regard to the 'film' that keeps running itself through the projector. The energy that preceded the Fall and built up to the point of the Fall is still inherent in your view of the illusion. Subconsciously the angelic children that were involved in the Fall still seek to demonstrate that their way of projection is correct. So, still within you, lies a subconscious desire to see the experiment succeed and to constantly reinvest in a projection which has consciously set you apart, as it were, from God.

Until you have addressed that disconnection from God and that state of disharmony that you originally created – until you project harmony back into the Field ...*the same pattern* will rise up like a peak on a graph and move towards conflict and towards points where matter attempts to destroy and reassert itself, but, because of the effects of the Fall, cannot do so effectively, as it can and does on an angelic level as a result of a conscious desire to bring forth, examine, then dissolve away concepts.

127

And so, because of your investment in the Field rather than in God, you pull yourselves – no matter what your surface intentions are – into conflict **time and again.** Sometimes pockets of conflict centre around some of the principal upholders of the Fall who find themselves, because of their insistence that the Fall experiment was correct, once again incarnated on Earth, seeking and attracting supporters. Sometimes there are minor conflicts. But always, unless halted by a reintroduction of harmony, of balance, those conflicts and minor cataclysms are progressing towards a repeat of the *major cataclysm* that we are trying to prevent at the moment. Do you see that?

Jane: Yes. So the horror of the trenches came about because of our continuing subconscious belief in the Fall experiment, and that belief gives rise to repeating conflicts around the world?

Joseph: Only when the individualisations of God **remember** that they are individualisations of God, and only when their contributions into the projection come from that angelic knowledge and reconnection with God *do the effects of the Fall fall away.* In effect, it is a matter of saying: 'I'm putting away this bad story and becoming part of the greater story that I once was.'

Everything you do is influenced from within, and your principal motives from within colour the projection. You have to have the right basis for sending out energy, and **the right basis is reconnection.** Reconnection then gives you that knowledge (not at head-centre level but at heart-centre level) that re-informs you that you are an angelic being and (whether you are conscious of it or not) that you are part of the Fall. That knowledge then frees you and gives you the ability to channel Light into yourself, into the world, and to reconnect with God so that God-harmony is the projection you are bringing outwards into your life and into the lives of others, rather than a belief in and a maintenance of the current negative illusion.

Does that make sense?

Jane: Yes, it does. Thank you.

Joseph: Another question, please!

Tony: Joseph, I would like to strengthen that 'muscle', as you put it earlier, to work from a heart-connection and to get it as strong as is possible in my lifetime. I know Michael visualises an 'armchair' within his heart that he goes to mentally every day as a meditation. Is that the right way, or are there other methods we can use in order to increase our daily awareness of working through the heart-centre?

Joseph: All of the ways that are given – whether it is Michael's or another visualisation technique – are ways of engaging the mind. The physical mind (as we have said in previous communications) is the 'enemy' and so, in the *initial* stages of attempting to connect with the God-within, the mind has to be given something to do. In the example of the 'armchair' that Michael uses, it places within the mind a 'situation' so the mind sees itself moving from its head-location into its heart-location so that it can it can divorce itself from the sticky aspects of the illusion around it. But *ultimately* (whether you use an 'armchair', whether you go out into the countryside or whether you just sit quietly) it is simply a matter of connecting with the God-within and of *knowing* that, whenever you ask, the call not only 'goes out' (it goes *in*, in actuality) **but is answered.**

Then it is a matter of becoming quiet. It is a matter of abandonment to that *connection-with-God* moment – not seeking a voice, a direction or a specific thing to happen (as the mind will do) but seeking only to commune and to be in harmony with the God-within.

To strengthen that 'muscle', you have to connect with the God-within constantly and allow the God-within to pervade your consciousness and the energy of the God-within to infuse you and direct you. Then, during your waking moments, you will be led by that energy to the signposts and indicators of what you should do in every situation.

So, the armchair is a lesser complexity for the mind, but the armchair or any visualisation is still a complexity – a *necessary* complexity because the mind has to have something to do. It has to say to itself, 'Now I am being taken on a journey to connect with God,' ...when, in effect, all you need to do (without the armchair or any form of visualisation *eventually*) is to sit, is to realise that connection and is to allow that connection to infuse you with the energy that you need and the expectation that your situations in life will be answered, addressed and evolved in a God-centred way.

Does that make sense?

Tony: It does, thank you, Joseph. Just an additional question about regarding our lives as a 'film' ...as a therapist, one of the things I do is to teach people to *disassociate* ...almost as if they are watching their life so they don't get the *feeling experience* it normally involves them in. Is that useful? Does that give people space in order to make that inner connection?

Joseph: Yes. If they embrace that concept fully, it is very useful. Your 'enemy' in this situation is the person's mind and the extent to which they can disassociate themselves from the illusion that you are showing to them. It is a new way of thinking. Remember that souls differ in the extent that they are buried in the illusion of the Fall. Some souls will respond and be able to see aspects of their life as separate from themselves, but others will find it much more difficult and will perhaps not even get past the *suggestion* that they should see their lives as a separate entity.

Strictly speaking, of course, the life is not a separate entity. It is contained within here [*pointing to the heart-centre*]. The life that you want them to see as a projection is an expression of their innermost desires and innermost beliefs. Were you to dig down through each experience *to the core* ...the block right at the centre would be **the effects of the Fall...** nothing more than the effects of the Fall, and a belief in that which is so unshakeable that it colours everything the person does.

So, yes, it is an extremely helpful aid. Anything that gives the mind something to do whilst you are addressing the core problem is an excellent idea. What I am suggesting is that you shouldn't be disheartened if certain people do not appear to respond to that visual imagery. It is dependent on how locked they are into their belief that they and their life – as expressed outside of themselves – are one unit.

You have to look at the triumphs rather than the disappointments. It is not being selfish to nurture those who will elevate themselves more easily and to spend less time with those who will not because, as you know, we are *one organism*. So, when you lift up part of that organism (i.e. the part that *will* respond) the part that *won't yet* respond is also lifted up to *a degree* so the day will come when that part *does* respond.

But, to directly address those who will not respond (and you will know when this is the right thing to do) at times you have to step back and say: 'I am not leaving you to yourself. I am not leaving you. I love you. I am not abandoning you, but I am lifting up those other parts of you that will enable you to eventually see.' Treat it as an experience rather than being a failure or a success. The failure or the success comes from the individual – not from the application of the attempt to elevate them.

Do you see that?

Tony: Thank you so much.

David: Joseph, when people think of changing themselves from within in order to change the world at large, I think a lot of people would probably consider that they couldn't make any difference at all. But, from your analogy of the film – if they are the characters changing themselves and the projection – then the other characters in the script have to respond because, in the idea of it being a play on the stage or screen, if they are saying different lines then the other characters have to respond differently, don't they?

Joseph: That is *absolutely* the point!

In film scripts there are a number of revisions that take place because some characters are perhaps not acting as effectively as they should within the storyline. So, revisions are handed out on different coloured sheets of paper to say, 'This is still the film, but in this act *this* has been changed.'

You are absolutely right and it is essential to say to each individual reading this book that they are an essential, vital and epic character. **No one who reads this book (and no person who doesn't read this book) is a 'supporting player'.** They are all central to the story because they have that power at God-level. You see, if they think they cannot influence the film ... they *cannot* influence the film. They are using that influence to put into the film the fact that they believe that they cannot influence it.

So, they have to understand that *every* choice they make affects the film. Even if they believe they cannot affect it, they maintain the status quo by their belief. Instead they have to believe that what comes from the God-within has absolute power to alter not only their character but the stories of the people around them.

You alter the story of the people around you by saying, 'Good morning'. You alter the story of the people around you by going into a shop and buying something from someone because you have altered the perception of that person for that day. You have been included in their life-story for that day ...and you have to understand that when you bring Light into yourself you infuse Light into their day as well. Maybe (if anyone is having difficulty with this) that is a better way to understand it. You alter everyone's day *simply by* being a presence in that day within that story. So, if you are taking Light and God-harmony with you, you alter the day of any person you connect with and interact with by bringing God-harmony into it. And, if there are enough instances of God-harmony within enough days then that God-harmony becomes a force that people have to examine because it occurs and emerges so often within their days.

And so, yes, *absolutely*, by altering yourself as a character within the film you *inevitably* alter the stories of the people who are around you in that film.

From the analogy of the film we are always looking for *the happy ending for everybody*. And so, on the days that you are discouraged and feel that the Earth is such a terrible, dark and oppressive place with no hope ...*be that hope ...be that Light ...* be that projection into the film. And know that – whether it is now or whether it is in a millennia's time – **there *has to be* a happy ending.** That film – if it plays seemingly forever and ever and ever – will *eventually* come to the end of its story *because of Light*. Then, the original story or 'prequel' will manifest itself and will play on this stage again.

Chapter Nine
Infinity

Joseph: Today I want to talk about a concept that is going to be extremely challenging for me to put into words because I want to speak about your *ultimate destination* – not the spirit cleansing spheres but *Infinity*, and to try and get across to you some of the experience of existing within Infinity.

Of course, you exist within Infinity *now*, but there is only a small portion of your consciousness that realises and can experience this, because there are layers of heavy matter and layers of mental suppression and mental confinement that encase you because of the Fall. In other words, it is difficult enough for us to talk about the spiritual realms and to put those into terms that you can understand – without us talking about a *further* step.

And Infinity, of course, is a further step. Infinity is the stepping out from the cleansing spheres that we have talked about at length in other communications ...a stepping out from those spheres *finally* back into your potential.

'Potential' is an excellent word for Infinity, because in Infinity you are surrounded by, and you exist as and communicate as *potential*. You are connected to the other souls who have escaped into Infinity, but you are also connected to the myriad of souls that were not a part of the Fall-experiment. You are reconnected to *what you are* ...you are reconnected to the *GOD IS* in full consciousness.

In Infinity you are aware of what is, what could be, what might be and what will be.

In Infinity you are integrated with your fellow angelic beings in a way that allows you to experience *almost totally* through their viewpoint on a one-to-one basis. In other words, you can link to one angelic being and experience their viewpoint almost totally ...or you can link to groups of angelic beings and experience their viewpoints almost totally ...or you can experience your viewpoint *totally* ...or you can share your viewpoint almost totally with those around you.

The confines of 'individuality', as you understand it, are broken and the shackles have fallen away. Although you are still *very much* an individual (and need to be an individual to contribute to God's plan) you are, at the same time, able to see the other person's point of view in 'high definition' or in multiple dimensions to experience what they have experienced and *intend to* experience – with all the nuances of their being and particular view on creation.

So, part of the joy of existing within Infinity, freed from the shackles of the Fall, is the joy of sharing and integration, but at the same time experiencing individuality.

Back to 'potential' ...existing in Infinity puts you back in the 'theatre of operations' where *you can create* – you can create individually, you can create as part of a group and you can create as a closer vibration of God. An aspect of your existence in Infinity is *to build* – to examine potential, to examine what could be and to examine how to create worlds.

And then, seeing that those worlds further the plan of God (which is to become more than He/She/It is through your experience) and – having determined that a world is within that plan and would elevate it – that world is then brought into being from the potential by yourself and by a number of others who then, for a period, extricate themselves from other aspects of

Infinity. They invest their perception into the creation of a world, for example, and then bring out from that world the potential of that world to enhance the potential of the angelic beings that have created it.

(And that, of course, in the normal course of things is what should have happened with the Earth before the plan went askew. But, despite recommendations that you should not go ahead with a particular plan, you did so and altered the scheme of things and became in disharmony with the rest of Creation and the rest of Infinity.)

So, a major part of your purpose existing in Infinity is to *create*.

Then, having created, a major part of your existence in Infinity is then to *investigate* ...to investigate the creations that you have put together ...to investigate possibilities ...and to bring out of the potential that you have given form *further potential* by going through experience within the worlds that you have created.

Can you understand that this, then, is an expansion of God? You are expanding the possibilities of God. God is investigating Himself by giving you (as part of Himself) free rein to create so that, by investigating that creation, you can bring out further potential ...further possibilities which are then also a part of God. So, Infinity can be seen as an ever-evolving, advancing and expanding area of potential – and, yet, 'area' is the wrong word because Infinity knows no bounds.

Consider that sentence: *Infinity knows no bounds.*

As you exist on Earth at the moment, you are bound by the physical body, as you see it. In spiritual reality you are not but, from your viewpoint locked into the effects of the Fall, there are boundaries to your physical body. There are then boundaries to the area that you live in – there are boundaries to the planet, as you understand it, and there are boundaries to space.

Not so in Infinity – INFINITY KNOWS NO BOUNDS.

From your viewpoint on Earth, you believe that everything has a beginning and an ending and that there is a journey to everything from point 'A' to point 'B'. That is the way you see things in a linear scale. That does not apply to Infinity. Infinity knows no bounds as you are beyond the concept of anything having a beginning or an ending.

Infinity *is* because Infinity is one of the highest expressions of God-energy, so Infinity simply IS. You cannot put Infinity in a box. You cannot apply the physical laws of physics to Infinity. Infinity is boundless ...and one of the most important things I have to say to you today is that phrase: **Infinity is boundless.**

Let us look at the steps ...if Infinity is boundless and you have within you – because you are a part of God – infinite capability then *you* **are boundless.** Doesn't it follow, if you are part of Infinity, if you are part of God and if you are part of that rich, boundless zone of creative potential *now* then all those aspects and capabilities are yours *now*?

I say this to you to open your eyes in a different way to the potential and the ability you have now to change things. There is no difference *except in perception* between an angelic being in Infinity creating part of a new world and you now (sitting or lying as you read this book) creating a new world. And, you do it in exactly the same way now as you do in Infinity ...you bring it forth by seeing the potential ...by imagining the possibility ... and, therefore, drawing towards yourself the creative elements and molecules that you need to bring that potential into reality.

Do you see then that all we have said thus far about bringing Light into the world to change your world, to escape the effects of the Fall and to recreate your world – everything we have said is there, not as a platitude, *but as a reality*, if only you will accept it, if only you will draw on your creative ability as an angelic being who is part of Infinity to change things?

You draw on the entire potential of God when you harmonise with God. And, I have said before that one person channelling the Light is the equal of thousands who do not believe in and turn away from the Light. Understand that if you connect to the God-within you connect to the angelic host, you connect to the potential of Infinity and, in the measure that you believe things to be true and in the measure that you see that Light going out into the world, *you change the world*.

I have spoken about Infinity today because the world stands on the edge, because *your* world is cutting itself off from that infinite potential and is withdrawing into a bubble of discontent and disharmony. Further and further it is investing in materiality. It is investing in technology. It is investing in the physical body as being the person that stands before you – when it is not. It is investing in skewed science. It is investing in a set of physical laws that are based on mistaken premises. It is investing in the glorification of humanity as a physical organism.

WRONG!

Wrong ...the world is teetering on the edge. The world needs people like you, who are reading this book, to reach out into Infinity. You will not be able to grasp, until you emerge into Infinity once again, the *actual experience* of Infinity but nevertheless you can grasp the potential of Infinity, you can grasp the power of Infinity, you can grasp the power of connecting to angelic beings and you can channel that power into this world to move it away from its material dream (as we have often said) before it is too late.

To go back to Infinity ...do *I* exist in Infinity? No (as I have explained previously) I do not *yet*, and [*smiling*] I have made the analogy of there being a 'hatch' in the ceiling of the highest spiritual sphere that can be opened, at a time when we have evolved and divested ourselves of the effects of the Fall, and we can step out into Infinity. I suppose that is a good analogy for the change in consciousness that comes to us as we progress through the spiritual cleansing spheres.

If I am not existing in Infinity, by what right do I tell you about Infinity?

I tell you about Infinity because, as I have progressed through the spiritual cleansing spheres and my brothers and sisters have elevated with me, we have spent part of our time (as progressing souls do) contemplating and connecting with Infinity. And, the first time you do it, it is *literally* a mind-blowing experience because it blows away from the mind all the concepts that it has held to be true up to that point. **A mind-blowing experience!**

But then it becomes something that, little by little, we can add to our concepts of how creation works and how we operate as beings. Little by little we acclimatise to the concept of Infinity. Just as today through this chapter, hopefully, I can allow you to connect with Infinity in that you will be able, in a more confident way, to channel Light into your world, we gradually become more and more aware of the aspects of Infinity within ourselves, and we feel *a pull* towards that state of being ...which is our natural state of being. It is the angelic state we were in before the Fall took place.

And so, two things happen as we progress through the spiritual spheres: gradually we become more aware of the potential and the experience of being in an infinite state but also, as we do that, *there is a pull that begins.* So, we find ourselves in beautiful spheres existing as part of a group soul with people we love and appreciate. We have created wonderful landscapes to exist in and we are in a state of bliss ...but *there is still that pull.*

And that pull grows stronger ...that pull elevates us ...makes us continue to strive for more ...and strive for more ...so that we elevate ourselves from one spiritual sphere to the next ...higher ...and higher ...and higher ...until the time comes when we can 'resist' (if that is the right word) Infinity no longer. And, that change of mind and change of state happens that takes us beyond that 'hatch'. It isn't a physical hatch – it is an analogy for a final change of mind that liberates us into being so much greater than we are at the moment.

As I have also explained in the past, we have visitors who, in effect, come through the 'hatch' to advise us and to illustrate to us aspects of what is waiting for us. So, my authority in talking to you about Infinity today is based on my own advancing and expanding experience of that state, but also on illustrations that are brought to us by beautiful, shining beings who are *our equals* – because when we step out into that infinite landscape that is what we will become *once again*.

It is not even a matter of *becoming*. It is a matter of re-realisation …of realising that that is where we began this journey (which also began with the Fall) and that is what we will become again so that we can go out into other physical journeys, having created the landscape of those physical journeys in order to experience and to bring the *implications* of that experience and the greater potential back to our God.

And, we do this infinitely. Having taken away the terms of 'beginning' and 'end' – there is only Infinity. There is only an endless opening …and blossoming …and blossoming …and blossoming of experience and growth.

The angelic hosts that exist in Infinity actually enhance themselves by the creative experiences they undertake. Having enhanced themselves, they enhance the group. Always there is this growth of experience – a similar growth of experience to that which you undergo as individuals from physical birth to physical death. There is growth, there is change, there is evolution and, here on Earth, it is a microscopic expression of what happens in Infinity. The growth that you should and do experience (either consciously or subconsciously) whilst you are here is a *tiny* representation of what happens to you infinitely in an infinite state.

[*Laughing*] ...How to explain the landscape of Infinity? ... There are multiple dimensions and multiple expressions of being and experience. You limit certain of them in order to go through those experiences. In other words, you draw away from the greater Infinity into a 'lesser-Infinity', as it were, to experience what you have created. But then you can, at any time, put yourself back into the greater Infinity and draw to yourself other aspects of experience ...infinite experiences within infinite experiences. So, you can concentrate on certain areas ...you can concentrate on colour ...you can concentrate on form ...you can concentrate on sound ...you can concentrate on a *blend* of these things depending on what you wish to experience and bring forth from Infinity.

Where is Infinity going?

No-where – because there is no 'place' in Infinity. The places are within your 'hearts', if you will, that you create, you bring towards yourself, you travel through and then you disperse – adding to Infinity the experience of having done so.

Where is God evolving to?

...This is a question that I cannot *fully* answer. It is not a matter of destination. You are not going anywhere – God is not going anywhere because 'anywhere' implies physicality. **But the experience, as we understand it, is the *key*.**

Experience is the key to understanding God and to understanding yourself – in that, at any point in your existence, you can look at what is happening through and around you, and understand that it is experience and that that experience is important. Without experience you do not grow. Without experience you do not bring the effects of you having grown, back to God. So, God is (in 'physical' terms) expanding, and you are the architects of that expansion ...*and that is what God wants*.

At the end of this chapter, it must seem a *huge* journey back from a liberated state (and I hope that in some measure I have brought you to a liberated state today) ...back down ...back down ...back down to your physical and mental existence. But, remember that physical and mental existence, which may seem small compared to what we have just discussed, is a trap that you placed yourself in. It is not a difficult thing to escape that trap – it is only difficult in the measure that you refuse to accept your greater potential.

By examining this chapter and what has been said about potential – your individual potential and, therefore, global potential through you – I hope that you will begin to *contemplate* Infinity at the very least. There are people around your world [*smiling*] who will not even contemplate the next step – will not even contemplate life after death and the cleansing spheres. I am asking you to take that step beyond the cleansing spheres now ...in feeling ...in whichever way you wish to imagine it (based in the description I have given you) in order to bring through more power, more potential, more Light to illuminate and change things for the better **because Light, of course, is one of the *major* attributes of Infinity ...the manipulation of Light into form.**

And, the manipulation of Light into form is something that each of you reading this book is an expert at. It is something that each of you around the world is an expert at because each of you is an angelic being, is an angelic child, is part of the angelic host. Contemplate that, add it to your concept of how to bring Light into this world, *and you will change things.*

You *must* change things.

Infinity awaits you. Infinity is within you – not the confinement that you have placed yourselves in, not the misery, not the suffering, not the small view you have placed yourselves in, but Infinity ...infinite potential ...infinite creation ...infinite joy ... infinite companionship ...infinite understanding ...infinite growth. **Which do you choose?**

Please ask questions whilst there is still the energy to answer them.

David: Joseph, what is the connection between potential and Light? I know people that read the books have some trouble in understanding 'the wielding of Light' – would it be beneficial to them to think of the wielding of *potential*?

Joseph: Let us see how we can better describe this. As an analogy, Light is a 'sea of potential'. It is a 'block of marble' with you as the sculptor. What will you make from that block? You can make anything, but you have to manipulate the marble and [*laughing*] have to, as some sculptors say, *release the form within* the marble to reveal the sculpture. So, the Light is the marble (perhaps marble seems too hard a surface as an analogy, but I suppose it is as good as any) and you are the sculptor. You look at the marble and you see within it whatever you want to see.

What do you want to see? Are you going to create a statue of a man? Are you going to create an abstract? Are you going to create a geometric shape? And then you set about with the tools at hand – your ability to wield the Light – and you shape the marble into whatever you want it to be.

Potential is *what can be …what might be*. And you need to use your ability *to dream* to see the better world that you want. When you do that you activate and draw towards you the aspects *within* the 'marble' that you want to *bring out of* it. It is simply a matter of applying – through Light – that vision of a better world over the current vision of the world. You can draw the Light towards you as a beam from a 'sea of Light' and then see it in your imagination being generated out from your heart into areas of the world that you want to change. See those areas illuminated. See them becoming lighter. See the greyness falling away from them. You can beam this Light into people's hearts and minds and into hostile situations …always seeing the good …always seeing your vision of what you would like the world to be *in the name of God*.

So, you are creating as you create as an angelic being but within the confines of the Fall. You are no less limited except by your perception. You are the sculptor. You draw from that sea of Light what you want to produce from it. And, not only can you draw from the sea of Light, but you can *project* it. You can project it to the people and areas of the world you want to surround with Light and you change them. You bring out a new 'sculpture' and a new vision.

Is that any easier?

David: Yes, thank you.

Joseph: It is a difficult subject – not to use but to describe. You are pulling that material from an infinite source of materials, and then shaping it in line with your vision for a better world, for better conditions for people, for God-conditions for people, for a restoration back to the state of things before the Fall. You are the manipulator. You are the sculptor. You draw on that infinite supply of Light and you mould it …you sculpt it …you apply it …you direct it …*and it changes things*.

Jane: Joseph, in Infinity where a group is examining potential, do they always examine a *new* aspect of potential or do lots of groups go through the same thing (similar to artists on Earth, for example, who like combining certain colours) as it is just the *experience* that they need to go through?

Joseph: That is an interesting aspect and one that is very true. You have art movements on Earth with a number of individuals who wish to paint or sculpt in a certain way, and so it is in the angelic host. Each angelic being is different and, at any point in their existence, each angelic being has various aspects of creation that they apply more than others. And, just as souls gravitate together into soul groups, they gravitate towards angelic beings of similar interest.

So, yes, there are individual creative efforts and group efforts but potential is infinite. If you examine your thoughts on any single day, you will see them switch around so many times to present you with different scenarios. Would you agree with that?

Jane: Yes.

Joseph: In just the confines of one twenty-four hour period your thoughts present you with *so many* different scenarios – thousands of scenarios sometimes. You can multiply that by Infinity with regard to potential, and [*smiling*] you can see that as an angelic being you will never get bored. You will never run out of things to do. You will never run out of new projects.

One of the points of the chapter is that – as you bring forth new projects and examine them – those new projects offer *more potential*, and so [*laughing*] there is expansion ...and expansion ...and expansion ...and expansion. That is one of the joys of being – in that there is no 'time' and yet 'all the time in the world' or 'all the time in forever' to examine, experience and enjoy as many different potentials as you wish to – both in angelic form and, moving through those potentials, in physical form.

Does that answer your question?

Jane: Yes. Also, does it mean that you are within your own soul group but can join other groups for specific projects?

Joseph: Yes. One of the joys of being is to see reflections of yourself in 'the other' and potentials of yourself that you have not yet examined. So, you exist within your soul group, you exist with your close associates and loved ones, but you are always 'opening the door' to new friends and new associates. And, you can, not only listen to their experiences, *you can experience their experiences* whilst still retaining your individuality. You can add their experiences to your own, if you so wish. Do you understand?

Jane: It sounds lovely, yes.

Joseph: I cannot describe to you the bliss and the joy of Infinity. You are so restricted here that it is almost impossible to convey the bliss that we feel in the cleansing spheres, and that bliss is nothing compared to the bliss that we are ascending to in Infinity.

Is there a final question?

Tony: What you say about potential having no limits and no boundaries is interesting – it makes me think that perhaps we are actually limiting ourselves by our thinking.

Joseph: That is exactly what happens …and limiting yourself is part of the potential because you are limiting yourself *perfectly*. You are drawing out of the potential of creation a *perfect limitation*. Do you see that?

So, there is no aspect of your existence on a physical level that is not infused with that potential. It is simply that the potential you choose is limiting; the potential you choose is confining; the potential you choose is blinkered.

What we are attempting to do is to remove those blinkers and say: 'Daily, you choose from potential and you create, but it is *just as easy* to create something positive rather than something negative …something expansive rather than something confining …something beautiful rather than something ugly …something giving rather than something that is taking from the world all the time.'

It is always a matter of choice. Whatever you choose to concentrate on you *create* – you bring out of that 'sea of potential' and you create. You might not see it today, but you will see it tomorrow because it is stored in your subconscious requests of what you wish to create. And you, as a spiritual being, work on that series of requests, and transfer potential into form.

We have to educate people into drawing from the potential *the right kind* of *experience* for them. From our evolved point of view (those words are not meant with arrogance – remember that we were involved in the Fall too) we see people daily choosing illness, pain, restriction, sorrow and misery, and they are pulling these things as an *expectation* out of potential. They expect them!

If you expect them, you draw them to you. It is a request. You are sending a request, like filling in a form, to say, 'I want misery. I want illness. I want lack. I want challenge in a bad way,' … because that is what you expect. You bring it towards you and you manifest it and, because you are limited by the effects of the Fall, you believe in the manifestation to the extent that it then delivers to you *more of the same.*

We are attempting to free you. It is freedom that we bring. One of the great messages of the communications is *freedom* … freedom from a way of existing that is limiting, that is painful, that is sorrowful, that is injurious to you. It doesn't have to be this way.

It really, really *doesn't.*

Chapter Ten
Energy

Joseph: I wish to talk today about *energy*. Much is said about energy – particularly in spiritual areas ...*'energies are high'* ... *'energies are low' ...'I need to send energy to this person' ...'I need to receive energy from that person'*.

But what is energy?

Energy is the means by which potential is given form.

Energy in its purest sense began with God ...began with 'first there was the word' and the 'word' was expressed by movement against the *wish* to express the 'word'.

Energy is volition and desire given form – nothing more than that!

[*Long pause*]

[*Addressing the circle*] I apologise for the problems in communication this morning. I wish to settle a little closer to Michael and to move into his vibration, so if you will send out your *energy* to me that will enable me to do so. There has been a great deal for Michael to think about over the past few days, and there hasn't been the opportunity to clear his mind as it needs to be cleared so that I can make an effective connection.

ENERGY

[Resuming the communication]

...So, I wish this morning to talk about *energy* and to explain the meaning of 'energy' and, as with many statements I have made in the past, this statement will seem strange to you [*laughing*] because energy, as you understand it, does not exist.

Energy does not exist.

Energy does not exist because it is not a tangible thing. It is given expression as a tangible thing but its basis is **within the heart of God,** where it emanates from. God, at the point at which He wished to examine Himself, gave 'the word', as it were ... expressed the desire to examine Himself through the individualisation of Himself.

And so, having fragmented Himself into millions and billions of angelic viewpoints, He then had to enable those viewpoints to express themselves and to grow and to change. The method by which He did this was to give His angelic children the ability to give form to their desire, volition and potential.

So, in your true expression as an angelic being, whatever you desire exists within you first as potential ...exists within the individualisation that you are, and exists within the individualisation of the other angelic children around you. And so, you have an individual potential – that which *you* wish to examine – and you have the potential and wishes of the other angelic children around you that you can either link into or stay separate from *according to your wishes and potential.*

The minute that you consider something the wish envelops you, the wish emanates from you and the wish is expressed by yourself and by the other angelic children who wish to participate in that particular adventure.

Inner desire then becomes an outer creative force drawing on the greater creative force of God. It is as though you are making a telephone call to God saying: 'I wish *such-and-such* to be delivered to me, so can you see that that happens, please?' And, the instant that that 'call' is made from within you the consequences of that 'call' begin to form around you. They form around you by you drawing on your potential as God *within* you and by the potential of God *outside* of yourself ...plus the potential of God *within* and *outside* the angelic children who wish to participate in your view of what you wish to create.

Energy is a manipulation of the creative forces of God.

And you might say: 'Well, the Earth is surrounded by and penetrated by certain energies.' ...And, yes, it is, but all those energies originated in the heart of God and in your core as an angelic being, and you drew those energies out and gave them form simply *by wishing it to be so*.

Having said that energy does not exist, we have to apply a better name to it than simply 'energy' ...and the better name I wish to apply to it is 'volition'.

Energy is volition.

Energy is the bringing forth of that which you wish.

God originally brought *you* forth as volition. He brought you forth by wishing to have various points within Himself by which He could reflect back experience to make Himself greater than he was before He created the individualisations. So, God's volition became the angelic children. Your volition as an angel becomes 'reality' around you as you experience it. Your volition as an angel also becomes further angelic children, as we have discussed in a previous book [*reference to the book on the Fall*].

What I wish to get to the core of today is that the complex energy fields you see around yourself and around the Earth are simply *solidified volition* because of the effects of the Fall on the angelic children who were trapped within the Fall. What I wish

150

to express today is the *simplicity* with which you can change things if you so desire. It is simply a matter of realising that what appears to be solid and what appears to be force within your matrix of reality is, in fact, simply *volition that you maintain by still wishing it to be so.*

If you wish to change things (and we have talked in all the other books about Light and the effect of Light on reality) you simply have to change the volition. The volition then becomes charged in a different way, and that different way manifests itself according to the acceptance of the changed volition within yourself and within the angelic children who are trapped within the effects of the Fall.

So, by changing your volition – the way that you *wish* to see things – you put a different charge into the fields around you. You sweep away the previous energy fields and you replace them with your changed volition.

It seems to be a complex thing to get across this morning, but to condense it into a nutshell, it is simply this ...what you perceive as energy is wish, desire or dream manifest around you. In sending out energy, your start-point is to change your volition. Do you want a better world? ...If the answer is *yes*, then you see and desire that better world, and in seeing and desiring that better world you change the energy-field around you that is compliant to your desires, and will restructure itself into what you wish to perceive.

Energy (as you understand it when you talk about 'healing energies', 'negative energies', 'positive energies') is, therefore, in reality, an interpenetrating field of desires *and nothing more.* Because you are creative beings, those desires are *eventually* given form around you, and coalesce into experience that you can travel through. (In fact they are given form on a spiritual level from the moment you perceive them – in the measure that you believe them to be true.)

But, the energy itself is a pattern of dreaming ...a pattern of desires ...a pattern of wishes ...a pattern of expectations that you live within. It is not the exchange of heat, or cold, or healing rays, or thought. **It is simply a matrix of dream.**

The pattern of volition around the Earth at the moment is to remain subconsciously in the state you were in when you decided that you would speed up matter at the point of the Fall. You are still dreaming that dream subconsciously as one united angelic force, as one section of the angelic host. On a subconscious level, you are dreaming that this is the way that you wish things to be.

What I want you to understand is that it is so simple to uncreate what you created. It is simply a matter of changing that wish, and then sending that wish out into the pattern of dreams that you call the Earth ...into the pattern of dreams that you call society ...into the pattern of dreams that you call reality ...into the negativity that you have created for millennia. It is simply a matter of changing volition and of accepting that the volition has changed. Then you draw from the potential of the dreams around you a different view, a different scene, a different landscape ...**but created by you.**

The reason I am talking about energy today is to strip back the complexity of approaching a different world and the worry of how you will accomplish it – to take away that worry completely and to say that *it is as simple as wanting something else ... desiring something else ...seeing something else ...and accepting something else.*

We have talked in the other books about sending out healing Light, but actually you send it out to those points you wish to change simply by changing your volition. If you change your volition, you become *a different dream* within the dream, and your dreams become different to the dreams that the other angelic children are still dreaming. The dreams around you have an attractive force, so when you change the dream within you, it resonates with and links with the similar dreams of those angelic children who also wish to change around the globe. And so, you penetrate the 'dream' that is the Earth at the moment with a different dream, which gathers momentum and strength, and grows according to the number of angelic children who believe and *wish* the new dream.

I hope this answers the questions that come up sometimes from readers of the *Joseph books* who say, 'How can I change the world? Am I being effective?'

Of course you are being effective!

Each angelic child has *equal* ability to change things.

Each angelic child has the equal ability to change things, and so you are not up against an *immovable* force because that force is just a dream. It is simply a matter of using your angelic creative power to create a new dream, and that dream then links up with all those others who are creating a new dream until the new dream becomes dominant.

What would you like to dream?

What would you like to dream? If I suggested that you dreamt, for example, that coming towards you was an elephant, you would instantly say to me, 'Joseph, that's impossible. That won't happen!' ...And there is the answer to why it won't happen because you have not dreamt that it *could* happen. You have not dreamt that it *will* happen. You do not believe in the dream that I have just set in front of you. I tell you, if you were to *truly* believe and dream that an elephant was coming towards you – **it would come towards you.** It could not do otherwise. You would draw it towards yourself from the greater dream of the angelic children via the force of your belief.

I would like you to test what I am saying. I would like you to imagine something that you want – not that you *need* – but that you *want* to see manifest around you, and I would like you to believe that that object or circumstance or potential will come into your life …*is* in your life …is yours …is around you because you are one of God's dreamers and it cannot be otherwise. Then, **I guarantee** that in the measure you believe in that dream (and that is the important aspect – *in the measure that you believe*) that object or circumstance or potential will manifest, arrive and be around you. It cannot be otherwise.

It cannot be otherwise!

But, such is the strength of the negative field of dreams around you that you say, 'That can't be!' because you are believing and investing in the negativity around you rather than your angelic potential.

The instant that you dream of something you draw towards yourself *whatever it is you dream of,* and you draw *yourself* towards *it perfectly* dependent on the degree to which you believe it is so.

Do you see the liberation in that examination of how you function as angelic beings? Because once you have proven to yourself that whatever you dream becomes reality around you, you can then dream whatever it is that you need and whatever it is that you want.

Do you want perfect health? It is yours as a birthright anyway as an individualisation of God but you have forgotten it. You can remember it; you can draw it towards yourself. If you want healing and perfection for others, then it is enough that you accept that perfection for them on their behalf, and you contribute to their breaking out of the dream by doing that.

You will not always have success because, remember that if you are trying to heal someone else, that person has the right to decide what they will bring out of the dream within and around themselves. But, simply by seeing them in a perfect way, you will send to that person an *overview of perfection* that will give them the opportunity (in their 'off-duty' moments when they are not investing in the Field totally) to tune into it and to recognise their own perfection and to become healed.

This, in effect, is what I am asking you to do with the world: to see the world in the way that you want it to be, and to see specific areas of the world that need healing as being healed ... as being Light-filled ...as having changed. And then you give the souls living within those areas of the world the opportunity in their 'off-duty' moments (when they are not investing in the violence, negativity or sickness of the dream) to actually link with your view of what they are. And, that view resonates deep within them because that is what they *truly* are ...joyful, creative beings – not destroying through violence and negativity, but creating in joy.

And so, by your pinpointing of areas to target with your belief in a better world, you help to change and illuminate it. You help to draw up those souls in the moments when they are not investing in a totally physical and mental view of how things are on Earth. You help to lift them up to what they once were so that they too can share in your dream. Then the dream becomes one and has changed from the negativity, upset and violence that you see today ...into the *original* dream, which is a creative dream of God for His fragments to go out and dream further creative dreams, and to bring back to Him the experience of having examined and gone through those creative dreams.

But, you will say on an everyday level: 'If I heat a kettle of water then the molecules become agitated and the water boils. If I go to the South Pole I have to wear certain clothing or I will freeze to death. There is an expression of energy that is hot in one example and cold in the other. There are all sorts of devices that we have on Earth that give out energy. We need energy internally to keep functioning on a physical level.' ...And, I have to reduce all that down to:

Yes, but only because you believe it is so.

Around the Earth you believe that if you put energy through a kettle it will become hot, and you have various physical equations that explain why this happens. There are various processes that happen on a physical level, but they are only on a physical level, and that physical level is the illusion that you have created in order to walk through the experience to take that knowledge back to God.

The simple act of a kettle boiling water happens because at one point you believed communally that it was so. If each of you around the world truly believed that you could heat your kettle without electricity *simply by thinking about it* ...it would be so.

What I am trying to say is that the energy systems that you believe through physics, through education and through trial and error on a physical level are not so. They are not fixed and immovable, and behind them is a principle of dreaming it as being so. If you wanted the kettle to boil water but the water to be frozen, you could do it in the measure that you believed it and in the measure that the angelic force trapped within the confines of the Fall believed it.

You have the potential to alter what you see as the 'laws of physics' because they only exist because you have invested belief in their structure on a physical level. Behind that physical level is dream ...is belief ...is volition ...is potential given form. And the potential that you have given form at the moment is the effects of the Fall.

I am not suggesting for a moment that you try to sit in front of your kettle and make it express frozen water. What I am trying to do is deconstruct your view of *what is* and of energy systems working in a certain way. Do you see that by believing that things work in a certain, immovable way you solidify them and, therefore, throw away further opportunities and other ways of looking at things? Through the effects of the Fall and through the solidification of certain systems that you believe in, you have thrown away your potential to change things.

You have thrown away that potential as an angel to say: 'I have created this world in conjunction with my brothers and sisters, but I am not totally harmonious with this certain aspect of it. So, in conjunction with them, I will withdraw this certain aspect of it simply by deconstructing it. Then I will create a better form that I will examine. I say it is a 'better form' but if I find it to be lacking in some way, I will deconstruct that and create an *even better* form.'

Do you see how you limit yourself by believing that your energy systems and the way things work on Earth are absolute? **They are not absolute.** They are only absolute for the amount of time that you believe in them as being absolute. You look at the formula and then apply it to the way things work. That is the wrong way round ...you have to apply the energy and then evaluate how that energy is affecting things.

But then, having looked at the energy and evaluated its effect on things, you have to be aware that that 'formula' for expressing how the action of the dream reacts on certain objects *is not absolute*. It is something that is perhaps absolute from twelve o'clock until half past twelve but if, at half past twelve, you decide to change things then that dream, expressed as what you would call 'energy', is able to be changed by you examining another way to do things.

...*Another way to do things* ...and that is something we are trying to give you – *the original way to do things*. If you don't like the 'system' at the moment – the energies that are interacting to produce your world – then you have to look behind those energies, go back to the original volition (which was the volition of the Fall to accelerate matter and the way that things were created) and you have to change that volition. You have to change the dream.

You are the source of the energy in your life. You are not at the whim of every ebb and flow of physical and mental energy. You are the instigator of that energy. You and every other person around the Earth are the instigators of the form of the Earth, of the way that the Earth works and of the way that you express and feel energies around you. And those energies are simply expressions of the dreams that you have had, maintain and believe to be true.

You have to dream a *different* dream.

Does what I am saying make sense?

Jane: Yes, absolutely.

Joseph: At this point, can we then examine this aspect further by inviting questions on the subject?

Tony: As we dream that dream and believe that belief, can that come into conflict with another person's dream and another person's belief?

Joseph: It is not a matter of conflict, it is a matter of which is the dominant dream and which is the dream that is invested in by the majority of souls. You are dreaming your dream initially as an individual, and it is your *right* to dream whatever dream you wish to dream. But, in creating a positive matrix and in creating an emanation of a better world, you are linking in two ways with the original intent for this planet. You are linking with the God-within and with the angelic host outside of this particular sphere ...but you also resonating and linking with all those others who wish there to be a better, brighter, more positive, more spiritual, pain-free, violence-free world. You link *automatically* with them because they are of the same resonance and vibration. It doesn't matter whether you know them or even know that they are there – you will link with them.

That dream of a restored world then gathers impetus, then gathers gravity, then gathers strength and becomes a Light that subconsciously (and, for some, consciously) can be seen and felt within the dream of the Earth. At that point those other souls who have not yet joined the dream are given the opportunity and choice, minute by minute, to become attracted to it and to become aware of it. They are presented with a different view and, as an angelic being on a subconscious level, they will look at that different view and evaluate it. It won't happen initially through the physical mind; it won't happen through the physical body – it happens on an angelic level at the core of the soul.

And there comes a point when that soul can either continue along its path surrounding itself with its dream of negativity, or can say, 'I like the new dream.' At that point they begin to dream the more positive dream and they join with all the other dreamers of the positive dream to change things.

It is not coercion. It is not force. It is not a bending of will. It is a presentation of a different way of living that is available for examination. The only way that that presentation can gather force is by becoming more luminous and more attractive than the dream that souls are dreaming at the moment. And at that point they become aware of it, and at that point they have a choice to either invest in that dream or to continue with their dream of negativity, violence, disease and lack.

Does that make sense?

Tony: Thank you, Joseph, yes.

Jane: A question asked by one or two readers is whether evil exists as a separate force ...or is it just a volition for destruction and chaos?

Joseph: An interesting question because *at its core* what you would describe as 'evil' is a subconscious realisation that you cannot strip down the Earth to what it was. Having created this scenario as a result of the Fall, you know on a subconscious level that you should by right, as an angelic being, be able to take away dreams simply by spiritual thought and by saying, 'I have had enough of this!'

You create and destroy by using the God-given tools within you as an angelic being that are skewed because of the effects of the Fall. And so, subconsciously you wish to take away that which you do not understand, that which seems to be in opposition to your happiness and to a harmonious way of living for you.

And, because you cannot understand it on a conscious level, this in many souls expresses itself as a wish to take away anything that is seen as a threat ...whether it be a person ...or an aspect of society ...or a belief that is held by a number of souls. So, driven from the subconscious to the conscious, is a desire to remove that which is not in harmony with the soul – and that (I hope) is an explanation of what evil really is.

At its core, evil is simply a realisation that you have got it wrong and need to get it right *expressed badly* ...expressed in the physical and the mental as a fear of 'that which is not of you'. So, you attempt to destroy it (as you would do as an angelic being but not through violence – you would destroy it by removing the dream of it and replacing it with a better dream). You cannot do that encased in physical matter locked within the effects of the Fall. So, from the subconscious to the conscious, it is projected as a skewed and distorted view of the need to eliminate 'that which is not of you' at this moment – whatever your dominant thoughts are.

And so, to a lesser or a greater extent, you can see it around the world. In its lightest form, you can see it in the gossip that takes place in the need to be superior to those that you see to be in opposition to you. In its heaviest and most upsetting form, it erupts as violence in its need to take away 'that which is not of you' through actual physical destruction of property or of people ...to eliminate that which you cannot understand.

Evil at its core is a *recognition* that you have got things wrong, but then you perpetuate the state of having got things wrong by reacting to that which you wish to take away from yourself *in the wrong way*.

Is that understandable?

Jane: Yes, that's great. With people who are sadistic, is that a kind of skewed aspect of the joy of creation …a warping of that creative joy through an enjoyment of destruction?

Joseph: It is an imbalance of the two aspects of creativity that are within each of us. In the normal course of things (as we have explained) you create a scenario and you examine that scenario. And, having taken from that scenario that which you need in order to further your understanding or experience, and having transmitted that back to God, you then collapse that scenario. You use equally the powers of positivity and negativity that lie within you as tools.

So, it is a distortion of the one aspect. It is a cry for help: 'Why are things wrong? How can I make them right?' It is a blind attempt to make things right in the wrong way. The soul is saying: 'I am unhappy. I am inharmonious and, therefore, I target these aspects of life …this person …that building …this society as being the reason why I am inharmonious. If I attack those aspects of life that I think are to blame I can restore harmony to myself.'

These actions and desires are going on at angelic level, and what we need to make people aware of is the fact that their expression of violence is, in reality, a need to understand that there is something wrong that can be put right by peaceful means …by recognising what they are …by recognising the God within them …by recognising that they are an angelic being …by recognising what first happened to make things as they are around the Earth …and by recognising that their violence will never solve anything. Or, I should say, *will never make them feel harmonious*, will never make them feel that they fit in, will never make them feel that they are part of the world and part of everyone else.

They have to recognise that imbalance within themselves and tackle that in a peaceful way by changing the dream rather than projecting it outwards as a need to eliminate those aspects that they see – either mentally or subconsciously – as being the reason for their unhappiness. They are inharmonious because of the effects of the Fall, and there needs to be more inward-seeking and recognition, which is why the angelic children who are trying to fight against the effects of the Fall should be dreaming a different dream to surround those violent souls with Light and with a different way of looking at things so that eventually they can make that choice.

It is back to the readers and those who recognise that they are angelic beings continuing to dream the different dream and pouring out sufficient Light into the mass-dream so that *literally* the souls, who are existing through violence and negativity, can see that Light, can feel the Light within them, can examine what they are doing and come to the right spiritual conclusions.

Is that sufficient?

Jane: Thank you very much.

David: I suppose, Joseph, everything you have said this morning just emphasises how change has to start with each of us individually and not to expect other people to put it right for us. The dream has to change within us first and then we can take part in a greater dream.

Joseph: It is strange, isn't it, that the ability to change and to seek change is seen by so many souls as the greatest threat to how they live. They know that they are living in the wrong way, that they are unhappy, that they are inharmonious, and yet they see change as one of those threats that is very often tackled in violent ways by such souls.

The ability to change, to dream and to create is the greatest miracle of God that has been bestowed on His angelic children. You have been given as your 'toy box' anything you desire – *absolutely anything* – simply by believing it is yours, by visualising it and, therefore, drawing it out of yourself and manifesting it around yourself. That is a wonderful, wonderful, *wonderful* thing …'I don't want to be ill – I am no longer ill.' … 'I don't want to be poor – I am no longer poor.' …'I don't want to live in a violent world – I no longer live in a violent world.' … 'I am making the difference because I am drawing on my angelic power and on the God-power within me. It is wonderful – I can do whatever I want. I am a wonderful, miraculous, creative being who can dream up and examine as many scenarios as I like.'

…And we are fearful of that and wish (as you have said) for someone else to take responsibility!

The way to retrieve that responsibility from other people is to recognise the God-power within us as the *wonderful* gift that it is. It is not a burden to create – it is a gift, a pleasure and a joy. It is not a burden to take control of your own life – it is a joy that brings you back in line with the God that you are.

So, I would say to the readers that they have to consider what has just been examined and that placing themselves in charge of their own dream is a joy. It is their birthright as an angelic being. It is recognition of limitless, infinite potential. Why would you then wish to allow others to dictate how that potential manifests itself? It is a wondrous, wondrous joy that should be taught to your children. Your children are creative beings, who can and will create a better world if you instruct them in the right way. It is a wonderful, wonderful thing to say to anybody: 'Here is the greatest gift that has ever been bestowed on a sentient being – **you have the ability to create whatever you can imagine.**'

But, of course, what the soul has to fight against is the fact that it has been coming back for millennia into a shared dream that believes *quite the opposite* …believes that it should always be someone else with the power …believes that it is subject to the ravages of time …and to violence …and to lack …and to disease that is everywhere just waiting to pounce on each soul. The soul has to combat millennia of thinking that the society it sees is 'reality' and that it can do nothing to change it.

There has to be a total turnaround of thinking to say: 'Of course I can change it – I created it in the first place. Of course, I can affect it – I am a dreamer as part of the host of dreamers that created the world we see now. If I don't like it, I must change it. Absolutely right, I must take *personal* responsibility. I must love myself enough to allow myself to remember who I am and what I am capable of. And, in loving myself enough to realise that …I then realise that I love everyone else enough to want to bring *them* to the point where they can remember too. And I do that by changing my personal dream and by putting out into the greater dream a different vision of what I want, of what God wants and what the world *needs* at this time.'

Chapter Eleven
Imagination and Creation

Joseph: What can you imagine? What are you able to conjure up in your mind's eye? I would like to look in greater depth at *imagination* this morning, and to reveal that imagination is your greatest ally in creating the world that you want to live in and producing around you the effects that you wish to produce.

Imagination is a *tool*, and it is difficult to convince people on Earth of this. Many times we hear you say, 'Well, I have no imagination.' Actually [*laughing*] *you have nothing but imagination* because, as part of the God-seed that you are, there is the facility to create ...**and the filter through which you create is your imagination.** You are using your imagination at various times during the day to conjure up images of what you believe to be true about yourself in a future state and images of what you imagine the conclusions to certain situations around you will be.

Is it not true that you see a news story – a hostage situation, for example, and you say to each other: 'That is going to go very badly. The hostages are going to be killed. They will never get out of that'? That to you is simply a statement (as you view it with your physical mind) but, in actuality, it is an activation of your imagination because you are concluding the situation in a visualisation. No matter how flatly you do that – whether you see those hostages coming to the end of their lives or whether you simply have a feeling that it is going to go badly for them –

you are, to a lesser or greater extent, contributing to that situation via your imagination.

You see, whatever you conceive of ...whether it is a trip to buy the morning newspaper ...whether it is flowers that you are going to plant in your garden ...whether it is a beautiful house that you want to live in ...whether it is a grave illness that you suspect you will contract at some point in your life because the trends seem to be pushing you in that direction ...*whatever it is* that you conceive of, the filter of your imagination begins to construct and pull it towards you from the creative molecules around you.

Imagination is the first stage in giving form to that which you desire.

You have to remember that you are an angelic being and, as such, you *created* in the past before the effects of the Fall entrapped you. In conjunction with other angelic beings you created worlds, you created landscapes and you created opportunities through which you could pass with a view to evolving spiritually and bringing greater possibilities and greater *understanding* of possibilities to your God.

You are an angelic being. You have not lost that facility and that filter is built into you. It is just that you have forgotten its potency and have forgotten that whatever you conceive of is not just an 'image on a screen'. On a physical level, from your limited view of the subject, you can liken imagination to an 'image on a screen', can't you? You can liken it to a viewing of something that you have conjured up which is placed on the 'inner screen' of your mind and is nothing more than that. ...Well, it is so much more than that *in spiritual reality* because that mental 'screen' is the first stage of *creating* that which you project onto it.

You cannot project onto that screen in isolation. In other words, you cannot project anything onto that screen without giving it power. Anything and everything that you project onto that screen – in the measure that you invest thought, hope and accepted conclusion into it – draws towards you the effects of what you have placed upon the screen.

So if, for example, you say to yourself, 'I would like a wonderful car,' [*laughing*] you have, pushing through the filter, your desire to have a wonderful car and you can see it on the screen. And you will say: 'Well, Joseph, I have wanted this wonderful car for twenty years, but I have never been able to place myself in the driving seat.' ...And the reason that you do not find yourself in the driving seat is that into the filter *you are also placing your belief that you cannot get the car.*

So, you create the car on the screen through the filter of the imagination, and you bring the molecules towards you that would eventually manifest the car within your personal experience, but, unfortunately, there is always a mix of believed conclusion in whatever you project upon that screen. So, you have already placed on a separate screen the image of the car as being *beyond* your grasp and, together with the placing of the car on the screen and the thought, 'I would love that car,' is the belief from your subconscious (and from your conscious mind at times) that you cannot have the car ...and the belief that you cannot have the car is stronger than the belief that you can.

So, ironically, you may bring to yourself pictures of the car that come through your letterbox, or you may bring to yourself a test drive in the car through some opportunity via a newspaper or by some other means, but, you do not actually bring to yourself the car because, through the filter of your imagination, you believe that you cannot have it.

The reason I am talking about imagination is because, as you know, the theme to all the books we have brought through so far is *the need to change the world*, and to change the world successfully you have to first see that world in your mind's eye ...in your heart's eye ...in your spiritual eye. But, along with seeing that world projected up there on your inner screen, **you**

have to believe in what you are seeing, and I have to first convince you that whatever you believe in and whatever you project onto that inner screen, you draw towards yourself *in the measure that you believe in it.*

Whatever you believe in and believe to be a conclusion with regard to world events (such as the hostage situation in the example I gave earlier) or with regard to the conclusion of financial affairs and political situations, you also *contribute* to ...you contribute to those perceived conclusions becoming reality.

So, in your meditative times, it is vitally important that you see the world as you want it to be *spiritually,* and that you have a clear view of a world where people are united ...a world where there is no lack ...a world where there is no illness ...a world where there is acceptance of and understanding of the God-within ...a world where there is acceptance of and understanding of the oneness of all peoples around the Earth ...a world where there is an end to pollution.

You have to see that world during your meditative times, but you also have to *believe* in that world. You have to believe in what you are seeing on your mental screen as being reality, as being not a film, not a hope, but *an inevitable conclusion* because you absolutely believe in it *with all your heart.*

That is how you will change the world. That is what happens when you send Light into the world. You send Light through that filter of your imagination to nations, to individuals, to situations, and you believe ...*thank you, Father – thank you, God...* **that the conclusion you wish to see manifest *is* manifest.** In doing that you draw towards that situation the changes that need to take place in order for your perceived conclusion (*which you believe in one hundred per cent*) to actually manifest itself.

And it is no use saying: 'Joseph, no matter what you say, I have no imagination.' If you had no imagination [*laughing*] you would not perceive yourself as a physical being. If you had no imagination you would not have a house around you, a car to drive, the illusion of distance, the illusion of space, the illusion of hunger, the illusion of poverty, the illusion of riches ...all these are things that you believe in through the filter of your imagination and create around yourself.

You may say, 'Well, I don't think visually.' Maybe you do not think visually on a physical level, but on a spiritual level it is the *only* way that you can think. The spirit is not interested in numbers. The spirit is not interested in words. The spirit is not interested in recording images of reality as text. **You create as an angelic being in visual terms by seeing whatever it is that you wish to create.** And so, you *have* an imagination. Perhaps the filter of your mental faculties and the way in which you approach things on a physical level makes you feel that you have little creative ability ...*but that is not so.*

And, however you want to project onto that mental screen ... perhaps you choose to see it (because that is the way your mind works) in terms of the written word, in a sentence that says: 'The world is now perfect. The world is now harmonious. We have escaped the effects of the Fall'...no matter how you do it, whether it is in words or images, you attract *similar molecules* to yourself which you then project out as a beam of Light into the areas where you want that change to take place. **You direct it – you direct your imagination.**

And I tell each of you that, freed from the constraints of the Fall, you are able to create worlds in conjunction with your heavenly brothers and sisters – with the angelic host. *You create worlds!* You created worlds before the effects of the Fall ...**and you create worlds *now*.**

You are no different except in imagining the way that things are. When you create poverty, when you create lack, when you create and perceive illness, when you create and perceive a world that is less than perfect, *ironically you do it perfectly* because you are using your God-given filter of the imagination to construct perfect situations ...perfectly *wrong* situations but, nevertheless, perfect situations.

So, it is a matter of understanding, first of all, that whatever you perceive to be true and extrapolate upon to imagine to be true tomorrow brings those recognition molecules towards yourself and outwards to the situation that you perceive to work in such a manner. In other words, your thoughts need to be guarded and monitored *very carefully* and, in all situations, you need to attempt to see a positive, spiritual and harmonious outcome. Then you project into those situations the right conclusion and the right creative power.

In fact, if you sit and look at your news stories correctly, you can contribute to peaceful situations coming out of violent happenings. You can contribute to restorative situations of health coming to those that are reported as being gravely ill. You can contribute shelter, food, warmth and love to those who are seemingly in situations where those things have been taken away from them by nature, by politics or by factions.

You can and *do* do it all the time, but you do it *negatively*. You can now see the problem with investing negatively in stories in your newspapers and through your media because you are already being stimulated via your imagination with the bias in those stories. You are being persuaded to create (not just to think but to *create* because you cannot think without creating) in a negative way by the spin that has been put onto world situations through the way that the media reports them.

What you have to do is rise above that, and if a situation looks dire then move away from it and, through your imagination, project *the opposite* of the dire aspects of that situation that you are being told to create. Filter in a different set of values and a different approach ...a spiritual approach ...a positive approach, and have the 'superhuman' strength (because you *are* superhuman in your reality as a creative angelic being) to say:

'No! This is not the way it is. *I* decide. **God decides the way it is** ...and *the way it is* is different ...*the way it is* is positive ...*the way it is* is constructive, is peaceful, is harmonious, and I believe *utterly* in that.'

You cannot stop being a creative being.

You cannot live without imagination.

If you understand that then it is a simply a matter of applying a different set of values to the filter of your imagination in order to promote and create the world that we are trying to get you back to.

In living in this way and exercising this ability to create a better world in your imagination, you may find that original ideas creep into your imagination at points during the day – ideas of who you were and of your time spent as an angelic being before the Fall. You may find that you 'feel' your ability to create worlds ...to create wonderful situations ...to create harmony ...to create colour ...to create Light. You will perhaps have flashes of a *deeper sense* as you strive for a better world.

And, yes, they are your imagination ...and, no, they are *not* your imagination.

Remember the imagination is a projector, a filter and an attractor of states of being – so it *is* your imagination in that you are able to sense what you were. But, it *is not* your imagination in that, when you sense these glimpses of a different kind of life and a different kind of power, they come from *what you actually are*. As you access that level of understanding, you can then project that understanding into your creations and imaginings on behalf of yourself, on behalf of the world and on behalf of your brothers and sisters.

You cannot un-imagine. You cannot wipe something out by taking it away or by subtracting from it. What you have to do is *superimpose* a different way, a better way, a more refined way onto the situations that you have already imagined individually and collectively.

Is it not true that you evolve *spiritually* throughout your life if you approach things in the right way from the spirit? If you look back at the situations that you no longer invest in, you evolve not by subtracting those situations from your life but by halting the imagination that you put into them and the expectation of gratification or connection that you have with those situations. You stop pushing imagination into them, you stop attracting those situations and you superimpose a new way of being.

Your evolution as a spirit to get you back to the point at which you recognise that you are an angelic creative being and do not need to return to the Earth is a series of superimpositions ... reviewing certain situations that you have invested in and imagined were right for you then superimposing a more refined situation on top of them ...and investing in that until such time as you superimpose a *further* situation on top of that which is even more refined than the one that you are letting go of.

This is what you have to do in order to change your personal world and to change the planet back to the state it was in before the Fall. You are rubbing out by superimposition – not by trying to subtract. You are, at points, saying: 'This situation is no longer of use to me or to anyone else. I see a better situation and I superimpose it through my imagination as a more refined way of existence, creation and perception.' And that is the way that you change things.

I hope that this chapter adds to your understanding of just how powerful you are when you spread Light from the heart-centre into your own lives, the lives of your loved ones and the situations around the world. Just how powerful Light is and just how powerful *you* are when you send that Light specifically and see it changing situations because, when you see it changing situations, you are drawing those winds of change to the situations through the filter of your imagination. You are actually setting up a different set of values.

I know on occasion people have asked: 'How can I send the Light out and is it doing anything? Is it changing anything?' **Of course it is!** If you are sending Light out into the world, then you are superimposing a more refined way of life onto the existing way of life of society. If you doubt that you are effective or if you invest in society as it is, then, through your imagination, you are reinforcing and continuing to solidify society and situations as they are at the moment.

Guard and examine your thoughts carefully and, if you find yourself daydreaming negatively or second-guessing the conclusion to a personal or global situation in a negative way, lift yourself out of that. Use the God-given filter of your imagination to superimpose upon your own thoughts of a negative conclusion a positive, harmonious and spiritual one. And daily, simply by thinking in this different way, you are changing things and negating the effects of the Fall by superimposing a better way of life for you all.

I must conclude by going back to the beginning, to the time of your creation as an individualisation of God, who said to you: 'I have imagined you. You are a part of Me. I have imagined you. I first had to think of you as being separate, yet not separate; individual, yet a part of the Whole. I imagined you into being and you are part of Me. And, having imagined you into being, I said to you: Go forth. Go out and imagine into being things on My behalf. Go out and create as I have created you – knowing that within you is that ability to imagine and bring forth whatever you want because you are part of Me.'

That is how God functions – by thinking possibilities into being through His heart, through His centre. That is how *you* function because you are part of God, and you bring forth possibilities through your heart. You are part of God and operate as God. You operated as God before you came here, before you encased yourselves in heavier matter, and you operate as God within that heavier matter but you believe the heavier matter to be the status quo.

It is time for a Light approach to living ...for bringing Light into every aspect of your life, into every aspect of your projections, and then you will return this Earth and yourselves so much more quickly to what it and you were originally destined to be in God's imagination.

Are there questions, please?

Jane: Joseph, could I ask something about drawing things to us through our imagination? I know what you have said is true from my own experience, but is there also the case where the opposite happens? For example, you have the hypochondriac who always imagines that they are gravely ill *but never are* and, on the other hand, the heavy smoker who arrogantly thinks, 'I will never get cancer – it will never happen to me,' *but it does*. Sometimes *the opposite* appears to happen to what people have imagined...

Joseph: You have to remember that you are in a matrix of thought and what has been said to you from the beginning of these books is that there will come (and we are working towards) a point at which there is enough change through Light put into the world that *everything* changes. You do not exist in isolation. You cannot exist in isolation because you are a part of everyone else and you are a part of the Earth that you originally created.

And so there are evaluations happening with your perception of yourself all the time, and into every life there is a mix of beliefs that affect the imagination of the individual. For example, the individual may consider himself or herself to be totally healthy but then is chipped away at by media reports on health ...is chipped away at by the mistaken perceptions of doctors and nurses ...is chipped away at by relatives and friends saying that surely something is going to happen to this person. And eventually (but not in all cases) the weight of 'evidence' through the imagination of others becomes heavier than the imagination of the individual.

What you have to strive for, in knowing how you operate, is a point of view that refuses to allow other values to permeate it. For example, you believe that you are one hundred per cent healthy, you believe that the world is one hundred per cent changed and bathed in Light and you believe that you are one hundred per cent powerful in doing God's work, and – through your inner strength and meditations – you do not allow in any other view of how things should be for you and your ability to project into the world at large.

Do you see that?

Jane: Yes, I do. Thank you.

Tony: Further to that question, at the Sanctuary I work with people who have mental issues, such as depression and anxiety, and they get so locked into 'I'm not worthy' that they can't imagine a positive future because of some inner voice telling them that there is no point imagining it because they don't deserve it. One of the ways we work is by suggesting something we call a 'well-formed outcome', where we try to get them to imagine what it would be like if they could have it. But there does seem to be this other factor always sitting on their shoulder that says, 'You are not worthy!' And I wondered whether inner silence, through which the imagination could then be more positive, would be a good thing to teach?

Joseph: First of all, the thing that sits on their shoulder is also the imagination. When they regard themselves as not worthy, they activate the imagination and the imagination *reinforces* that sense of being not worthy. No one stops imagining – they do not say: 'I am not worthy so I am not capable of imagining.' They imagine that they are not worthy, but then they reinforce that view of being not worthy – either on a conscious or subconscious level – indefinitely, and it is that, as you say, that needs to be broken.

Various soul groups sit to work with individuals on Earth for healing purposes. What they do in attempting to elevate the person is to, in effect, 'sit around them' and each of those souls project an image of perfection towards the person to the point that that image of the person as being perfect (or certainly improved) is more powerful than the less-than-perfect image the person has of themselves ...and at that point things begin to change.

It is difficult if you have someone so entrenched, but I would repeat what we have said in earlier conversations about the need to elevate those who can be elevated first. That is not a selection process; it is not saying: 'This person is worthier than that person.' It is knowing (because you are part of the same organism) that, as you elevate those who are susceptible to positive change, you also lift up those who find it difficult to let go of their concept of themselves as, for example, being not worthy.

In other words, you elevate as many people as you can, which adds, through their changed consciousness, a greater sense of well-being and harmony to the mass consciousness ...which then makes it possible for the next 'layer' of people to be elevated to the point where they are out of the doldrums and that negative view of themselves through their imagination. Do you see what I am trying to get across?

It is always a matter of elevating those who are ready – not because you are ignoring or turning your back on those who are not yet ready – quite the opposite! It is a spiritual principle: you elevate those who are ready and, in elevating them, you give them power to elevate more people. And, as they join together in the belief in a better way of living and a more effective way of healing, they draw up from 'beneath' them (as it were) those who up until this point have not been able to elevate their own thoughts.

Here is a different way of thinking: at its core you have to treat 'healing' as healing *everybody* and if you are healing one person *here* and one person *there* you have to understand that that person *here* and that person *there* is actually an aspect (perhaps a 'bruised toe' or a 'broken knee') of the whole organism. So, you are not healing anyone in isolation. You are healing the *whole* situation. You are healing the effects of the Fall, and you are healing everyone by healing that aspect of everyone that you see as an individual before you.

So, you have to bear that in mind when you are healing that you never heal in isolation. You are placing back into the whole a revised vision of health through the person you see as an individual and have lifted up.

Does that make sense?

Tony: Thank you so much.

Joseph: We are low on power. Is there a final question?

David: Briefly, Joseph, could you just give us some ideas about using the imagination? Is it something you should constantly do, or do you imagine and then let go so that you are not constantly tweaking and changing – making things unable to manifest?

Joseph: That is an excellent point. An excellent point! If I can expand on that …you cannot help but use the imagination. The imagination is your true method of thinking. If you were to see your angelic counterparts communicating with each other, you would see them communicating through Light, through colour, through images and through projections from the imagination. That is communication as it takes place on a spiritual level, and it is also communication as it takes place on an individual level within the effects of the Fall.

You cannot help but imagine. It is how you perpetuate your vision of yourself and how you perpetuate your vision of others. It is difficult because, if you want a certain outcome, you revisit that outcome at various points, and it is like scratching an itch or returning to a wound to see if it has healed. But of course, as you say, in doing so you can lessen its effect because the mere fact that you revisit a situation to see how it is doing implies that you are not satisfied with how it is doing. It implies that there is a negative aspect that you have to revisit to see if that negative aspect has re-established itself.

In a perfect creative situation you see a situation through the filter of your imagination as being perfect, and then you get on with other tasks in your life. Of course, it is difficult to do this because it is not just *you* who will feel that the situation might fail. There is also the projection of everyone else's imagination suggesting that things are different to the way that you have projected them through your imagination.

And so *gratitude* is a great sustainer of the imagination and a great empowerer of the situations that you have placed into the collective consciousness through your imagination. For example, you may feel yourself pulled back to a situation in slight doubt but then say: 'Thank you, Father, this is as I have left it. I don't need to worry about it. I put it back into the ether and I know that everything is fine ...that You are working through it ...that You are perfect ...that I am perfect ...and, therefore, the outcome is perfect.' By doing this you push away the irritations and the stings and bites of the surrounding thoughts from society.

So, yes, to be most effective in imagination it is best to visit your projection just once, to see it as perfect just once and to release it.

However, because you are living in a society that is skewed and because you are part of every other person you meet (or don't meet) throughout your life, their thoughts work to chip away at your belief in your vision and your determination that your vision is true. So, at points where *inevitably* the world gets in a little and tries to shake your absolute belief in what you are constructing, **you can give thanks.** You can give thanks to the creative power of the angelic host, the universe and the God-within that your vision is stronger and more perfect than the visions of those around you who want to maintain the effects of the Fall.

Chapter Twelve
Memory

Joseph: I want to talk today about *memory*, and to examine memory in a different way ...to look at what memory really is and how memory can be changed to your advantage in your striving to alter yourself to absorb more Light and to alter this world to absorb more Light and to reset itself.

I haven't given you a statement that is a shocking one for some time, so here is a statement that, hopefully, will shock you:

Memory does not exist.

That is a classic Joseph line: *memory does not exist!* What you perceive as 'memory' is, in fact, a delving into the 'showcase of experience' that you have placed around yourself since you became individualised from God.

That 'showcase of experience' does not end. This minute that you are experiencing at the moment, which appears to shift into the past as you view it, *does not end*. It is simply you moving into a new area of experience that allows the experience that you have already experienced to become (from your point of view) the 'past'. But, because everything is alive, **the experiences that you move through are also alive.** Therefore, when you move past a point of experience, because that experience is linked to you and because that experience is alive, whenever you move *back* into that experience you are not experiencing memory, you are experiencing something that is as alive and vital as it was (in relative terms) the first time you visited it.

Is it not true that most people visit memory (as they perceive it) in one of two ways? They either go 'back' to an experience because it is joyful for them or because it is painful for them. They revisit a part of their infinite experience but, because it is alive, that part of their infinite experience *still has the same effect* on the point of experience that the person is going through *now* as it did when they first experienced it. In other words, when you revisit a point in your experience that you call 'memory', you take out of that *living* experience *the experience once again*.

If there is no past and no future but simply a moving tableau of experience and you perceive different experiences in order to grow and take those experiences back to God ...**then all experience is NOW.**

All experience is *now*, which from a spiritual point of view, takes away your traditional view of memory. A memory is nothing more than selecting from your present experience of everything (that you can wander through as an evolving soul) a point that you choose to experience again. That experience is filtered through the physical brain where there is a numbing effect because you expect to 'move on'. You expect to go into today ...into tomorrow ...into next week ...into next month, and, because of that expectation, the full impact of revisiting your memory or points of experience is, to some extent, lost to you.

Through the physical mind you sample certain aspects of revisiting the experience, but what does actually impact on you *totally* is the circumstance of that point of experience. If it was a sad experience, that sadness is *totally* revisited. If it was a happy experience, that happiness is *totally* revisited. And so, by selecting your memories, you are having an effect on your physical body and physical mind because of the strength of the points of experience that you choose to revisit. Therefore, from an earthly point of view, the logical conclusion would be that memory is dangerous.

Memory is *not* dangerous.

Revisiting the experience is not dangerous. What *is* dangerous is revisiting the experience without learning from the opportunities that that experience has brought to you. In other words, you should be revisiting the experience without the experience pulling you down or causing you pain.

And, in order to do that, there is a *vital* tool that I introduced you to many years ago and have asked you to use throughout all of your experiences and projections into this world and into your own perceived futures ...and that tool is **Light.**

When you visit an experience that you call 'a memory' you are back in that experience, and here is another statement: **you are still able to *influence* that experience if you know how to do it.** So, what you should do with memories – with those points of experience you choose to revisit and relive from the ETERNAL NOW – is to take in with you something that can change the negative aspects of that experience ...and the thing you can take in to change the negative aspects of that experience is Light.

We choose to revisit those memories that cause us harm and we revisit them *habitually* almost. We choose to revisit them because there is almost a comfort in revisiting something that we are familiar with. But what you have to avoid is the jagged angles of those experiences harming you, and re-energising them and taking them forward into new experiences with you as a viewpoint of the world.

As you revisit experiences, and in your meditation, as you seek out those memories, bathe them in Light – bathe *every aspect* of those memories in Light. As an example, if you had an altercation with someone and revisit that point of your experience, you bathe yourself in Light, you bathe the person you had an altercation with in Light and you bathe the memory of the location, the feelings and every aspect of that memory in Light. You then take away the *negative* aspects of it.

So, in a very real way, you can rewrite your personal history, because your personal history, when bathed in Light, becomes a more acceptable history. It becomes a place that you can still visit, yes, but in bathing those memories in Light, you see their *true* purpose. You illuminate their true purpose and you realise that their true purpose was to teach you something, to teach the other person something, and for everyone involved to gain something out of the experience. You 'switch the light on' so that you do not visit your memories in darkness. You visit them in Light and, in visiting them in Light, you do not change the experience but you change its impact on you at *this present point* in your experience. So, you can safely visit memories without loading yourself with the negative aspects of those memories and carrying those negative aspects forwards.

Having spoken about personal memory, *there is a greater implication* in what I have said to you this morning because, at the core of each human soul, there is that point of experience that came when you decided you would speed up matter and immerse yourself in the effects of the Fall.

There is a *core* memory.

That core memory manifests itself *constantly* through each soul on a subconscious level, and, in the way that consciously revisiting negative memories actually attaches those wounding aspects of the experience to you once more, similarly you *subconsciously* revisit that point at which you decided you were right to speed up matter. And you carry through, as a subconscious thread into your present experience, the conviction – based on that original experience – **that you are *still* right.** In doing that you then (to a lesser or greater extent) attract towards yourself daily the consequences of harmonising with the 'correctness' in your subconscious mind of having taken that decision.

So, all the consequences of plunging yourself into the effects of the Fall revisit you. Instead of progressing as a being of Light and building new constructs and harmonies through your thoughts, you pull towards you *more of the effects* of that core decision being carried with you into the present.

Therefore, the same Light-tool needs to be employed by you in going back along that 'corridor of experience' to the core decision, and your core decision (whether you are consciously aware of it or not) needs to be bathed in Light.

You need to 'reach' back down that corridor to the point at which you said: 'Yes, this is what we are going to do. This is what *I* am going to do. This is a better way to create'. You need to bathe that decision in Light so that eventually, through the amount of Light you have brought back to that point, you can see on a subconscious and conscious level …that that wasn't the way to go …that that wasn't to your advantage …that that was a decision that has influenced *every* individual and societal decision that has been made since that point. You therefore transmute your original decision by bathing it in Light to the point where you say: 'I was wrong!' [*Laughing*] …'**I was wrong!**'

And, at the point that you illuminate that decision with enough Light, you free yourself from it. The circumstances of your life become more positive, more constructive and more harmonious, and you find that you are an even greater asset in the change that must come to everyone …the change back to the realisation that you are part of the angelic host …the change back to a wonderful, bountiful world that no one harms …the change back to a time when you look at each person around you, recognise that they are an angel and that you cannot hate them – you can only love and harmonise with them because they are part of you.

So, we have quite a complex notion today. We have spoken in the other books about transmitting Light into the world, transmitting Light into yourself, transmitting Light into your present and transmitting Light into your vision of a harmonious future. And that is what you must at all costs do – that is a vital, *vital* tool for change ...and it is the *only* tool for change that will work ultimately.

But what I am suggesting today is that you can also move around your infinite corridor of experience. You can move backwards and forwards along it, and at certain points you can use that Light to change – not your memories – but your perception of the effect that those memories have had on you, which will make you healthier and more receptive to spiritual inspiration.

Then, having done that, you can also reach back ...and back ...and back to that point at which you changed the world by changing your mind about how you create, and bathe that experience in Light, too, in order to free yourself from the subconscious imperative of *still being right* that you colour all of your todays and tomorrows with. And that subconscious imperative (as we know from the earlier books) individually and collectively creates and maintains the world that you *don't* want. By moving along the corridor of your experiences and flooding those experiences with God-Light, you can free yourself from your decision made at the point of the Fall, and so create the world that you *do* want now and tomorrow.

So we are, in effect, today examining a transmission of Light into the *present* ...a transmission of Light, through visualisation, into the *future* ...and now a transmission of Light into the *past* – into the past that is still the 'present' and still has the energy and power to transmute the individual and collective decision to plunge yourselves into the effects of the Fall.

The ultimate transmission of Light along the corridor of memory is not just to work to release yourself consciously and subconsciously from that decision to speed up matter, but to send out Light to all the other angelic children trapped within the effects of the Fall.

Imagine: as you move backwards (and 'backwards' is only a relative term) to that point at which as an angelic child you decided to speed up matter and change the world, if you infuse that point with sufficient Light to relinquish that decision ...see that decision as being skewed and let it go... whilst you are meditating at that point *surely* you are also reaching that point in the experience of *all the other angelic children*. And so, by working to release yourself, via Light emitted down that corridor of memory, you also work to change, lift and illuminate the experiences of others.

So, we are talking about changing people's minds today but also about revisiting the point at which they mistakenly created the Fall, and giving them enough Light to examine the decision for themselves in their own memories and to change that decision at its source.

You can now see the power of Light working on many different dimensions ...to change the construct you see around you at present ...to change the construct you want in your 'future' (as you perceive it from your linear perspective) ...but also to bring Light back into that *original decision* so that you can free yourself from it and, by working to bring Light into the darkness, can free those other souls who have not yet reached the point that you have reached in wielding Light and remembering your angelic heritage.

Finally, at the end of each day, it is an excellent idea to view the situations that have happened to you as 'experience' ... experience that is always accessible and will never be lost. But, before placing that experience into your corridor of memory, send your Light into the events of the day so that you don't have to revisit that experience to alter and amend it later. Place it within that corridor of memory *already liberated by Light* and seen simply as an experience, an opportunity to grow and a harmonious state of events, so that when you revisit it in memory it uplifts you and doesn't pull you down.

Work always with the Light to infuse yesterday, today, tomorrow, yourself, others and the world. Work to liberate the world at the point of the Fall and to put Light into that decision so that, at this point in your experience and everyone else's experience, this thought comes to mind: 'Maybe there is a different way to do things.'

...*Maybe there is a different way to do things*... because if you illuminate the core decision of your fellow angelic children to such an extent that they see subconsciously (and it will only be subconsciously at first) that that decision was wrong, then you place into their subconscious *in this present timescale* a flexibility that hitherto wasn't there. It gives them an ability to look at the way they react to society, to politics, to violence, to sexual matters, to finances, to the world, to nature, and to have the strength to say: 'There is another way! I can look at things another way. I might not know what that way is yet, but I sense it and I have the strength from somewhere to say *what so many people on Earth can never say*, "I WAS WRONG." I am wrong. My decision is wrong. How can I put together decisions that are *right* ...right for me ...right for my fellow men and women ...right for the world ...how can I do that?'

And then inspiration floods in because we can subconsciously add the weight of our conviction to theirs to show them a better way and to suggest that they seek out more understanding of themselves spiritually, which opens up the floodgates to an influx of Light that changes things.

I feel elated that I have attempted and managed (I hope) to bring through a very complex subject, which has weighed heavily on me [*laughing*] and I invite your questions.

Tony: My question is in two parts, and the first is: are there things we can do in physical form so that we can handle more Light? I have (perhaps crazily!) been practising looking into the sun in the early morning to try to get the inner imprint stronger to 'lighten' my ways. Are there things we can do in physical form that can increase the Light that we can handle?

...And the second part to my question is on a completely different tack: as a therapist I work with people who revisit their memories all the time and, for instance, if they have lost someone close to them, it is the *emotional content* of that memory that hurts, so the person tries to block the memory to avoid the emotional pain. By doing the opposite of that and putting Light into every aspect of that memory, could that not engender anxiety, panic attacks and things like that?

The two parts are very different, but I would appreciate your comments on both.

Joseph: In answer to the first part of your question, you do not ingest Light ...you *transmit* Light. It is not a matter of, as you mentioned, looking at the sun or looking at bright aspects of the world (although that is an aid to visualisation) but, as a spiritual mechanism you do not ingest the Light. It is not that you take in Light to give it out. It is that you go to your core and *find it there*. Because you are part of God and God is (at one level) Light, **there is within you an *endless* well of Light**.

If you were to imagine that there is a well at your heart-centre with a bucket that can be lowered into the well, when you reverse the handle to bring the bucket back up that bucket would always, always, always be full of Light – *always* because that is the nature of what you are. You are drawing on your own resources.

If it helps in visualisation with regard to what I have said about memory, for example, you can see a scene with perhaps yourself and somebody that you have had an altercation with, and you can see it as it was – with perhaps you wearing dull clothes or standing in a rainy, overcast street. You then visualise that incident becoming brighter, as though you can 'stop the film' (which you *can* – you can stop the film at any point) and see that incident becoming brighter, and brighter, and brighter, and whiter, and whiter ...until you can hardly see the individual aspects of the scene you are looking at. And then, you also *feel* that Light infusing the aspects of the past memory and every molecule of that situation with Light. And you hold that vision – not straining, not troubled, but rejoicing in the fact that you can feel, see and immerse yourself and the past in that Light. Then, as you put that memory away and let go of it, just see the whole scene becoming a sea of beautiful White Light.

The Light that you are transmitting, by the way, is pearly white – not like the light from the sun, which is yellow. The Light from within is white, is pure, is cleansing. You can feel its healing properties; you can feel its warmth; you can feel its restorative properties and that is what you must seek in your meditations and your bringing out of the Light. But the Light is yours. It is *your* Light on an angelic level and God's Light on a God-level that you are transmitting. It doesn't come from anywhere on a physical level.

The physical level, of course, is the end illusion. The physical level is the result of your transmission of Light collectively on a lower level than God-perfection. What you are seeking to do is to infuse tomorrow with Light on a *higher* level of God-perfection so that it becomes a brighter, lighter and more illumined place. Does that make sense?

Tony: Thank you very much.

Joseph: Regarding the putting aside of memory, which is a way that many people choose to avoid severe memories in order to 'move forwards' as they see it, there is no putting away. The memory remains on a spiritual level. It is only a blanking-off on a mental level that is taking place.

Ideally in such circumstances, it would be a matter of having a team of people who would sit around someone (as we do) who is stricken by experiences that they continue to suffer from, and *gently* guiding them and giving them the strength, through Light, to move back into that experience. *Gently* …it is not something that can be done rapidly. It is not something that can be done if there is any kind of resistance to the Light and to revisiting that memory.

This is a *vast* subject. Also remember that in an ideal situation, having identified the memory causing the problem, healers can sit between visits without the person being consciously aware of it, to illuminate that memory on their behalf so that they have the courage to revisit it.

On a spiritual level in one of the lower planes you would find elevated souls sitting around a person who has to face a memory to de-clutter it and view it as what it really is, and they sit around them and send them the Light to give them the strength to do so.

You see, a lot of the problem with illness is that it is based on a skewed view of memory. ...A husband or wife has 'gone' from a physical point of view but not from a spiritual one. *They have not gone*, and from a spiritual point of view, even within the person who is grieving, *that knowledge is there*. That knowledge is there when they relax the physical mind. That knowledge that the spouse has not gone is there but, because they put up barriers within their *physical* structure, pushing it to one side, they suffer and become ill.

In an ideal world, a complex series of events needs to take place and, hand in hand with the healing and Light-transmission (which will allow the patient to visit that memory calmly to see the events for what they really were) is the need for the patient to understand *spiritually*. This is why eventually you will need a healer and a spiritual philosopher in your healing centres. They are both 'healers' – the healer is attempting to get the person to review the memory causing the problems, and the seer is explaining what is happening on a spiritual level in a way that is understandable to the patient.

Your view of healing, like everything else on Earth at the moment, is limited and is (forgive the phrase) one-dimensional, when it should be multi-dimensional.

So, yes, you heal through Light but what the Light does is give the patient a *true* sense of the situation because, when they receive a true sense of the situation *spiritually*, they heal themselves. It makes sense. It may not make sense consciously, but it makes sense to them *subconsciously* and healing takes place. That is what the Light is doing …it is replacing one view of themselves with a better view of themselves which makes them able to see things as they really are and to restore themselves.

But, in order to do that *fully* in a physical healing situation, there has to be an explanation to the patient of process with regard to Light. There has to be an explanation to the patient of process with regard to their approach to the 'sore spot' within themselves that is causing the problem. And, there has to be an explanation with regard to the patient on a spiritual level as to what is really happening. When you combine all those aspects with Light-healing you have healing and a cure.

Does that make sense?

Tony: It does. Thank you very much, Joseph.

Jane: Joseph, could I ask a question about memory in the spirit realms with reference to the life review where we have to go through *every single thing* that we did on Earth? What really worries me about that is our having to go through all the tedious bits again. With the spiritual highs and lows and the good and the bad that seems OK, but I don't want to have to go through all the shopping and washing up again. I wondered if perhaps, during that process, they compressed the mundane bits and concentrated on the important spiritual aspects of your life?

Joseph: It is not a matter of compression. It is also not a matter of your timescale with regard to how you perceive events changing on Earth. From the point of view of a guide or an angel, in looking at someone's life, you would see that life as a 'map', with points on that map that give off alarm signals. …As an analogy, you would see flashing lights along certain points on a map and be drawn towards them. The angels and guides (who are also angels, of course) link together with that person to 'zero in' on those *key* points that need observation and study.

The *whole* of the life cannot help but unfold itself, but the perception of time when viewing that life is very different from your perception of time here on a physical level. A very contemporary analogy: if you watch a film and there are certain points in that film that you find tedious and other points where the action takes place, do you not have mechanisms now that allow you to fast-forward to the crucial parts? And yet, if you are watching the screen, the whole of the film is still going on in front of you at an accelerated speed. Do you see that?

Jane: Yes.

Joseph: So, that is the closest analogy I can give you and, from our point of view when reviewing a life with a soul, we already know because we can see it – it is not that we have been given instruction – we can *see* that life and we can see the areas most in need of review and attention and contemplation of what has happened in those particular circumstances by the soul. And, to those particular circumstances are then sometimes added the different views of other people who were affected by that soul's actions. Does that make sense?

Jane: Yes, that's a relief.

David: Joseph, is it actually easier to revisit past experiences and put Light into them in the cleansing spheres? Is that another good way of saying that it is best to quit the Earth?

Joseph: There are, of course, specific spheres of contemplation that we have spoken about in past communications [*reference to Your Life After Death*] where people go to do exactly that, where people go to very calmly and very slowly address certain of their experiences and bring out of those experiences the 'honey' and the meaning with regard to the evolution of their soul, and to examine aspects of their being through the experience they had.

What I am concerned with today is giving you a method by which you can become more whole *here on Earth* as the angelic being that you really are, and a method by which you can look at memory in a different way – not as something that is there to plague you but as something that can be revisited to *appreciate*.

If you put Light into past experience, as I have suggested, and you remove the abrasive nature of that past experience when you experience it again then a *sweetness* comes out of the most difficult experience. A realisation comes out of the most difficult experience that this was not, in fact, a difficult experience, but was a teaching and learning opportunity.

Now that is transformation. How many people do you know who revisit memory negatively and who build their future based on a negative revisiting of memory? If you remove that negativity by giving the soul an ability to view those memories for what they really are, you illuminate the whole path of memory and, by doing so, you also illuminate the path that (from your point of view) lies 'ahead' of that soul. You completely change the outlook of that soul and you bring that soul more in line, as a physical and mental being, with the angelic child that they really are. You strip away the layers of constriction and restriction imposed by the effects of the Fall, and you bring the soul closer to its real state.

With that realisation of change there also develops an ability to change the world more effectively, to transmit Light from a brighter point of view, to be more effective in the transmission of Light to change the world back to the state it was in before the Fall and to 'de-claw' those souls who are still hell-bent on their violent ways based on that core belief that you now have the ability to illuminate on their behalf and make them more flexible. Do you see that?

David: Yes, thank you.

Joseph: I must at this point release Michael. It will be a sudden...

Chapter Thirteen
The Voice of God – the Still, Small Voice

Joseph: I want you to consider the voice, and I want you to consider words, and I want you to consider how little of intent and true meaning is conveyed by the voice and by words. I want you also to consider that there was a time (and there still is a time that is masked and *is* within you) when the voice would be the *true* voice …a voice that was not spoken to manipulate the air between two people …a voice that came from within …a voice that was an instant connection …and a voice that conveyed, without sound or words, the *total intent* of the person who was delivering that message.

What you convey in words via the voice is but a small portion of your capability with regard to spiritual communication. If you consider for a moment how little of yourself is able to be expressed through the voice and how complete a being you are but how little of that completeness is projected by words, you will begin to understand what I mean.

As the spiritual beings that you really are you are capable of total communication, total transference of meaning, total transference of purpose and total expression of soul, spirituality and angelic intent, but that ability is within you – masked and struggling to get out. It is that ability that I have spoken about throughout the books delivered thus far …that ability to change the world, because your intent and *spiritual voice* transmits all your focus and ability to change things, whereas the physical voice and words convey so little of that.

So, what I am saying to you is that when you transmit Light, when you imagine a better world, when you imagine better people in that world (i.e. people better able to express their true selves and their spirituality) **your imaginings and your direction from within are your *true* voice.**

Your transmission of energy carries within it *intent*, so when you focus on an area of the world or an individual and send out Light via your true voice, you are also imprinting your intent over the current view of the world that that point of the world or person may have at this time. In other words, you are saying: 'Here is my wish for a better world …I imagine it …I see it …I construct it …and I place it over the darker vision of the world or darker view of a person that exists at the moment.' You are not saying this in words – you are saying this *in intent via the soul.* You are saying this via your angelic abilities, and your angelic abilities are so much stronger, so much more purposeful and so much more focused than your earthly voice and earthly words.

But, I want to move on from that ability you have to change things by using your inner voice – to expand on the theme of 'voice and communication' and talk to you about *God's voice.*

Inherent within every aspect of the universe and every subdivision of God, within every individualisation of God and every angel, but also within every planet, within every part of the landscape, within the rocks, the mountains, the skies, the trees and the animal forms **there is a constant communication** …and that communication is order …that communication is reassurance and suggestion of purpose from the God-within.

God – if you imagine God at the centre of all communication – gently and lovingly sends out transmissions of suggestion, of order and of creation to every aspect of His incarnations …to the planets ...to the devas ...to the angels ...to the angels clothed in heavier matter ...and, yes, to the angels who have fallen and who are encapsulated within the bubble of the Fall (although within the bubble of the Fall it is difficult for them to hear that constant transmission).

The transmission from God is always creative perfection. The transmission from God is always creative suggestion. The transmission from God is always perfect vision, perfect health and perfect geometry. That transmission from God permeates every 'seeming' individualisation of God.

It is a pulse that permeates ALL.

It is a beat that transmits order ...but order that is available *only* through free will and by harmonising with that order. In other words, that transmission from God says: 'I am Peace. I am Perfection. I am Creation. I am Love. I am Harmony. But it is up to you to use that communication – to listen to that communication and to tap into it. If you choose not to – that is fine. That is also part of My Creation through you. If you choose to link into the transmissions that I send out, you will find that you have no worries, no cares, no need to worry about the path you are on because the path will be infused with My creative ability and My creative wish for you to explore yourself, each other and the universe around you in harmony ...*and you will expand*. And, in expanding, I will be able to send out more of My transmissions to you, and you will be able to bring back transmissions to Me that will refine the communication that I send out to you.'

In this way, through deva activity, for example, the connection to God and His transmissions allows every creature and creative aspect brought forth by the deva to be in harmony with God. This is what is meant by *never a sparrow falls* without God knowing and that *the hairs on your head are numbered* because in the natural order of things, by linking into the transmission from God, all is taken care of – the animal is in the right place and the hill is in the right place, and the deva has the energy and power to bring forth creation perfectly.

And you will say: 'Why, Joseph, if the animal is in the right place, is it then eaten or attacked by another animal?' You have to remember that the communication coming from God has been polluted *by choice* by the angelic children because of their decision, which created the bubble of the Fall that you are living within. But, in normal circumstances outside of that bubble, deva and angelic activity brings forth the most splendid, wonderful creations you are able to imagine (and many that you are not able to imagine) because of that link into the voice of God.

The communication of God that spreads outwards from God also *links everything to every other thing* so that there is harmony not only between God and angelic child, but there is harmony between angelic child and every other angelic child ...and the angelic host ...and the animal forms ...and the landscape forms ...and the planets ...and the stars ...and the universe.

Everything is in perfect harmony.

I bring you this vision of perfect harmony today because it seems appropriate, at this point in our communications, to boost your vision of what is possible and to bring you an indication that you can have (if you wish) further health, further harmony, further success and perfect creativity simply by listening for the voice of God within.

It is said in spiritual literature that there is 'a still, small voice' and it is *the still, small voice* that should be the title of this particular chapter, and should also spark a recognition and understanding – because there *is* a still, small voice that loves you and uplifts you constantly during your lives.

But, in order to listen to the still, small voice, you have to be still.

And you have to realise that it is a *small* voice even though it comes from God. It is a small voice in that it is a humble voice saying to you: 'Here is a *suggestion* ...here is a suggestion for a better way, for a perfect way, but only will that suggestion be of use to you *if you wish it to be.*' **...If you *wish* it to be.**

God comes in at the core of each being quietly, *subtly*, with a suggestion, and the suggestion is: 'Listen to Me if you so wish. Connect to Me if you so wish. But, if you make that connection, then harmony is what you will project, harmony is what you will connect to, harmony is what you are capable of and restoration is what you are capable of with regard to the effects of the Fall. It is simply a matter of connecting to Me and listening to Me.' **...Listening to the complete harmony that emanates from the Godhead.**

You therefore have, as manifestations of God, a very powerful voice for change. The voices for change that you see in your world that are surrounded by protest placards or on a soapbox or extolled by megaphone have only a tiny percentage of the power of the voice that you, sitting in your living room or office, have if you choose to work for God. You have a powerful voice that you send out in the form of Light to change things. So, the Light that you are sending out has a message within it: 'This is the way it can be. Doesn't this feel better? Doesn't this feel wonderful? Isn't this what you want to be a part of? Remember this is where you started and this is what you can get back to.' ...And you get back to it simply by projecting the Light and going within to that perfect voice.

As an individualisation of God you, too, give out communication. It doesn't matter if you seal yourself away in a room and say nothing for six weeks – **you are communicating all the time.** You are sending out your 'voice' and spiritual 'words' so it is important that you understand that your 'voice' and 'words' should be the best at all times. You should endeavour to make your spiritual voice a gentle one and not a judgmental one. It is important that you should endeavour to make your spiritual voice a peaceful one, a healing one and a harmonious one so that if you, for example, are speaking words of peace and harmony or being nice with people on the surface *that should be reflected within too.*

In fact, it should be a greater degree of harmony that you send out than with your physical voice. It is no use using words that are hollow. It is no use using a voice that is a deceptive one. It is no use sending out a veneer only. **You have to be *within* what you purport to be *without*.** What you purport to say and what you purport to believe in has to be *truly* what you believe in and *are* within.

Then your physical words too will bring comfort, harmony, peace, upliftment and *energy* to people because the voice within (the voice that radiates from God which you radiate outwards) is permeated with an energy that says: 'I know nothing of disease …I know nothing of corruption …I know nothing of violence … I know nothing of disharmony.' That energy, if you infuse it into your physical voice and words, actually uplifts people and – even if they are just listening to your physical voice or simply in your presence – you make a difference to them. You permeate their lives, you permeate their circumstances and, *most importantly*, you permeate their viewpoint with that Light-energy.

They need energy to change because the energy they are running on is polluted, is dark, is of the Fall and of the Earth since the time of the Fall. You have to present them with the energy that will clear and replace that pollution of the Fall, and give them a 'chamber' within which they can review their position and see things differently – which they cannot do at this point because of the effects of the Fall.

So, today's contemplation has been on communication and the 'missing voice' in many people's lives on Earth, and that missing voice isn't missing at all – *it is within*. The voice of God brings constant guidance. There is never a situation in which a soul, from the viewpoint of God, is required to suffer.

God never wants a soul to suffer ...ever, ever, ever, EVER!

I want you, please, to listen to this with regard to your views on reincarnation and with regard to your religious views on a judgemental God: **God never, ever, *ever* wants anything but harmony for His individualisations of Himself.**

And, the way never to suffer is to tap into those communications on a daily basis ...on an hourly basis ...on a *constant* basis to make them a part of every day that you live on this planet. Realise that the God that is communicating with you, *is you*, wants only the best for you and, for each situation that you are in, is able to guide you into the next step to either make it more harmonious or to extricate you from the situation if it is harming you and making you suffer.

Were you to see this planet with spiritual eyes, you would see waves of energy washing against its shores – waves of energy from outside the planet and waves of energy from within the planet. Those waves of energy come from God but, for the most part, they dissipate because of your decision so long ago [*reference to effects of the Fall*]. They wash against the shores and dissipate ...and yet there is still the Earth ...and yet you still exist ...and yet there is still a landscape for you to move through because *at core* that communication of God is maintaining the structure of the experience that you are a part of at this moment.

There is an arrogance that says: 'We maintain the fields and skies; we control aspects of the planet; we control our own lives and are able to operate on the physical body to restore health to people by sorting out the physical.' And [*laughing*] all of that is untrue because the *ultimate* power comes from that beat of Creation that comes from the Source. If that communication did not come and manifest itself at core within you **...you would not exist.** None of the things that you feel are so important ...your advances in medicine ...your advances in science ...your advances in construction or the ordering of governments and society… would exist because, if you strip away all those things that you consider to be so important, what are you left with?

You are left with yourself, you are left with God and you are left with the Love and communication that exists between you. And that, ultimately, is all there is **…is all there is.** It is back to nothing existing except as a tool to allow you to move in consciousness closer to your God-abilities within.

[*Laughing*] I am sorry doctors …I am sorry scientists …I am sorry architects …I am sorry solicitors …I am sorry teachers … but much of what you place so much store in and believe to be immutable and solid *is a mere fabrication.*

It is your communication with God that allows you to perceive, to move forwards and to have any effect on people at all. The power that you believe is so important in your lives that you have gathered in a 'basket' and 'locked in a room' *as yours* doesn't exist except within you as a communication from God. It doesn't exist! Shake yourself and understand **…it doesn't exist.** And, the moment you realise that is the moment that *true* power is given to you …God-power …the power that restores …the power that harmonises …the power that builds out of nothing splendours that you will one day see.

And, I pray that that 'one day' will be sooner rather than later, but that is up to you. It is up to your perception of reality and, if you shake your perception of reality, you are on the path to visiting and moving though *such wonders* that the amount of excitement, bliss and creativity you will experience you cannot comprehend at this moment. That is what lies ahead for you. That is what was part of you before you came here after the effects of the Fall. That is what the angelic hosts and the expression of Love in other spheres enjoy. It is only here where you have locked the door for a little while and the chamber is dark. We are handing you the key – take the key and unlock the chamber.

...Change!

...Communicate!

...Listen to the voice!

...Give out the voice of God!

[*Pause*]

Are there any questions, please?

David: Joseph, you don't actually need to be with other people to talk to them do you?

Joseph: The communication is constant. The communication orders where you should be according to the voice that you are giving out. So, the shoals of fish that are so ordered *are so ordered* because they know where they should be in relation to God and to each other. The birds in the air that flock and wheel and never crash into each other do so because they are listening to that voice.

You are absolutely right – there is a constant communication from each individual, whether or not they are in actual *physical* contact with other individuals. So, the hermit sitting on the hill or the person locked away in an iron room is still in communication with the rest of the world and with the rest of Creation. You cannot be otherwise than a communicator with the rest of Creation. There is no isolation.

This is the greatest joy too because, in your iron room or sitting alone on your hill, you can communicate purposefully and consciously with the rest of Creation on this level, and you can make that *vital* difference that needs to be made. You can send out the Light, you can send out God's purpose, you can send out your vision for a better world, you can send out harmony and Love to those that are plunged into darkness of the soul at this moment, and you can change them. You can create within them the conditions so that they can hear that God-communication.

Ultimately everyone that changes is listening to the God-communication, is retuning their 'wireless inside' to that channel that is the God-communication and saying: 'Ah, yes, that is who I am. Isn't this harmonious? Isn't this peaceful? Isn't this healthy? Isn't this wonderful? Now I know what to do next because I am not worrying about what to do from the head-mind but am working, in conjunction with the God within me, to illuminate each step.'

Does that answer the question?

David: It does, thank you.

Jane: With the animals, even though they are in heavy matter and are within the Field, is the reason that they can hear the pulse of God because they don't have a head-mind but are linked through just the heart-mind?

Joseph: It is exactly that, and it is also because the devas that emanate the animal forms have not been polluted (as we have said in the past) by the effects of the Fall. In one way, they are trapped within the matrix of the Fall, but in another the devas have elected to continue to supply a landscape against which you can measure yourselves.

So, the pulse from God flows into the deva. The deva then makes a conscious decision, connected to other devas, to create a matrix against which the angelic children can measure themselves (and that, originally, was in conjunction with the angelic children *consciously*). Then the pulse of God from the deva goes out to the facets of the deva that manifest themselves as the animal forms.

The deva works in the same way as God, i.e. God bringing forth individualisations of Himself with a separate but linked consciousness. We *all* work in the same way but the deva's specific purpose is to bring through the evolutionary forms that can eventually house an angelic spirit so that that spirit can have adventures in different playgrounds. So, as the deva gives out the pulse of being to the various animal forms, those various animal forms are also individuals, but they have a keener group-mind than you do. Do you see that?

Jane: Is the pulse a pleasurable communication for the animal? Sometimes you see an animal just daydreaming in a field and you wonder if there is a pleasant experience going on there.

Joseph: This is a reversal of thinking from the perspective of many people, but there is a greater intelligence with regard to God-intelligence inherent in an animal than there is in the human form. So, the animal is aware of itself existing on two levels. It is aware of itself being in the landscape of the Earth but is also aware of itself being part of God-Creation and part of the purposeful creation of the deva.

It is simpler for an animal form to relinquish its physicality than it is for a human being because there is the dual mind — there is the individualisation mind in the animal but there is also the link to the deva, the link to every other animal, the link to Creation and the link to God. So, at the end of the physical body, there is a relinquishing to the purpose of God and, therefore, less trauma in most cases with animal forms passing than there is with the human form because the human form has the troublesome mind that has constructed a view of how things should be at the end of physicality — very often with the view of there being nothing at the end. Does that make sense?

Jane: Yes, thank you.

Tony: As a psychotherapist, I have noticed working with people that there are other inner voices — very strong inner voices that at any opportunity will come in and give an opinion to that person, and can be very specific about things going on in the world and how they relate to those things. This makes it very difficult for

THE JOSEPH COMMUNICATIONS: FROM HERE TO INFINITY

the individuals to listen to the still, small voice. Is there anything we can do with these (I would imagine) man-made inner voices that seem to have such strength and can overlay that quiet voice?

Joseph: It is a difficult area. The *key* to connecting to the God-within is not through thinking. It is through sensing. It is a matter of relinquishing the thought that causes the inner voices that you talk about.

The connection with God is an acceptance. The connection with God is a simplicity. The connection with God is a matter of 'melting away', as it were, physical thought for a time so that the purpose of the communication is sensed, is entered into, is appreciated by the soul, and that is not necessarily a conscious thing initially. You are all listening to the voice of God *at this moment* but you do not realise it. What I am suggesting is that people who wish to change circumstances *consciously* connect with the God-within but that is not always possible initially.

What you have to present to people who are wishing to banish the inner voices is a relinquishing of the inner voices through not accepting them and by not becoming an antagonist with those inner voices. The way through the inner voices is by just observing them as a viewer rather than being a participator in those inner voices and their effects.

You have to present methods by which (as with hands-on-healing or absent healing) the patient is brought to a state where they become detached from the situations that are causing them harm. It is (as you will have learned over the years) a process of detachment: 'I detach you from this belief. I detach you from this ingrained perception of the world. I give you the power to detach yourself from them.' And the moment that they are detached from them, they connect to the God-within …to *that* voice and they heal, realising that they have never been ill in the first place, realising that those inner voices are nothing more than 'ghosts in the fog' and that when you connect to the Light-within they melt away.

Does that make sense?

Tony: It does make sense. Once an individual understands that it is a voice and not them, can they pray for help in detaching from that particular voice?

Joseph: Yes, always healing has to come though volition. You always have to wish to be healed and to be whole, and the voices that you speak of are often very seductive. As we have discussed before, they often give the individual a sense of being, a sense of individuality and a reason for attention to be focused on them. What they have to connect with is the God-within and then there is all the Love that they will *ever* need ...ever ...ever ...ever as a constant supply. But [*laughing*] they don't want to relinquish the inner voices because they believe that *those* are their path to attention and love from outside. It is Love from *within* we are trying to make them aware of.

So, yes, in praying for them you pray that they are able to hear the God-within and (as we have talked about for many years now) you can project enough Light into their inner being so that they have the strength to listen to *that* inner voice and not the other 'voices'.

My view on healing is that the best healing is done by stealth. The best healing is done either when the patient is distracted or is not even in the room because then they have no barrier that they can automatically put up against that healing.

You would surprised if you were to appreciate how many of the people who are 'dis-eased' or unhealthy actually cling on to that disease and lack of health as a purpose and focus for their being that otherwise wouldn't be there. In many people's cases this is down to the fear of an existence that (in their perception) must come to an end and is slowly ticking away day by day. So, they need a purpose and in many, many cases ill-health gives them that purpose because it focuses (as they see it in their subconscious) the love and attention of others on them, and fixes them in time and in space *as something that cannot possibly die* because there is so much attention on them. Do you see that?

Tony: I do. Thank you, Joseph.

Chapter Fourteen
Spheres of Influence

Michael's observations: Towards the end of this chapter, in the questions section, Joseph matter-of-factly reveals in a single sentence something quite startling about himself and the Communications (with regard to how we measure time). This concerns just how long he has been involved in his and his soul group's mission to quite literally enlighten us and the world using the Communications as a means of rectifying the cataclysmic plunging into spiritual darkness that happened at the time of the Fall. You can't miss his statement – it's in bold capital letters – just as you can't fail, having read it, to feel humbled by Joseph and his group's dedication, patience, and love for each of us, and also shocked by the implications of his words. All the more reason to understand, assimilate, adopt and practice the advanced Light-transmitting method described by Joseph in the chapter below...

Joseph: The title of this chapter is 'Spheres of Influence' and I wish today to extend and enhance your capabilities with regard to healing the world and your brothers and sisters in it.

I want you to consider what I have said in previous books regarding the way that souls from higher realms link to the lower realms whenever you endeavour to raise yourself *spiritually* or to sit (as we are doing this morning) to increase spiritual awareness. And, as I have said in the past, this begins with a circle of like-minded people on your level that is then linked to a circle above that one on a spiritual level ...and a circle above that one on a higher spiritual level ...and so on ...and so on ...so that the intent, Light and *purpose* – God-purpose and purpose from the higher spheres of the spiritual realms – can be channelled down in order to be picked up and used either as energy or information by the circle sitting at an Earth-level.

It has often been asked of me by those reading the books as to how to be *effective* when sending out Light, and I have, to this point, suggested that Light be beamed out from the heart-centre into the relevant areas of the world and into the hearts and minds of those you wish to elevate and into the situations you wish to change.

I now want you to try to appreciate the fact that, when we link with you and you link with the higher circles, those in the spiritual realms not only form a circle around you but, in fact, form a *sphere* around you. Freed from your need for gravity, when we are operating mentally and through the spirit-heart, if we form a circle, we form a circle not just along a vertical plane, but also along the horizontal plane, and along every plane in-between.

So, there are a great many spirits that join you from the higher circles, and these spirits, in effect, channel energy to you but also form around you **a complete circle or sphere of intent** ...of their intent and of your intent. This circle of energy and spiritual-mental purpose actually excludes the effects of the Field and the effects of other people's negative vibrations during the time that you are sitting spiritually. The sphere is, therefore, a protection for you but is also an *inspiration* for you, and within that circle – that sphere – you are divorced for a little while from the effects of the Earth so that we can transmit energy to you, which is then translated as 'information' by your seers and channellers.

What I am now suggesting you do is take up *that image of the sphere* so that when you send out Light from your heart-centre, you not only see that Light illuminating the brothers and sisters that you wish to elevate **...but you also see it encased by a sphere of Light** *at the other end of the communication.* So, you yourself are encased in a luminous, uplifting sphere of harmony, and the beam from your heart-centre and its target are also encased by a sphere of high spiritual intent.

If you consider what this means **...it means that your Light-sending has far more power.** It has far more depth and far more ability to change circumstances because, when it reaches the person or situation that you are attempting to uplift, that person or situation is given a chance to absorb the effects of that Light through being encased within a protective sphere of energy from the higher spheres of intent. The person or situation is given an atmosphere within which to grow and change. So, if a person is at the point of 'twilight' – the point between listening to and acting on the effects of the Fall or listening to and absorbing Light from the higher spheres – then they are given a better chance for change by being removed from the effects of the Field during the time that you are sending out Light to them.

I am explaining this to you because, from this point onwards, I want you to have **an 'advanced method' of sending change out into the world.** And don't forget that, if you send Light to the whole planet, you can see *the world itself* encased in a luminous sphere of Light that separates it from any darkness and lower vibrations. This gives it the chance to change ...for growth to be enhanced ...for Light to take root ...for spiritual values to connect to the heart-centre and make themselves heard ...for the intuition of all the people on Earth to be heightened for that time that you send the Light to them encased within a sphere of Light ...and for that intuition to bring them *true* spiritual values – God-values that they have forgotten for so long.

So, I would ask that in your Light-sending from now on you become aware, when you attempt to send Light out and connect to the God-within and to the higher spheres, that *you are already surrounded by help and intent* – because another aspect that is asked many times is, 'How can *I* do anything?' And the physical mind says: 'Well, you are alone in sending Light out. It is a big world and there are so many people ...how can *you* possibly make any change? How can *you* possibly change the hearts and wills of people – *just you*?'

It is *never* just you.

You are never alone. No one is *ever* alone.

You are connected the moment that you wish to send Light out ...first of all to the God-within (And what more powerful source is there than your Creative Source?), but also, as you sit with intent to change and uplift things around the world, you are joined by a 'circle' (which is, in fact, a sphere) of mental-spiritual activity. This is not to say that the spirits involved in connecting to you are totally involved in just surrounding you. You have to understand that there is the ability to 'multitask' from those spirits that join you, but whenever and wherever there is a point of Light on Earth that wishes to expand that point of Light on behalf of others, there is a pull on part of the consciousness of spiritual workers and angelic sources on so many different levels of Light ...**a pull that is *answered*.**

It is answered by some spirits who are totally dedicated to this cause with one hundred per cent of their consciousness. And it is also answered by others advancing into the angelic realms by *a portion* of their consciousness because there is that desire within their consciousness for a change on Earth (and we have touched upon this in other books). So what I am saying is that, as spirits progress towards the ultimate escape sphere and beyond, there is always a portion of them (because they are linked to everyone else on Earth) that wishes to make that change on Earth. That is part of their make-up and core desire, so they apportion a percentage of their life energies, their creative energies and their conscious and subconscious energies to making that happen.

So, when someone sits on Earth, you have spirits above them who are fully aware of what they are intending to do and who join them in full consciousness for the sole purpose of adding Light to Light. But above that, as you get into the more rarefied spheres of existence, there are also those spirits performing their wondrous tasks as part of group souls interacting with each other as they grow more God-like (as they remember more about who they are and let go of more of the effects of the Earth plane) that add a part of their consciousness to the sphere of intent that surrounds the person on Earth wishing to change things.

My point in all this is that no one sitter is ever alone. Every sitter wishing to send Light out into the world is joined by *hundreds and thousands of souls* ...hundreds and thousands of souls who wish the Earth to remember what it is, who wish the lost children to remember that they are angelic beings and who wish the effects of the Fall to be put aside and transmuted for good. So, when in the past I have said that one person transmitting Light is equal in strength to many, many souls who are unenlightened ...**this is why I have said it.**

I hope this explains why you are not alone. You are channelling an *immense* amount of power. It is as though that power is *around* you and is crossing space and dimensions to get to the point that you wish to send it to, but, remember you are also channelling the most powerful force that you can, which is the God-force *within* you, and that you are a part of God-intent.

So, you have spiritual intent joining around you as a sphere, and you have within you the dot within the circle, the God-power that is capable of changing things. It is capable of nothing else because God *is* change and experience and you are saying: 'Father, I wish things to be as You want them to be on Earth. I wish things to be as You want them to be within the hearts and minds of those who have fallen.'

How can you fail?

How can you *ever* fail with such weight and Love and harmony behind you?

I am describing this *advanced* method of healing and changing the world to you at this time because in the spiritual realms we have become aware in 'recent days' (as you would measure it) of a further entrenchment into the heavy thoughts and perceptions and into the lack of Light that is a result of the Fall. The whole intent in transmitting this information to you is to bring enough Light into the world to change it before it is too late, and that is a very important phrase **...before it is too late.**

Recently the *collective* mind of humankind (not the individual mind but the collective mind that the individual mind contributes to and draws from) has scored a little triumph, has scored a 'goal', has decided that it has entrenched people successfully through the manifestations that have been erupting around the world at this time ...through the violence that has been erupting ...through the materialism that is becoming more glamorous to people ...and through the thoughts for revenge that reverberate around the world and draw on the Field's energies to promote further violence.

We have, therefore, become concerned with the timescale of being able to put things right on Earth during this current cycle. That is why I have advanced the Light-sending technique and explained it, I hope, more fully today, to say: 'If the world seems dark in coming months and years, remember that it is an illusion. Remember and exercise daily that immense power that you have and immense ability to change things from within and without. Concentrate on the Light-vibration that you are sending out, concentrate on the help that is always there from the spiritual spheres and concentrate on the perfect vision of the Earth and its people that you must hold fast to at this point.'

Am I saying that the end of society is assured?

No!

If I was convinced that the end of society was assured, I would retreat from this information, there would be no further chapters and I would turn my back on *this* cycle ...to return in millions of years' time when the Earth has presented a new playground for the children of the Fall to attempt to work their way out of the effects of the Fall as the pattern presents itself once again.

I am not doing that.

I, and the souls in the group that I am a part of ...and the souls that are above us ...and above that ...and above that ...have become *more aware*: I spoke earlier in the chapter about only a percentage of awareness being dedicated towards the Earth, but of late *a greater percentage* of awareness has been turned towards the Earth because collectively we can feel the pull that says: 'If mankind doesn't change then we are heading for the end of the cycle *again*.' As a result of that pull, there is more dedication at this time and you are, therefore, **more powerful at this time than you have been up to this point.**

What we have to say within our hearts is, 'Yes, the end is nigh!' But [*smiling*] 'the end that is nigh' is not the end of society and the planet but the reverse of that ...the end of the Field being set to negative *is nigh* ...the end of the vicious cycle of violence and revenge *is nigh* ...the end of the children being lost and not knowing who or where they are or how to behave as aspects of God *is nigh*.

...And that is what I want from you. I want *courage* from you. I want *dedication* from you. I want *focus* from you. I want *discipline* from you. And I ask you, on behalf of millions and billions of souls, to send out the Light *daily* with the new knowledge that I have given you today.

You see, the nature of creation is to create *spheres*, and you exist, at the moment, within a sphere of polluted energy. But, within that capsule you are all parts of God and, therefore, you are able to create your own mini-universe – your own sphere of Light within the effects of the Fall and within the effects of the Field. If enough of you do this and enough of you make souls aware, as you send out Light to them, that they are now within *their* own mini-universe of Light too, then there will be so many spheres of Light nestling, joining and harmonising with each other that the sphere that is the Field and the effects of the Fall will pop like a balloon ...like a dream ...like a cloudy soap-bubble ...*and will be gone.*

Remember that you are protected. Remember that you are able to protect others by sending out Light and seeing that Light enveloped in a sphere around them, and never doubt that you are *changing those hearts and minds*. **Never doubt!** Even if it was the worst case scenario ...even *if* (and this is not so) it was the end of the cycle, through your efforts you would have delivered enough Light to certain souls and to certain situations by channelling it daily that, when those lost children arose again in the theoretical next cycle, you would have given them a head start. You would have given them enough Light to begin to consider and embrace *earlier on* in that new evolution encased within physical matter the fact that they are spirits ...the fact that they are part of God ...the fact that they are angels ...and the fact that *this time* they need to change. So you cannot lose.

By channelling the Light you cannot lose.

You win either in this scenario which you have changed, or you win in the next scenario by fuelling the 'batteries' of those lost children who must reincarnate (if the cycle came to an end and the effects of the Fall were still there, they must be drawn into physical matter again because there is nowhere else for them to go). You would have given them enough of a head start and fuelled that 'battery' to the point that they could consider earlier on in the cycle that the world is not as it should be, that there is a connection to a greater world within and that, as a result of that connection, they could *this time* change things.

Are there questions, please?

David: Joseph, in wielding Light is there one target, as it were, that works better than any other? Should we send Light to the world as a whole, or perhaps some people would want to send Light into a war zone or to a set of individuals who are ill – what's the best way of doing that ...or *is there* a 'best way'?

Joseph: Your personal preferences, as you have just said, come into play whenever you are sending out Light, and every person who is enlightened on Earth will have a different set of preferences. To one person it will be to end war, terrorism or violence; to another person it will be to uplift the lives of children or those who are in drought and famine conditions; to another person it will be the nature aspect of the world that will need to be uplifted. Through free will, you have the right to choose for yourself which of those aspects (plus others we haven't mentioned) are priorities for you.

It doesn't matter, because (linked to what we have said today) your intentions from the God-heart are enhanced by the intentions of the spirits that join you in the 'sphere of Light' that you are seated within whenever you wish to send out Light. You are joined in those circumstances by *higher* intentions ...by pure, *pure* intentions. Not that your intentions are not pure, but what I am saying is that, as the spirit progresses, it becomes aware of the *complete situation* on Earth, and so, yes, longs for a change to the situations that you specifically wish to change (because that is part of the whole) but, as an intent, wants the whole of the Earth to change.

As you send out Light (i.e. Light enhanced through links with those spirits from the sphere of intent that is placed around you and which you then place around the people and situations at the other end of your channelling of Light) the specific intentions that you wish to sit for are addressed. But there is also an 'encoding' within that Light to address *all* the circumstances that need to change ...everything that needs to change within the Field ...everything that needs to change within the minds of men and women ...everything that needs to change within the landscape ...everything that needs to change within the plan. And so, you strengthen that intent wherever you send the Light. Do you see? You cannot help but strengthen the holistic intent of those who wish (including yourself as a channeller of Light) to lift the Field out of its negativity and lift the children out of the effects of the Fall.

You are sending a code; you are sending a core message that has within it other messages, and those messages do not affect the free will of the brothers and sisters that you are sending the Light to. As we have said before, it has to come to a point where they – of their own intent and fuelled by that Light – become spiritually aware again. But, as they become spiritually aware, the Light-within that they are now wielding has within *it* certain preferences and considerations that they become aware of. It is like delivering a 'wonderful book' that they immediately open, but there are other 'books' on other subjects delivered in the same brown paper parcel, and, having enjoyed the first book, they cannot help but look at the others and say: 'Yes, I need to do something about this situation and that situation.'

Does that make sense to you?

David: That does indeed, yes, and if, for example, one person is working to put Light into the Earth itself and another person to put Light into areas of famine, those all join up because in the background there are thousands of souls working behind them.

Joseph: There is the *one* intent. The one intent is the *same intent* no matter how it is spread out ...whether you wish to elevate a terrorist so that that person is no longer a terrorist ...whether you wish to elevate a rain forest so that that forest is verdant and productive again ...whether you wish to elevate someone who is locked into depression and upset ...it is the *same* intent, and the intent is for everything to reset. The intent is for the effects of the Fall to disappear and for the souls locked into the cycle of coming back to repeat the same pattern to be freed and for the individuals to remember, for the landscape to remember, and for the planet to remember its spiritual heritage.

215

It is down to remembering spiritual heritage, and, at the moment that that takes place, all thoughts of violence, all corruption, all power-seeking and all exploitation of the planet *cease instantly*. So, you are addressing aspects in your Light-bearing, and each aspect is a part of the whole and needs to be healed for the whole to be healed ...and the whole needs to be healed for the aspect to be healed, **but it is the same intention.** It is the same set of circumstances that need to be healed and, carried within that Light, is an ability to uplift people and situations to the point where they see the whole pattern and heal it themselves.

David: Thank you.

Jane: Joseph, you were talking about how, if the world did come to an end, the Light-sending would still help people in the *next* cycle. In the event of a next cycle, could they not somehow regulate the number of fallen souls coming back, because the more people 'in the dark' there are on the Earth the worse the effect of their negative thoughts on the Field? So, if a higher proportion of elevated souls from the cleansing spheres (who are wanting to help anyway) also reincarnated at the same time, wouldn't that be a more effective way of helping the others to see the Light through their positive influence on the Field? Is there something that stops that from happening – such as free will where you can't prevent the people in stasis from piling back in?

Joseph: You have the *truly* enlightened people who wish to move on from the Earth plane, and with each cycle there have been a number of souls who have escaped, first of all, the Earth plane and then travelled through the cleansing spheres and escaped out into the angelic reality. So, with every cycle (*and I must stress again that this cycle is not yet set as coming to an end*) there are a number of souls who escape.

We have also explained in the past that the souls who are more entrenched in the effects of the Fall and who see that as the only reality are pulled back into that reality because they have not prepared themselves for anywhere else. What we always attempt to do at the beginning of a cycle is to prepare those souls awakening from their slumber between cycles by giving them *enough* **Light to have a chance to remember.**

Then, Light has to connect with Light, so there are certain members within the new society that will be connected to the spiritual realms from the beginning of that new cycle by the amount of Light they are able to draw on within themselves. Those are the *sensitive* members of society, and thus *our* cycle begins again at that point because, at that point, we have to connect Light to Light to begin the process of bringing through the information that we are bringing through *now* to extricate souls from the effects of the Fall. Do you see?

Jane: Yes.

Joseph: There has to be preparation, and I say this not with weariness, but from your point of view, to bring an aspect of weariness into it …can you imagine what it is like for us to see the cycle beginning again and to have to wait …to be in glorious surroundings, yes, but to be dedicated to bringing those brothers and sisters out *again*? We have not gone through the 'escape hatch' that I frequently talk about, and we have to wait …and then *we have to begin the cycle again*!

…This [*smiling*] is not the first time I have brought this information through.

THIS IS NOT THE FIRST TIME I HAVE BROUGHT THIS INFORMATION THROUGH.

I do not wish to bring it through again.

But *if I have to*, I have to.

It is an excellent question because I hope it highlights in readers' minds the need to *this time* make sure that the cycle is not a 'cycle' but a beginning and an end that leads to the re-establishment of the previous matrix for the Earth rather than a repeat of the cycle of the Fall.

This chapter more than any other requests dedication and requests that those who read this become 'Soldiers for the Light' (and I am hoping that this book will go out more than ever to those who have been prepared by the other books and are willing to do something) so that the cycle ends, yes, but not in the tragedy of the beginning of another cycle and a repeat of the effects of the Fall …but ends in that *this time* we re-establish the Earth as the paradise it once was, and that the souls, who have chosen suffering over bliss for so long *this time* choose bliss and the dream ends.

Do you see that?

Jane: Yes.

Tony: The group have recently been talking about what we can do to expand awareness of the books and to do it in a way that allows Michael to conserve his energy for your transmissions. We were thinking of having a study evening at the Sanctuary where readers could ask us questions to get deeper insights into the spiritual meaning of the books. We have sold thousands of books and there are a lot of readers who are asking us to do additional things. Would a study group be too left-brained? After listening to what you have said today, should we start with group healing in the Joseph way – would that be a better way for us to expend our energies rather than a study group?

Joseph: Perhaps 'study group' is the wrong word and 'a meeting point' is a better term – where people can meet you as the group that you are and can better relate to the books because they can see that the members of that group are *just like them*. That would be a start-point for a meeting but, as a result of that meeting, it would also be helpful to see that the members are able to answer questions and to clear up any grey areas (I find that an amusing phrase ...'grey areas'... because we are talking about Light and it *is* the grey areas that we are attempting to clear up).

I feel that that would be a good start-point without imposing too much on people, and I feel that that could be something that is a regular event (and may also be a regular event at other venues, if it goes well). It brings people a sense of family, which it is difficult to do through the books. We bring them a sense of 'family' in that when they read the books they are surrounded by that intent that we have been talking about today, and are surrounded by people who are attempting to uplift them, educate them, inspire them and help them to send out the Light, but unless they are used to seeing or sensing psychically, they are very often not aware that there is anyone with them, which is why I addressed the question that sometimes comes up of, '*I am alone – what can I do?*'

It is a good point of contact and, of course, we will be there – not to take over Michael as I am doing today, but to answer those questions by inspiring him and inspiring you, as members of this group, to encourage those Light-bearers in the exercise ahead of them. So, a regular meeting point is, I feel, a very worthwhile idea.

What is also a worthwhile idea is to have, as you have said, a group that sits to send the Light out because, of course, that group will be instantly joined by ourselves and by spirits from higher realms to do as much good and to uplift as many people and as many situations as it is possible to do during the time that they sit.

It is very difficult for us to comprehend your methods of communicating today because they are on the very edge of the Fall. They are tinged with the effects of the Fall, and yet we must use them. You have to appreciate that many people who will visit your meetings have never seen a spirit or connected to a relative who has passed into the spirit realms, and so they need that point of contact. So, yes, we are *wholeheartedly* behind and interspersed with your efforts to broaden the 'appeal' (because that is what you have to do) of *the Joseph Communications* to make them more visible to people. Then, it is our hope that the people who attend the meetings and the Light-sending sessions talk to their relatives, talk to their friends and talk to other organisations to spread the word.

There is a cautionary note to the chapter today, of course, and that cautionary note is that *there isn't all the time in the world left* in order to make things right in this cycle. And so, over the coming months and years (with your permission – which you have already given as spirits on another level) we are accelerating your ability to communicate the existence of *the Joseph Communications* to a wider audience, which we hope to be global.

Does that answer your question?

Tony: Yes, and further to that can we make today's chapter available ahead of the book and tell people about this way of healing?

Joseph: The book seems thus far to have been a random collection of essays on various topics but, when viewed as a whole, you will see that it has been a preparation for this chapter. I would *rather* that the book is made available as soon as possible, and you will see the connectedness of the chapters once they are put together. The information that this book contains is a preparation for this chapter and the chapters that are yet to come. There are not many and I have not yet decided how many ...it is probable that there are just a further four chapters, but in those four chapters I wish to expand on the themes that I have covered today. I don't wish to tire Michael further or to put into his mind what those subjects will be, but they are a building of this theme that I have brought through today.

I would say that the other books and the communications you have had thus far are doing their work. **They are doing their**

work. What this book is, is a booster to that work for those who have become aware of the information, have absorbed it and wish to be of more help.

The communications are layered. There are communications for those who wish to have the fear of death taken away, so those readers will take out of those communications *just what they want* and will stop at that ...but at least they have become enlightened. Then there are communications for those who wish to see a better world personally or in their family group, so those readers go deeper and begin to apply the meditations and the Light-bringing exercises to their lives.

And, then there are those who will make this *a lifetime commitment* and take from the communications a need, a desire and a love to send Light into the world and to each man and woman in the world on a daily basis. They become wonderful, wonderful 'soldiers for the cause' because, even when they are applying themselves to other tasks, their motive is identical to the motive of those higher spirits who join them from their spheres of influence in that *they are sending out Light constantly*.

They are sending out Light constantly because they have built it into their schedule of soul tasks. So, they may sit for only ten minutes a day, but they are also sending out Light from the whole of their remaining existence on Earth ...during the day ...during the night when they are asleep ...*especially* when they are asleep and the physical mind is switched off.

So, I would prefer the book to be a motivation for those people and a further awakening. Each book is intended to be a further step and awakening ...here is how you operate ...here is what you can do about it ...here is what happens to you after death ...here is what happened in the Fall ...here is what you can do about it in an *enhanced* way. Each book should be a wake-up call and an awakening spiritually. That is what they are intended to be.

Tony: Thank you.

Chapter Fifteen
The Dedication of Energy

Joseph: It is with gratitude and a sense of companionship, friendship and humour that I join you this morning. I want to talk about energy in a different way this morning because I want to talk about *the dedication of energy* and an aspect of energy that you have probably not considered before. I certainly don't feel that I have mentioned it before in any of the earlier Communications.

I did, however, mention in the first book – **Revelation** – the means by which you can create a chair, for example, out of nothing and then put that chair back into the proto-matter around you ...to pull it back whenever you want it, and to put it away again whenever you want to. I also talked about the consequences of creating a chair. *Whatever you create has consequences* because you have brought it into being, and there is an interplay between that object and the rest of the objects within the plane of reference that you are operating on.

However, I want to take that further and I want to make you aware that *everything* that you create ...be it a thought ...be it a chair ...be it a painting ...be it a building ...be it a method of dealing with an aspect of society... contains within it, not only what it is (i.e. not only it being a building or a chair or a concept) but a 'personality-charge'.

Each object contains within it a part of you or a part of the group of people who have created it because, in your role as a creative angelic being, whatever you give form to *has intent within it*. For example, the angelic host creating the Earth created it with the intent of the Earth being a playground or zone of experience for angelic beings, so that the angelic beings visiting the Earth could pass through it, pick up on those opportunities woven into the creative structure of the Earth and benefit from them on their journey through the physical plane of the Earth.

You still operate as angelic beings, so whatever you create contains within it your intentions. Now, you might say: 'If I am creating a chair my intention is to create a chair.' And, yes, it is, but on a greater level you also have intentions with which you approach the Earth, with which you approach others and with which you approach yourself on a daily basis. These are, for the most part, subconscious intentions but, nevertheless, they exist. For example, you might see the world as a wonderful place and want to contribute to that wonderful place on a daily basis. You might treat the world with suspicion on a daily basis and expect the world to deliver to you less than satisfactory experiences. You might approach the world with anger and expect the world to deliver to you circumstances which justify that anger.

Each individual on Earth has a different approach to the world, has a different approach to society and has a different approach to others. For example, do you love others on a daily basis, do you hate others on a daily basis or do you treat others with indifference on a daily basis? There are so many different aspects with which you can approach what appears to be your 'outer world'. Of course, you can also approach *yourself* in different ways ...you can say, 'I am not a worthy being' ...you can say, 'I am a tremendous being' ...you can say, 'I am an average being' ...you can say, 'I am an ill being.' Because of your subconscious choices towards yourself, towards others and towards the Earth, with *anything* that you create, you place those underlying themes into the creative matrix and into the matter that has formed because of your wish to create something.

223

So, for example (going back to my favourite analogy of the chair) I can, as one person, create an angry chair; I can, as one person, create a welcoming chair; I can, as one person, create a defective chair; I can, as one person, create a chair that is superior in its feel to other chairs. So, every object contains the subconscious wishes of its creator. And we are not just talking here about chairs, buildings or hard matter that you can see and react to ...**we are talking about thought as well.**

If you are applying a thought to how you want to structure a relationship or how you want to create society (as just two examples) every thought has within it a subconscious layer of themes that flavour how that relationship or how that approach to society reacts to you and to others and reacts within the Field of consciousness of mankind.

So, *nothing* is neutral.

The painter puts love into his painting, but the angry chair-maker creates chairs that have within them a signature – not only of being a chair – but of being angry until ...*and this is important*... **until such time as the resonance within those objects is changed.**

So, an angry chair remains angry; a depressive building remains depressive. That energy maintains itself – just as the physical structure maintains itself. The chair maintains itself as a chair until, through entropy, its molecules break down *partially*. We know that they cannot breakdown totally as they should do outside of the area of the Fall because of the effects of the Fall. But, until that chair breaks down through entropy, its signature of being an angry chair continues. And, the molecules that cannot disperse themselves completely once the chair breaks down, also have within them the radiation of anger until such time as the theme of those molecules is changed.

This is why we stress the importance of placing Light into the world.

I hope this 'illuminates' (and forgive the pun) the need to put Light into society ...Light into objects ...Light into thought-patterns ...Light into other people because, in bringing Light into those objects, into those people, into those situations, into those concepts, into those buildings *from beyond the Field* – from the God-within – you rededicate the molecules within the objects to make them more God-like. You reset them to a state that is close to the one they would have had – had they been created from outside the area of the Fall, in dedication to God and angelic intent.

You see the urgency and dire need to place Light into this world on a daily basis and to build that into your structure as part of the radiation of vibrations that you give out. Within the Field of human consciousness are contained all the physical objects that you see and all the non-physical concepts that you live by ...your approach to government ...your approach to illness ...your approach to structure in society ...your approach to each other ...your approach to yourselves. And, all these things contain within them the *intent* of their creator or creators.

They contain within them the intent, for example, of the chair-maker, but they also exhibit and contain the intent of the souls who maintain this level – yourselves – as a collective creative force. So, the chair from the angry chair-maker has within it the vibrations of anger that have allowed that chair to be created in the first place *plus* those molecules of anger resonate and attract to themselves *more anger* from the Field of consciousness around them.

So, we have to 'turn the hour-glass right over' and we have to place Light-vibrations into objects, into buildings, into each other, into concepts, into the way that we view society so that those begin to resonate with God-consciousness and with angelic intent, rather than with the lower vibrations of the Field of human consciousness at this time.

In examining this chapter, therefore, you have to also examine what *you* place into the world apart from Light [*smiling*] because, in placing Light into the world, you are also surrounding that Light with your intentions ...and your intentions might not be as noble as the intentions of the Light-core that you are sending from your heart-centre.

So, at all times you need to look at the underlying approach that you have to yourself and to this world, and to say to yourself: 'What is my motivation? How do I see people? Do I see people in a neutral or (*better still*) in a loving way, or do I see people with a bias? Do I put a spin onto my thinking so that I expect people to react to me – and me to them – in a certain way? Do I see the world as being a dark and angry place, or do I see the world as being a world of potential and a world that will blossom back into what it was before the time of the Fall?'

So, you have to approach *yourself* with Light too, and it is an excellent exercise on a daily basis – or certainly on a weekly basis – to sit within the sphere of Light that I described in the previous chapter and *to bathe your intentions in Light*. Bathe your intentions in Light and ask the God-within to illuminate your subconscious and your conscious minds so that you know what your viewpoint is towards the world.

And, what is revealed to you in those times of bathing yourself in Light *may surprise you* because you will find that emerging from your heart-centre into your physical mind is sometimes *shock* ...shock at the way that you approach people ...shock at the way you approach yourself, but also an angelic maturity that gives you the strength to say: 'Well, perhaps I am less than perfect in the way that I am operating currently within the matrix of the Field. I am perfect as an angelic being, but I have surrounded myself with beliefs and approaches that are less than beneficial to myself, to others and to the Field of human consciousness.'

It is a brave thing to bathe yourself in Light. It is a brave thing to listen to the God-within. It is a brave thing to realise that perhaps your approach is more biased than you think it is. Perhaps you are the equivalent of the chair-maker who is making exquisite, beautiful chairs but is placing within those chairs an underlying theme of anger, reproach, judgement or limitation.

This exercise of sitting within a sphere of Light and feeling the Light well up from within you, integrating with and illuminating every part of your being and your mind is not a judgemental exercise. It is not something that you should do with the view of *what a terrible person I am.* It is something you should do with a view to remembering that you are a perfect angelic being and that in the Light you can illuminate the dark corners ...**and in illuminating the dark corners, the dark corners disappear.** They disappear and they make you a far more effective vessel and transmitter of the Light that is needed in all those areas where people don't realise that they have dark corners.

Having sat for yourself, you can then transmit the Light out into the world knowing that that Light is always effective. Do not misunderstand me – *it is always effective* no matter what your biases towards others and yourself, but, you can make it *even more effective* by harmonising in a greater way with that Light through the sweeping out of those tendencies that place vibrations into your connections with the world that are, perhaps, less than illuminating.

Then, having sat in your sphere of Light, you also have to regard your world in a different way because you are surrounded on a daily basis by material objects. You sit on those chairs; you drive cars; you exist in buildings; you walk on roads; you shop in stores – but all of these areas and objects have within them vibrations that might be less than you would admit into your house, were you able to tune in to them.

You would not, of volition, buy an angry chair, would you? And so, you have to get used to blessing and putting Light into the objects around you. If you buy something new, bless it and dedicate it in God's Light before you use it. Before you step into the car, just place your hands on it and infuse the car with God-Light before you drive it. On a weekly basis, go through each room of your house and spread Light into each room to rededicate the objects within your house in the name of the Light and to create for yourself a 'fortress of Light' within which you can operate as a harmonic God-being, as a harmonic angelic being.

This, of course, also applies to the food that you eat, to the liquids that you drink and to the clothes that you wear. And you will say: 'Joseph, this sounds like a terribly complex undertaking. It sounds like I have to be conscious, minute by minute, of where I am, what I am doing and what I am reacting with on a material level.' ...And, yes, *you do* but remember that at first you might have found it difficult to meditate or to give out the Light. These things become second nature once you practise them and are aware of them. It only takes a second on almost a subconscious level to make sure that the surroundings you find yourself in at all times are of benefit to you and to the people whose lives you touch.

And *I promise you* that, if you dedicate your houses, your cars, your objects, your clothes, your food and your drink with Light – if you infuse those things with Light – then you will have a more harmonic life, you will have a healthier life, you will have a more inspiring life and you will have a life during which you can make so much more of a difference to the Field of human consciousness whilst you are here.

So, there are great benefits in recognising that what you see is *just the surface* of all objects and that contained within all objects are the dominant traits of the people who have created those objects. And that, of course, applies (as we have said) to the non-material aspects of society, society itself, and the way in which society is run because those are constructs. The plans that people put into, for example, creating a police force or an army or a structure of government become solidified in the ether. They become structures that, to angelic eyes, are every bit as real and as solid as the buildings, and the chairs, and the crockery, and the cars and the roads.

They are structures that are created by individuals or by groups of individuals, and then those structures are given intent ...*are given intent*. And that intent is not always the intent of the surface. The plan for government, for example, is not always the surface plan for government that might be written down and put in a folder. It is that surface plan, yes, but beneath that surface plan there are the layers of intent from all those people who have put together the plan in the first place and are maintaining the plan by giving it energy on a daily basis. So, the plan can be self-corrupting – do you see?

The plan can be self-corrupting dependent on the strength of the vibrations that are interwoven beneath the surface of the plan. So, if there is a plan which on the surface looks to be sound and for the good of people, you have to send Light into the structure as well, and then it will change because the structure will become what it was intended to be. If the people who created that structure in the first place had good intent, you can restore that good intent, or perhaps allow that good intent to emerge for the first time by putting Light into your concept of the 'concept' of government ...into the concept of a peace-keeping force ... into the concept of a police force ...into all these concepts that exist and are as permanent and solid on a non-sensory level as the objects around you materially.

It is important to bathe *everything* in Light.

It is important to bathe the people around you in Light as well because (as we have said in many of the books) in bathing people in Light, you bring to the surface of *their* consciousness those aspects of themselves and those intentions from themselves that are less than harmonic with the intentions of the angelic being that they really are. Then they have the option through free will of discarding those intentions once they have identified them.

Remember that, as an angelic being, you cannot create without intent.

229

You cannot create without intent – whether you are making a painting or a piece of furniture – *whatever* the object is. And you may say, 'I am just putting this together,' but there is an intent with it. There is a conscious intent in making a painting or a stick of furniture – but there is also a *subconscious* intent. What is that subconscious intent? How do I regard that object? Is it neutral?

NEVER!

Never is it neutral.

There is [*laughing*] the old phrase of a 'Friday afternoon car', is there not? …'A Friday afternoon car' because on a Friday afternoon the intent is to get away from the process of manufacturing the car, and so, by its very intent, that car has within it the capability of breaking down more often than an identical car that has been created on another day. Do you see?

Everything has intention. As an angel you cannot create without intention. Your original intention is to bring experience to the Godhead. So, your original intention is pure and blissful and enlightening. Your original intention is to create spheres of experience but spheres of *uplifting* experience, *harmonious* experience, *evolutionary* experience …not the experience that you are having currently around the world. And, you have to understand *that* to strengthen your ability to be a creative force for God-Light in this world at this time.

I hope you see that this book is concluding and has given you, throughout its chapters thus far, the means of *enhancing* your ability to make a difference in the world and make a difference to yourself and to the people around you, because we are still on that knife-edge, Dear Reader. We are *still very much* on that knife-edge of existence on this physical level, and that 'knife' can fall either way. What we are trying to do immediately is to make sure that it doesn't fall at all for the time being, and to make sure that *when it falls* it falls on the side of the Light. We don't want it to fall on the side of the darkness, but that is all to do with intent and rededication of this world and the intentions of the people who live on this plane, and it is all to do ...as I have said in many of the books... **it is all to do with *you*.**

That difference is made by *you* – not you alone but it is made by you ...and you ...and you ...and you around the world. You have to look at this world in a different way, and I guarantee that if you look at this world in the way that I have suggested today, if you look for the intentions behind physical objects and the intentions behind people on a subconscious level, you will begin to see them. You will begin to see the world as it is, and seeing the world as it is will not bring you down in your approach to your Light-bringing but will make you more effective as a Light-bearer.

Are there questions, please?

Jane: Joseph, is creative intent as strong a force as subsequent 'user-intent'? For example, you might have a chair made in the eighteenth century by an angry cabinet-maker but if that chair was then loved by the first owner and cherished by subsequent generations, could the love bestowed on it later be stronger than the original creative anger?

Joseph: At the point of creation the subconscious wishes of the creator are placed into the object and, in fact, that is the *strongest vibration* held within the object because the object is a temporary illusion placed around an intent. So, the intent is always there. Now, until the intent is changed by rededicating the spin of the molecules and by rededicating the way in which they react with the rest of the plane around them, that intent remains a constant. But, as you have correctly said (and the theme of this chapter is, indeed, about loving things better because Light and Love are the same thing, of course) in loving the chair, you change the concept of the chair and change its awareness (because everything is alive) of what its intention and purpose is.

This can be done by placing your hands on an object and seeing the Light streaming from your hands into every part of the object. This can be done by talking to the object and explaining to it that you love it, that it is an essential part of God's plan, that it is a part of the Light and that it is in the atmosphere of your own loving home and is part of a community of objects that are dedicated to the Light and which exhibit Light. By doing that you then change the original intention of the chair.

As to which is the greater force – the original dedication of anger or the later dedication of Love – that is dependent on the force with which you place the Love into the object. Remember that the chair-maker may not have necessarily known that he was spreading his angry view of the world into the chair in the first place. So, in that case, there is this undercurrent of anger. What you are trying to do is replace that undercurrent of anger with a bright rededication of Light so that every aspect of that chair (not just the undercurrent) is loved. The chair then becomes what it was originally at core, which is Love. It remembers (as we have asked you to remember who *you* are) ...it remembers what it is as an original creative intention. Do you see that?

Jane: Yes, thank you very much.

Tony: Can I ask a question further to that, Joseph? The anger is the emotion that was built into the chair by the craftsman, and emotions and beliefs are less tangible than a chair but they are what drive human beings. We have minds that are constantly chattering and a lot of the time the thoughts are unproductive, and I have this image of them bubbling up and spilling into the Field. Is there a way that we can catch these thoughts? Sometimes we make judgements in our minds that are not productive, so if we spot them can we neutralise those thoughts that we have just released into the ether?

Joseph: There is an interesting phrase there ...'if we spot them'... and that is the most important phrase in your question because, if you spot them, you are already elevating above them. In spotting them, you are recognising them. If you cannot spot them, you have not come to that point at which you recognise the need for change. Do you see that?

Tony: I do.

Joseph: So, it is a matter of – *in Love* – infusing yourself with the God-Light and the God-power which is your birthright ...not your birthright as a physical being but your *original* birthright as being a point of view of God. And so, you sit in Light and you bathe yourself in Light *and you love yourself*. You are not looking, in those circumstances, for anything that is counter-productive or disharmonic. You are simply, in God-Love from the heart-centre, bathing yourself in Light. That Light then has the effect of strengthening, protecting and armouring your original state of being and bringing that original state of being more to the fore through your heart-mind and through your physical mind.

As a result of harmonising with your true self you then, in the times when you are not meditating to bathe yourself in Light, become aware of areas that need to be changed if you are to be at your most effective in becoming a channeller for Light and a bringer of harmony into all circumstances and into all people whose lives you touch. And so, it is a process of sitting in the Light *non-judgementally*. This is not a process of judging but of *discovery*. This is a process of discovering the inner you – *the original you* – and, through bathing that 'original you' with Light, allowing the strength of the 'original you' to look at the layers of the 'surface you' and to say: 'Those aspects there are now no longer what I choose to harmonise with.' Does that make sense?

Tony: Thank you.

Joseph: None of this is judgemental. None of this is looking at yourself and saying, 'I am a terrible person.' This is looking at yourself through the absorption of Light and saying: 'I have been wearing 'clothes' for a long while that don't suit me any more so

233

I need to change them. I need to put on some other clothes ... clothes of Light. I have discovered habits in my life in the way that I think that *now* need to be modified because I no longer think in that way.'

It is a process of letting go, but in order to let go you first have to discover what you need to let go of. And you find that out by going within, by bringing Light into your being and becoming what you originally were and what you *still* are, which then sheds – like unwanted, shabby clothing – all those surface aspects of yourself that have prevented you, prior to you undertaking the Light exercises, from operating more as the angelic being and less as the small earthly personality. Again, is that clear?

Tony: When we are created as human beings, do we then have those essences built into us over and above genes and the stuff we know about? Like the anger in the chair, do we have an emotion built into us even before we get here?

Joseph: 'Built in' is the wrong term; we have to examine what we have said in the past about re-entering this arena of skewed vision with regard to the effects of the Fall on the God-consciousness within.

You have *by choice* – whether that choice is because you wish to be a Light-bringer in the darkness or because you want to re-experience the effects of the physical plane that is the Earth – **you have *by choice* come here.** You come here as an angelic being, but you are automatically clothed in the consequences of the Fall through your physicality once you come here. Also (as we have said before) you resonate with aspects of your past lives here. The themes of your past lives that have not been sorted out on a physical level resonate with you again, to a lesser or greater extent, depending on who you are and the strength of your angelic vision and angelic purpose whilst you are here.

Those emotions are not built into you. Those emotions are part of this physical framework, and have to be recognised as such and let go of. We have to remember that the whole purpose of *the Joseph Communications* is to make you aware that this illusion is not as it should be and this creative area is not as it was originally created to be (which is the point of today's chapter).

We could just as easily talk about the Earth as talk about a chair. So, what we have in the Earth at the moment are the underlying currents that are the effects of the Fall that constantly and repeatedly bring to the surface in people the baser consequences of having speeded up matter so long ago ...that repeat the violence ...that repeat the power-struggle ...that repeat the selfishness. But those things are *surface*. They are not what the person is about at core, and what we have to get back to is what the person is *at core* – which is an angelic being.

In recognising that you are an angelic being you let go of all those attitudes. These are not emotions – they are attitudes. They are a combination of attitudes that are filtered by the emotions so that you react to the world in a certain way. They are viewpoints, and they all go back to the one big viewpoint at the time of the Fall: 'We are right. This is how we are going to do things, and from now on this is a better way to create' ...*which obviously it is not*. Does that make sense?

Tony: Thank you, Joseph.

David: Where does intention actually arise from? Is it from the angelic core of our being and, if so, why would it be laced with anger? Or is it that the intent is more pure and then gets stepped down as it approaches the physical plane and becomes affected by our attitudes and so forth?

Joseph: The intent is always at creative heart to create for the joy of creation ...to create so that what you create can be experienced by others ...and to create arenas within which angelic beings can *play* (because at that level of creation it is play and is recognised as play) in order to bring to the Godhead the experiences that have arisen and presented themselves because of those arenas.

At angelic heart, the creative act is always one of pleasing God ...of pleasing the angelic host ...of pleasing the individual as an angelic being ...of furthering the creative process ...and of furthering the experience of the individual and of God by presenting new vistas and arenas within which angelic beings can play, discover bliss and take that bliss back to the Godhead.

Because of the effects of the Fall, you are a layered being. People on Earth are not aware, for the most part, that they are angelic beings. The reason is they have layered themselves in fields of physicality and materiality. The chair-maker does not usually say, 'I am going to create an angry chair'. He says, 'I am going to create a chair', but because that chair is an extension of himself, as he creates the chair and it exists on a lower level of energy (the chair has to exist on this plane within the sphere of the Fall) those aspects of himself that are of the Fall and of this lower physical level imprint themselves onto the chair. They cannot do otherwise because the chair is part of himself and is simply an expression of creativity. And so, the chair picks up the dominant physical and material vibrations within the aura or sphere of influence of its creator.

Now, we have majored upon the creativity of someone who creates an angry chair, but the contrast to that is someone who is blissfully in harmony with their angelic self and is a loving and Light-giving being, who creates a chair that has Light within it, that has a resonance of Love within it, that makes everyone who sits in it feel wonderful, feel comforted, feel warm, welcomed and safe. This is the difference.

You have to be consciously aware of who you are and be *spiritually* consciously aware of what you are putting into whatever you create. After a time that then becomes a *subconscious* theme of Light (just as the anger is a subconscious theme). And there will be times when you are making something or addressing something, and you think to yourself: 'Wait a minute! I have just tilted that a little bit. I am putting my own biases into it when I should be putting a God-bias and an angelic bias into it,' so whatever it is (whether it is a chair or a concept for the benefit of society) it will operate at its highest level within this sphere of degraded, skewed matter.

And, if you have enough angelic viewpoints creating objects of Light, creating an approach of Light towards all aspects of society and creating an approach of Light towards each other ... then the effects of the Fall are nullified.

Does that make sense?

David: Yes, it does. Thank you.

Chapter Sixteen
Paper-Thin

Joseph: I have an unusual chapter heading for you this time and it is 'Paper-Thin' ...*paper-thin*. Now, what on Earth is Joseph talking about ...*paper-thin*?

I am referring to the fact that on Earth you gather in houses, in forts, in castles, in communal buildings, and you believe that, once you have shut your house door, you are perfectly private and are safe with your own thoughts. I have to tell you, at this point, that **you are never safe with your own thoughts** – at least not on the level of physical mind, because the walls of your houses, your castles and your communal buildings are no protection against the *communal thoughts* that link to *your* thoughts minute by minute, day by day.

The protection that you feel is around you on a physical level is paper-thin because, whatever your dominant thoughts are on a physical and mental level those thoughts connect with and attract *more of the same vibration.*

There is no such thing on a spiritual level as an isolated thought.

On an angelic level (and remember that you are angelic beings) your thoughts connect to thoughts of similar intention from within the angelic host, and this is an accepted way of being – *this is the God-way of being.* You are intended to be part of a community, and so your thoughts are expressions of intention and expressions of the ability to visualise and bring forth potential. Once you have, as an angelic being, determined what you want to bring forth, your thoughts connect to similar thoughts from the angelic host. Similar angels, who wish to bring forth the *same thing*, and who are interested in the potential that you are proposing, cluster and gravitate towards you so that they can enjoy, put forth and investigate the same potential with you ...and you with them.

So, your thoughts as an angel are a message, an invitation and an intention, and because of that message, invitation and intention, *similar intentions* cluster around the indicator that you have put out into the matrix of angelic thought.

You are no different on Earth.

You are an angelic being *at core* now, and your thoughts attract in the same way ...as a request to examine potential... so your thoughts on an earthly level attract similar thoughts. The moment, for example, that you become angry about something, your thoughts attract, seek out and bring towards you *similar thoughts of anger* from those who are subconsciously angry in a similar way at that particular point ...and *also* from the Field, whose intention it is to maintain itself at a negative setting and to hold you in thrall to its intentions. And so, every angry thought attracts further angry thoughts.

Every thought of sadness attracts similar thoughts of sadness, because those similar thoughts of sadness come from other angelic beings encased in matter, who subconsciously recognise your invitation to partake in sadness and gather around you – and you around them.

I want to get to the core of this chapter, which is to say that there is no such thing as a single, isolated thought and that the barriers of your individuality, which you perceive on a physical level are *actually not there*. They are only there as an illusion, and you cannot have a thought in isolation because every thought resonates with similar thoughts and intentions from around the world and from around the universe.

Unfortunately, because of the effects of the Fall, your thoughts on a *physical level* harmonise with similar negative thoughts from within this bubble of skewed creation and, from the point of physical mind, are not able to connect with greater, more constructive and more elevating thoughts. This is why you have to come to the point of heart-mind in order for your more noble thoughts to have greater power.

We have talked in many of the books about the need to connect with the heart-mind, because at the heart-mind you connect with God-mind and you connect with angelic-mind. I have to stress this again today, and I hope the first part of this chapter explains why it is so important to go to heart-mind rather than head-mind.

Head-mind thoughts connect with similar thoughts from around the world and from within the Field.

Heart-mind thoughts connect with angelic thought and with God-thought.

In your intention to change the world and to illuminate yourself, you have to *always* operate from the point of heart-mind. You have to isolate yourself from physical thought by withdrawing into the heart-centre and *there* stating your intention for yourself, for the world and for the people who live in this world. Then, those intentions are connected to and given greater power by angelic thoughts and the thoughts of the spirits who have, to a certain extent, relinquished this world and are proceeding away from the effects of the Fall through the spheres of cleansing towards Infinity.

So, your heart-mind thoughts have great power because, just like your head-mind thoughts **your heart-mind thoughts are not**

thought in isolation. They are 'thought as intent' and, because of that wish to see the world in a certain way and to transmit Light into it, are then connected to the similar wishes of spirits, who are working to raise the world out of its present conditions through Light-based intention.

What you also have to consider is that many times your thoughts are not totally your own. Now, that is an astounding thing to consider, isn't it?

...Your thoughts, at times, are not actually *totally* your own.

Let us go back to that example of anger. When you become angry, you link with similar thoughts and intentions, but you are a single angel and a single point of intent at the moment that you have the thought. But, once you have had the thought and are entertaining it, you then join with many, many other similar thoughts and intentions ...so your anger is given force. And your anger can be fuelled, maintained and sustained not by your original thought, but by the thoughts that elevate that anger in your mind and psyche, *into more than it was when you thought it.*

So, it is important always to go to the heart-mind when you find yourself troubled ...when you find yourself saddened ... when you find yourself angry ...when you find yourself despairing ...when you find that you feel as though you need to turn away from the world and don't want to contribute anything more to it... because the original thought, yes, can have been yours, but then that initial negative intention is *magnified* a hundredfold ...a thousandfold ...a millionfold and is sustained by the fact that it is connected (as it was originally supposed to do in the way you operate as an angel) to similar thoughts that *fuel* it.

And, there are energies out there that *wish* to maintain you in a state of anger ...wish to maintain you in a state of sadness ... wish to maintain you in a state of depression and despair, because it serves their purposes for you to be in thrall to the Field and maintain the Earth and society as it is today – i.e. dependent on the energies of the Field.

So, what I am suggesting is that the next time you feel 'under the weather' ...or angry ...or sad ...or resentful ...or revengeful, examine how much of that thought is yours and how much of it is coming from the Field and from the minds around you by transferring in meditation from the head-mind to the heart-centre and *asking*: 'Father, why am I angry? Why am I depressed? Why am I sad? Is this solely *my* thought?'

And, as you bathe yourself in the energies of the heart-centre and connect to the Light, you will find that it isn't. You will find that that anger lifts, that depression lifts, that sadness lifts and *dissipates*, and you are left in a state of peace so that you can re-energise yourself and turn that initial thought of negativity around into something constructive ...into a wish for Light and peace for yourself and the world. That will then attract the higher minds from the cleansing spheres and the angelic spheres and will allow you to turn what was a negative situation into something very positive, uplifting and transforming for yourself and for this world.

We are always there, ready to help.

There is a misconception that the spirit worlds and cleansing spheres are far away, that it is extremely difficult to contact them and that they can only be contacted through mediumistic activity and through deep meditation.

We are on the other side of that paper-thin barrier that you have placed around yourself ...*always* ...from second to second and from minute to minute.

The instant that you *think* of us and the instant that you connect your intentions with our intentions **we are there** (not just there outside the paper-thin walls of your consciousness but within them) adding our Light to your Light, our intuition to your intuition and our intentions to your intentions to make sure that you are balanced and whole and that you are the most effective vessel you can be in holding and transmitting the Light so that this world can be transformed.

There is always, always, *always* connection to us, but, from your point of view, the walls that you have put up and invested so much energy and belief into seem like impenetrable barriers. So another thing I wish you to do as a result of this chapter, please, is to not regard yourself as being in isolation any longer, and to understand that the walls that you perceive as being thick and around you (both the material walls of your homes and buildings and the walls that you perceive and place around you to protect you from other people) *are not what they seem.* They are only solid because you believe in them as being solid. And you can still protect yourself from the energies of the Field whilst letting in higher inspiration and higher intent.

If you examine some of the negative 'spark' thoughts that we have talked about today, we can banish them instantly. If you are angry – why are you angry? You are an eternal angel …you are an infinite spirit …you are connected to Love. That is the way out of anger: to remember that you are connected to Love, you are connected to God and you are connected to us. It is simply a matter of changing your mind and changing your thought-process.

If you are sad because you feel isolated and lonely – you cannot be lonely because you are eternally, infinitely connected to each of us and to the God-within. And, if you go within to the heart-centre and take your loneliness and sadness in there to examine it and let it free, we will connect with you. Even though you may not see us, you will feel that you are a part of a family, you are loved, you are nurtured, you are balanced and there is nothing to fear.

If you look at a thought of depression – a thought of depression is only there because you are reacting to the Field around you

243

and are subconsciously missing your spiritual status and spiritual home. So, once again, retreat into the heart-centre taking that depression with you, and allow the energies within the heart-centre to bathe that feeling and the depression will disappear. You will be filled ...not with *hope* ...but with a *certainty* of positive action taking place around and within you on our part and on your part because of the connection that you are making again to us.

There are no barriers.

If only the people of the world understood this: there are no barriers and there are no thoughts taken in isolation. Yes, you are the originator of your thoughts in that if you are presented with a variety of different emotions and thoughts in front of you, minute to minute, you say: 'I choose this one.' ...'I choose that one.' ...'I select this one.' ...'I select that feeling.' ...'I select those circumstances.' But they are communal – they are not originating from you.

You are the *chooser* within a field of glorious angelic thought.

Minute by minute, you decide what you want to harmonise with ...whether it is the *bliss* of existence within God's Creation, or whether it is the dark *despair* of a viewpoint coming from an isolated position within the Field and not acknowledging any spiritual upliftment whatsoever.

So, you are choosing. The moment you choose, yes, the initial choice is yours, but then *that choice has consequences*. That choice brings towards you similar thoughts from other choosers. You are linking into a 'pool' or a set of vibrations that signify different emotions, intentions and hoped-for outcomes. You do not do this in isolation.

Every intent on Earth has, beneath it and behind it, *similar* intents.

If only you understood this.

If only everyone on Earth understood this then, knowing that they could go within to the heart-centre and choose *something else* consciously, they would be able to step back from their anger …step back from their potential violence …step back from their need to get even …step back from their sadness …step back from their despair and depression – and fill themselves with Light and choose from that 'table of potential' in front of them uplifting thoughts …transforming thoughts …strengthening thoughts … balanced thoughts.

Then that range of thoughts that creates disharmony would wither because no energy, no choice and no volition would be put into it. And so, anger would shrink as a concept across the world; depression would shrink as a concept within individuals; sadness would be banished – because they would simply be old-fashioned ways of thinking that are no longer tuned into, individually and communally. Instead, that 'table of potential creation' in front of each spirit would be an uplifting one: …'Today we are harmonious.' …'Today we are creative.' …'Today we are more than we were yesterday.' …'Today we are builders in the right way.' … 'Today we are lovers and healers of the Earth.' …'Today we are part of the angelic host with limitless, bright, blissful potential in front of us.'

There are no barriers. *You* create barriers.

There are no isolated thoughts. You choose what you wish to think and how you wish to feel but, at the moment you do so, you magnify whatever it is you choose and wish to feel via *either* the God-potential and angelic potential within you …or the limited and negative desires of the Field. They say, don't they, 'Guard your thoughts!'

…Indeed! Guard your thoughts!

Guard them carefully. Recognise that they are *not ever just your thoughts*, and if you find yourself in a blind fury or a deep depression remember that the fury is 'blind' and Light can be put into it, remember that you can be lifted from the depression through Light and remember that you can visit the heart-centre to bring out the best parts of yourself.

This is not a negative chapter. It may appear so and be frightening for you to consider that you do not ever have a single thought in isolation, but it is not about frightening you. It is about making you *aware of that fact* so that you can use your thought-process as a tool to create a more uplifted you, a more uplifted society and a healed and Light-filled Earth.

Your thoughts are tools.

Do you see? You are not your thoughts – you are the *chooser* behind those thoughts. Your thoughts are tools. Angelically your thoughts are 'a flag of intention waved about in the air' that is seen by those of similar intention who then gather around that flag and wear its colours.

You are not your thoughts – you are the chooser of thoughts. You can choose different thoughts, and it has been my intention all along in gathering this book together to give you better ways, to give you further explanations of *how* you can tap into the Light and why you *should* tap into the Light, and how you can create that *better world* simply by choosing ...and seeing ...and dreaming ...and selecting that better world.

Bearing in mind what I have said about negativity, you can now see that, if you choose *the better world* from that 'table of potential' in front of you, you choose to link with all those people on Earth and around the Earth in the cleansing spheres who also wish that better world. What power of thought you have then!

What power of thought for change!

Back, finally, as we end this chapter, to 'isolation' because many of you have asked in contacting us [*reference to e-mails received by The Band of Light*] how you can sit for the Light, what you can do by yourself and whether you are making a difference. Can you see now that you are never by yourself? The minute you think something you are not by yourself, and so when you sit from the heart-centre, when you sit for the Light, you connect with millions ...billions of souls who also want to sit for the Light, who also want to see that better world in front of them *now*. And, I have said before that one person sitting for the Light is the equal of thousands of people sitting in fear and in connection to the Field **...now I have explained why**. I hope this makes sense to you.

Are there questions on this topic, please?

David: Joseph, does silence have a role to play in turning from the communal thoughts of the Field to the heart-mind?

Joseph: Your natural setting as an angel wishing to create is one of quiet expectation and quiet contemplation of what you wish to bring forth. And, there is the ability to connect fully to the angelic host in whatever the potential is that you wish to bring forth or to de-select from the angelic host your *individuality* for a time in order to contemplate. This does not mean that you are disconnected from the angelic host. It means (as we have talked in previous books about going into the no-thing) that you have selected for a time to examine your *own* wishes, to examine your *own* being, to examine your *own* part that you are going to play in the potential that you intend to bring forth.

In becoming silent and becoming contemplative, you become the *opposite* of what the Field is, and [*smiling*] you become the quiet oasis within the cacophony of noise, intent and action that is the Field. So, you are quite right – in becoming silent and contemplative you take that first step to divorce yourself from the Field. **You become of a different vibration.**

But, you also have to consider that, even at that point when you become contemplative and quiet, you link with other souls who are contemplative and quiet and wish to withdraw from the Field. So, you are already adding power – even at your contemplative, quiet stage – to the potential for Light and the potential for positive change that you are about to bring forth. It is an excellent means of preparing yourself for the Light-bearing and Light-sharing that you are about to bring forth.

You must also understand *ironically* (if that is the right word) that, even at that point, you are still connected to the angelic host and are still making decisions. You are *deciding* to become silent, you are *deciding* to become contemplative, you are *considering* those states of being in thought and, by doing so, you connect with similar thoughts of silence, peace and contemplation. You are connected with another set of values, but they are the values that you wish to bring out by going within to the heart-centre. This question (for which I thank you) reinforces the concept that you are never alone ...even when you are – you are not.

...Even when you are – you are not [*laughing*] because, in choosing to be alone, you link with everyone else who chooses to be alone. It is a state and a choice from that 'menu' of potentials and it links you to similar intents – to choose as an intent *I wish this*. The minute you wish something, you draw it towards you and you draw towards you other souls who are wishing the same thing because they are on the same waveband. It is like they have entered a room that says, 'I wish silence.' They are drawn to that room simply by wishing it but they are all connected within that room. Then they come out of that room, wish something else and find themselves in another room, which contains every other soul that wishes that particular state of being.

Ultimately, on an angelic level, this applies to every point in Creation; this applies to every point in the universe; this applies to every point in the *universes*. So, you could say, on an infinitesimally small level, you are drawing silence to you from everywhere. You are drawing every point of silence and contemplation to yourself from *everywhere* – that is your potential. It is only here that your potential is stifled, dampened and diminished by the barrier you have put up as angelic children that we call 'the Fall'.

Does that make sense?

David: It does, thank you.

Jane: Joseph, could I just ask for clarification on head-mind thoughts, because I think you said that head-mind thoughts attract other thoughts from *within* the Field. If people have positive head-mind thoughts – such as artists and musicians – are they only linking with other artists and musicians on the Earth, or do they connect with similar thoughts from the spirit realms as well?

Joseph: If I could draw a *diagram* of the human being and could circle the thoughts of the mind, if the mind is having an everyday thought then that mind draws from the Field around it – particularly if that mind is not aware of or doesn't believe in any form of spiritual concept. So, there is a circle there where that mind is which connects to circles that signify the other physical minds of the people around the world who are encased by the Fall.

When you choose *positive* creative thoughts – for example, artistic and musical thoughts – then there is a circle for the physical mind and another circle here [*indicating the heart*], which is the heart-mind, and 'tendrils' come up from the heart-mind through the body into the head-mind. There is an instant connection. Now, this is not always a conscious thing but because you are ennobling yourself by examining your potential to create beauty and to work with love and with Light you pull up, irradiate and infuse the mental faculties *for that time* with thoughts from the spiritual centre **...with thoughts of what you *truly* are.**

It is then a matter of the strength of the heart-mind thoughts versus the strength creatively of the head-mind thoughts as to which wins in the expression that finally comes out as art or music. Because, if you look at art and music, you will find that some examples of art are dark and some examples of music are discordant. You are drawing from the heart-mind but then the head-mind infuses, masks and mingles with, to a lesser or greater degree, those thoughts from the heart-mind and translates them into its vision of art or its vision of music or its vision in other areas of creative expression. Do you see?

Jane: Yes, thank you.

Tony: Most people on Earth live in partnerships of some kind, and there's a percentage of people who understand spiritual concepts and are working for the Light ...but then they can go home and, for example, get very niggled at their partner 'for stacking the dishwasher wrongly'. Many couples can have a lot of anger within their relationship, so am I right in assuming that that anger must be very damaging because negative thoughts aimed against somebody else will actually do harm to that person?

Joseph: Yes, every creative wish constructs ...or deconstructs... and every creative wish pulls towards it a set of creative building blocks which *eventually* form into something on a physical level.

I think we have to go back to what you mentioned with regard to couples. You have to understand that there are two types of couple. There is the couple who are on a connective mission and a harmonious vibration. And then there is the couple who, as a result of choosing to incarnate, have been brought together for a relatively small amount of time (one lifetime, perhaps, or certainly less in the case of many couples today) to examine and make the most of confronting those conflicting emotions *positively* and to transmute them. In effect, we have to go back to the book that describes how the Lords of Karma work [*reference to* **Revelation**]. They have been put together so that, in ideal conditions, they can raise themselves out of those detrimental emotions by learning to work in harmony. **But, they would not have to learn to work in harmony in this seemingly brutal and violent way** *had they not first decided to reincarnate.*

It is another example of the most potentially beneficial circumstances being woven into two life-paths in order to raise those two life-paths above the pull of the Field, so that they can recognise their angelic inheritance again. Then *hopefully* (Please, God!) when they move on from the physical realm, they will make the decision not to revisit this plane, but can investigate positive potential by moving through the cleansing spheres and, at the end of that process, escape through that 'hatch' that I always mention …into Infinity and back into bliss.

It is very difficult for us to watch the eruptions of anger that are constantly bursting throughout the thick layers of the Field. As an analogy: it is like seeing boiling water with the bubbles rising to the surface and bursting – except they are not transparent as you would have with boiling water …they are blackened, red, angry and sore.

And, yes, there is always an effect of anger on the person that anger is directed towards. First of all, it makes the person *more* angry but it also disturbs the vibrations around them. It restricts them, it holds in and masks their creative potential and it does put up a barrier, which, strangely, *is greater than paper-thin*. It hobbles them, it imprisons them and it attacks them.

Anger *within* in response to anger *without* actually lets the anger into the physical body and into the physical mind. If held unchecked for a long period of time, that anger that is being fed from without speeds up the physical body (even more than it is speeded up because of the effects of the Fall) and begins to deteriorate the organs. **It begins to deteriorate the organs!**

So, the greatest protection that anyone can have (and we could talk for days on this subject) is to go to the heart-mind and send out Light as a response to the anger and to send out Light as a response to the restricting vibrations that are being sent towards them ...then that anger cannot take hold. You have chosen another way. From that 'table of possibility', you have said: 'I am not choosing to receive the anger. I am choosing to give out Light. I am choosing to give out harmony.' And the anger cannot do any damage in those circumstances.

It is always best, and I would advise couples of *any* connection (whether it is a love connection or a business connection) always to take their anger away the moment it starts to flare up, and to go into a separate room to deconstruct it. That would be sound business practice, for example, and you would find that businesses would flourish if that happened. It is a difficult thing to suggest to people – to go into another room, to be calm and to look at that anger and to say: 'I have sparked off an angry response. I can withdraw from this. It might seem like my choice to originate this anger, but it can also be my choice to negate this anger now, to turn this anger around and to turn it back into Light' ...and then to bring that back into a negotiating arena and negotiate from a point of Light and harmony.

If this were done in peace talks and in theatres of war, if people would withdraw from their anger every time it arose, they would find that they would then connect with the God-within and with the angelic host ...and peaceful, harmonious and *lasting* solutions would be found to conflict.

It is as simple as that and all the wars that have been fought, all the lives that have been lost on this level and all the torment that has gone on ...and continues to go on... could be negated *now* if people would only take their anger within, infuse it with Light and let go of it.

Choose something else. Don't choose the anger. Don't choose the despair. Don't choose the sadness. And, ultimately (as we have said in all the books) don't choose that view of the world that continues the anger …continues the negativity …continues the Godlessness …continues the disharmony.

Choose always the harmonic view – and we will talk of this later [*reference to chapter seventeen*]. Choose always the God-view. Choose always the angelic view and transform this world. And the anger will then wither from that 'table' and will be put aside as something that is not required anymore in the future potential of the Earth and the people who live in it.

Does that answer the question?

Tony: Thank you so much, Joseph.

Chapter Seventeen
The Radiating Soul

Joseph: There has been much said about *ascension* in various magazines and books, and I have touched upon the subject in previous volumes, but I want to talk today about the *real ascension* – the real evolution of the soul that can take place whilst you are *here* on this level of consciousness. And so, I want to strike out the word 'ascension' and substitute the term 'the radiating soul'.

The radiating soul – because we have talked in this and previous books about how you can help others, how you can send out Light to the world, to other souls and to violent situations and how you can diffuse the effects of the Fall, but we haven't spoken about *yourself* – about *your* destiny in an ideal world ...and it is an ideal world that we are working towards through the meditations and through sending out Light.

There is an evolution that can be compared to ascension – not ascension that takes you away from this world and separates you from others as though you are somehow 'superior' and they are somehow 'inferior', but there is an ascension or elevation of the soul that takes place when you begin to transmit Light because, in transmitting Light, you begin to see that there is a different way to live.

Initially, that different way to live manifests itself in those times when you send out Light, when you meditate, when you bring into sharp focus those areas and inhabitants of the world that you perceive as needing God-change, as needing to be brought back to a knowledge of who they once were and *still are* within that shell of dark vibration that they have placed around themselves.

But, as you do this, a change will slowly come to you in the way that you deal with your life, in the way that you perceive yourself and in the way that you perceive others. You will find yourself, for example, on a particular day, saying: 'I should not be angry about this situation. I should not be aggravated by this situation,' because the molecules around you actually become aggravated as does your perception of 'self' as a result of anger, with aggravation moving you away from spiritual harmony, and you will instead say, 'Bless you, Brother,' or, 'Bless you, Sister'. You will find that, as you are talking to someone on a quite mundane level, you are also sending out blessings and Light to them in an effort to elevate *their* Light to a point where they, too, can realise that they are a spirit, and that they, too, have an opportunity to shine and to send out Light themselves.

You will look at your thoughts and realise that your thoughts are a mixture of your own perceptions of this world and an admittance into your consciousness of the thoughts of others and the thoughts of the Field. You will be able to slowly disentangle those thoughts that *are not* of you from the thoughts that *are* of you and that come from the core. In other words, in transmitting Light you begin to take steps back to who you were and who you are *at core*. You begin to illuminate, not only others but yourself and, in illuminating yourself, a change comes over the way that you view your life and the lives of others constantly.

So, the radiating soul – the ascending soul – makes a hymn of their life, makes a miracle of their life and makes a glorification of God manifest in their life in the way that they treat others. And slowly, ever so slowly, as you send out the meditations and the Light, you will find that *you* too are changing because **you cannot elevate others without elevating yourself.**

[*Laughing*] A word of caution here, however, because the path of elevating oneself through elevating others is not an easy one. The path of elevating oneself through elevating others makes you step back from the world and see it as it really is. It makes the scales fall away from your eyes and, from the viewpoint of the radiating soul, you will never be able to view your former life, your former activities and your former integration into society in the same way. You will look at your life and see it, as you consider society and your part within it, as difficult. You will look at conventional religion, perhaps, and see your connection to it as difficult. You will look at the way that other people skim the surface only of their spiritual consciousness and see that as difficult. You will see the way that they live their lives as difficult *and you will feel out of step.*

And, this will be a situation that you will not be able to reverse during the rest of your physical lives. You will see only the difference. You will see the glory in people, you will see the potential in people, but you will also see that they are steeped in a way of life, a society and a reaction to each other that is *alien* to you.

If this happens to you, then ...*hallelujah*!

And you will say: 'But, Joseph, you are talking about *disquiet*. You are talking about a way of life that sets us apart from communion, from companionship, from integration, from sharing the worries and woes of the physical world.'

Not at all!

Not at all ...through the Light-meditations and through viewing the world from the point of view of the radiating soul, you will have placed yourself in a different sphere of consciousness altogether. You will be in a sphere of consciousness that connects you to all the other souls who are attempting to bring Light to this world, and, subconsciously, every minute of every day, you will be helping in ways that you cannot imagine.

For example, you will become a lantern for the Light when you are sitting at your desk writing ...or sitting at your table eating ...or sleeping ...or watching your television ...or working on your devices because your motivation as a spirit has changed. Your major core-themes will change from the core-themes of survival, self-protection and the acquisition of power, status, comfort and safety. Those core-themes change because you realise that you do not need any of these things, and you realise that you are a spirit and, as a spirit, it is your choice now to radiate harmony wherever you go ...[*smiling*] you cannot help but do this once you become a radiating soul.

The other 'unfortunate' effect of becoming a radiating soul is that the Field will sense you immediately. The Field will *target* you immediately. So, not only will you feel out of step with society as it is and with the life that you perceived as being so right for you before, you will also find yourself on the receiving end of more aggravation from others and of more unwarranted attacks, verbally and mentally, from others. It will be as though you have to move yourself away, lock your doors and keep yourself in a quiet area reserved for yourself in order to feel safe. When this happens to you, however, it is a reason to rejoice – *to rejoice* because you are doing the work that you need to do as a lover of your brothers and sisters, as an angelic child re-awakened to change the Earth and to change others.

So, it is a paradoxical situation – you have elevated yourself, you are elevating your conscious and subconscious thinking to help uplift others ...and yet you seem to be rewarded for this by verbal and mental attacks from people and by seeing the world in a different way that is alien to you, that feels threatening and that you can never be a part of again. It is asking a lot, isn't it?

But a lot is at stake ...a *huge* amount is at stake.

For one thing, by choosing *not* to transmit the Light, you are *perpetuating* the state of affairs here on Earth. You are contributing to and being a transmitter and receiver for the effects of the Field – the negative energies that permeate this level and keep people subjugated with regard to their spiritual heritage.

So, you have to consider the rewards for all of mankind and for yourself as an angelic child when you decide to elevate yourself by sending out Light-meditations into the world and by viewing its trouble spots in a vision of Light to uplift and change those areas. We are asking that you connect to your spiritual heritage *wholly*, and this happens when you send out the Light-meditations. It cannot help but happen, to a lesser or greater degree, because you cannot channel God-energy to illuminate a spot out there in the world without also illuminating *yourself*.

And your goodness and love in doing this elevates and changes you from within. **That Light that you send out is also sent back to you.** It permeates the atoms of your physical body, permeates the atoms of your physical mind and permeates your soul so that you *remember* ...re-'member' ...connect once again with the Godhead, with your angelic parents, with the angelic host and with all mankind. You connect to the best aspect of all mankind.

So, forget what has been said to you about 'ascension' in various texts ...much of which is – and, to use one of my favourite words, *nonsense!*

NONSENSE!

THERE IS NO ELEVATION INDEPENDENT OF OTHERS.

There is no escape to another dimension, allowing your brothers and sisters to wallow in the mire of the Field whilst you have transformed into a beautiful 'butterfly' and left them behind. You cannot transform into a beautiful 'butterfly' until your brothers and sisters have transformed into 'butterflies' too. That is not a restriction that God has put on you; it is a restriction that you have within yourself, knowing what you really are. As an angelic being, you are a part of every other angelic being and you cannot leave your brothers and sisters to suffer. At core, you do not want your brothers and sisters, or indeed any aspect of the universe, to suffer.

And so, when you begin to elevate yourself in the right way as a radiating soul, you are radiating out energies of Love and peace and harmony and Light to all others knowing that this is the way it should be. But we can only truly ascend in the cleansing spheres when every soul has been elevated out of the mind-set and physical effects of the Fall.

I wanted to talk about *you* today. You have been selfless in reading these books. You have already elevated yourselves, to a lesser or greater extent, by considering the information that these books have given you, but I wanted to concentrate on you and *the effects on you of giving out the Light.* There is no physical reward (and you would not wish a physical reward) and there is no mental reward, **but there *is* a spiritual reward.** And, in changing others and drawing on the God-within and the Light-within that we add to, there *is* the reward of elevating yourself as a consequence of that process.

The world, Brothers and Sisters, needs radiating souls ...needs souls who can walk into a room and say nothing but make others feel better ...needs radiating souls who can converse with someone and make them feel as though a great weight has been taken off them ...needs radiating souls who can enter areas of negativity, areas of anger, areas of violence, areas of lack and elevate those situations *simply by their presence* ...needs souls who work on a subconscious level (and on a conscious one) day and night to make things better, to re-integrate the angelic children who were cut off at the time of the Fall from the rest of the angelic host and need to be reconnected. **Those souls are *needed*.**

Radiating souls are needed – not souls who selfishly say: 'I deserve to be elevated. I deserve to ascend. I deserve to be taken away from this society', but souls who recognise the family that is suffering at the moment on the Earth plane and wish to elevate *the entire family* away from that way of thinking.

There *are* also rewards in that you will find *other* radiating souls connecting to you through a letter, through a phone call or through a connection in that you discover someone on a particular morning in conversation who thinks exactly the way that you do. This cannot help but happen. As you radiate Light, you give out a 'signal' to others who are radiating Light and the two connections pull together until you meet.

So, there will be compensation in that people will appear in your life who are jewels of Light – not, perhaps, the tens of shallow friends you had before who did not fulfil you, other than being there to converse with at times and feel distracted by. There will instead be 'shining jewels' and permanent connections placed into your life so that you can do the work, be supported and can converse regarding spiritual matters, whereas before you sat in isolation and gave out Light by yourself.

So, recognise that there is a metamorphosis happening with you when you begin to send out the Light. You change the charge of your physical molecules, you change the charge of your mental power and energies and you change your heart-centre to reconnect with the God-within – the power of which then irradiates your physical, mental and spiritual frame and brings you a harmony that you then radiate out to others.

This harmony also brings you the benefits of health and peace of mind (which seems a contradiction when we said earlier that you will feel that you are out of step with others). Nevertheless, you will find that you have a peace of mind in that you can withdraw from the chaos of the world, which up to this point has invaded your consciousness as seemingly part of your own thought-process. You can step back from those thoughts that are not yours, and you can retreat, re-group and strengthen yourself from a point of view that has nothing to do with the baser elements of society, thought, or the intrusions of the Field.

You will also find that, as a radiating soul, you can step into that Light mentally in your meditations and draw the Light into the molecules of your body and mind so much more easily to put right anything that seemingly is wrong within your physical or mental frame. In other words, you can heal yourself by being a radiating soul and connecting to the God-within because the molecules of your physical and mental frame are *more receptive and responsive* to the Light than perhaps those of a soul who has not reached this position would be.

You will also find that, your thought-processes on a physical level are more receptive to the fact that you *can* change things – not only that you can change things by sending Light (which is the point of the books we have brought through thus far) but that *you can change things within yourself*. You will be more receptive to the fact that you can heal yourself, that you can elevate yourself, and that, by connecting to God, you can banish, from your mental and physical fields, conditions that would otherwise have overwhelmed you and pulled you down to the point of illness or perhaps even physical death. So, there are great rewards *personally* for being a radiating soul.

This is one of the most important chapters in the book because it gives you some idea of your potential. We have spoken before about your potential with regards to being able to change this world, but we have not spoken of your potential for changing yourself, for elevating yourself and for becoming (if all goes according to plan and if enough of you send Light into the world) the next stage of *physical evolution*, manifesting as a return to a time when you are *consciously* angelic beings travelling through a physical sphere.

The next spiritual point of evolution is for *everyone* to be a radiating soul...

You might think that is something that is unobtainable. **It *is* obtainable!** Remember the power of the Light. Remember the energy that you can wield and bring into this world and, as more souls elevate to the point where they radiate Light twenty-four hours a day, then those souls link up and the matrix of the Field changes, as we have said before. That is the goal: to change the Field back to what it was …a Field of harmonic vibration that then removes the scales from everyone's eyes so they see once again their spiritual heritage as angelic children.

I would also say, in closing this particular chapter, that as a soul radiating the Light you make it easier for us in the cleansing spheres to reach you. You make it easier for us to comfort you, to advise you and to connect with you – either through your intuition or directly, if you are sufficiently evolved with regard to spiritual communication. And I promise you – *I guarantee* that in the times when, as a radiating soul, you feel out of step, you feel that society and the world is not worth looking upon, **there is always someone from our spheres with their hand in yours …** *always*. You are never alone …Light …attracts Light …attracts Light …attracts Light. Amen!

Are there questions, please?

Jane: Joseph, could I just have clarification – you said that you cannot escape until all your brothers and sisters escape, so presumably the ones who have gone on into Infinity are still linked in some way to the rest of the angelic children who have fallen?

Joseph: Yes, we have touched on this before in that there is a choice at a particular time as to whether you go through the 'hatch' (that has been so eloquently and perfectly portrayed in the last few days [*reference the book cover designed the previous week*]) or whether you remain to more actively pursue the reunification of the angelic children and the lifting of them out of the mire they have placed themselves in. But, as we have said before, once you go through the 'hatch' there is still that connection and still a percentage of you that senses and works on the need for *all* the children to get through the 'hatch'.

There is a great pull, you see, and as you elevate yourself through the cleansing spheres there comes a day when it is very, very difficult not to go through the 'hatch' because there is so much beauty, so much potential, so much bliss and there is the call of your angelic family. But, you do not and cannot totally ignore those who are still suffering on the Earth plane. There is a link forever (as there is a link forever with you and all of the angelic host) and you go through the 'hatch' but you monitor and you send through Light, which has to be filtered because once you have gone through into Infinity you are able to absorb a great deal more of the Light-spectrum. You filter through help …no matter what you are doing, no matter how you are creating and where you go.

So, it is true to say that, until all the angelic children have escaped from the effects of the Fall, those souls who have 'escaped', as it were, from the cleansing spheres into Infinity are still restricted *to a degree*. Not that it pollutes or upsets the rest of Creation, but it limits their potential to a degree because they have not truly escaped. There is a thin filament that links them with the angelic children on Earth, and in the back of their minds is the worry that things are still not as harmonious as they should be on the Earth plane.

Do you see?

Jane: That's perfect, thank you.

Tony: Joseph, you were saying that, as a radiating soul, we become very visible and attract the negative forces of the Field. As a therapist, I see the Field as *enlarging* negative emotions in people (for example, turning fear into terror and annoyance into rage) so that it affects the way they are living their lives. If we are a radiating soul, does that mean that the Field sees us as a whole, as a specific target, rather than simply homing in on those negative traits that might be within us as emotions?

Joseph: The Field sees you initially as a threat, as a point of Light. The Field is of one density and you become of another density. The Field, therefore, sees you as an irritation within itself, as a 'tummy ache', as 'an itch that needs to be scratched' and as an alienated part of itself that needs to be re-integrated. The Field attempts to surround those points of Light – the radiating souls – with more of its intention. It is the only way it can think of to subjugate the points of Light that it sees within itself. So, it surrounds the souls with more of its intention – which is to keep the points of Light, the whole of the world and the angelic children contained within it *set to negative*. And so, as a result of it concentrating on that 'itch', that 'ache', that 'pain' (as it sees it), it gives *more power* to those souls who are predisposed towards negativity. And they are directed via that power of the Field to those points of Light to cause trouble *if they can*.

That is how the Field reacts to points of Light …but *conversely*, the way that radiating souls react to the advances of the Field is different to the way that a non-illuminated soul (i.e. someone totally immersed in the Field) would react. They still receive the attacks but they react to them in a different way. They recover more quickly because they do not react with anger, for example. They do not react with irritation or with thoughts of revenge, which would connect them with more points in the Field. So, the attempts by the Field to smother that Light slide off and cannot gain purchase. Do you see that?

Tony: I do.

Joseph: They cannot gain purchase and so protection, in being an illumined spirit, is provided simply through being what you are …in that you have reached a point (otherwise you would not be a radiating soul) where you react *differently* to the vibrations of the Field. You are slow to become angry, and if you become angry you step back from that anger and diffuse it. You are slow to wish any harm on people and find that virtually impossible. Instead you are sending out a wish for every being to be at maximum potential, to be harmonious, to be healthy and to be creative.

When a molecule of action from the Field reaches a molecule of your physical or mental being *the two do not fit together*. You will feel the effects of the attack; you will feel that difference in vibration, but that is good because it *is a difference of vibration*, and if you were not illuminated you would feel nothing. It is the fact that you feel the difference that signifies that you are doing the right thing and that you are giving out the Light.

It is true that the Field is 'food' for souls. **Spirits need food in the form of energy.** It is like a choice of menus – which menu do you go for? Do you go for the menu of Light or do you go for the menu of darkness? If you go for the menu of darkness then, yes, those aspects of yourself that are strengthened by the Field become accentuated, become more violent and become more twisted. But, if you are choosing (and forgive the pun) the *lighter* diet – the diet of Light – then it is more difficult for those formerly affective molecules of the Field (i.e. formerly affective on the person before they began to invest in Light) to have any effect other than, because you are more sensitive through elevating yourself, you realising that they are there. You will feel the attack as a difference in vibration.

And, of course, there is the reaction, which is totally opposite to how the Field would react, in that, when those attacks take place, you send out Light to them. If you illuminate the attacks and the source, you push away from the source those darker molecules from the Field. So, when you send back Light in response to an attack, you chase away from yourself the negative molecules of the Field, and you also chase away *part of their power* from those people who, consciously or subconsciously, are attacking you. Do you understand that?

You lessen their effect, and today it might be that you lessen their effect but tomorrow – if you are joined by a million brethren who are sending out the Light – you not only lessen their effect but you begin to change *their* molecules from molecules of the Field to molecules of Light, *and you raise them*.

265

This is why it is so important to always send out Love and harmony in response to negativity.

Chase away the clouds of the Field, and then that 'itch' becomes a body-wide itch ...something that the Field has to address in so many different directions that it dissipates because it doesn't have the energy to do it effectively, and then Light changes the Field.

What we are *ultimately* working to do is not just change the individual souls **but change the Field itself** ...illuminate the molecules of the Field so that the Field, which is a sentient presence, becomes aware that the Light is a better way and that it has nothing to fear, so that 'petulant child' I spoke about so long ago [*reference to Chapter Twenty of Your Life After Death*] suddenly realises that it can let go of the way that it has been acting and that there is another way which is more creative and more harmonious. Then you will see not only a change with every soul, but a change right around the world.

There is that tipping point when the world becomes illumined again too, and then the cleansing spheres will dissipate, Infinity will only be a 'phone call away' and you will have re-established yourselves as God's angelic children into the sphere of creativity and potential that you created so long ago and then polluted.

Is that a sufficient answer?

Tony: Yes, thank you so much, Joseph.

David: Joseph, a quick question about practice – if people are radiating Light, they could radiate Light, say, into a war-zone and they might not appreciate that it is having an effect. If they were to start by projecting Light into more personal events, such as some upset at work or in a family, then they might see some sort of result which would confirm that what they are doing is actually working. Would that be better?

Joseph: That is a very good and interesting point. We advise that souls send out Light into war-zones and into the most violent areas of the Earth because those are the areas where the Field is the strongest and where the Field can generate vibrations that can, not only be sensed throughout the war-zone, but can be sensed by the rest of humanity. So, we advise that you send out Light, which for many of the readers of this book will be *at a distance* because they are fortunate not to be living in a war-zone.

Yes, it is splendid proof for a soul, on a daily basis, to first of all recognise the occurrences where the Field is having a 'field-day' (again another pun – I apologise) and to look at those various eruptions of negativity and conflict and see that they can make a difference by injecting Light into them, but also to recognise that there is *a need to do so,* because isn't it true that it is sometimes fascinating to watch people arguing? Or to look at violence and think: 'Well, I have nothing to do with that but it is somehow interesting.' It is interesting because the Field is plucking at you and is drawing you to be a part of it or, at the very least, an observer of it.

Instead of being an observer of it, change so that you are an active participant ...but not a participant in a dark, threatening and negative way... a participant that injects Light into every argument and every altercation. In business and commerce, there is no situation that cannot be solved if Light is injected into every aspect of what looks like a conflicting situation. Everything can be solved and everything can be worked out to the benefit of all concerned if *enough* Light is sent into the situation.

See what happens if you inject Light, silently and without anyone noticing into an argument at work or into a domestic situation. See what happens if you find *yourself* rising to the bait in a domestic situation and then pull yourself back into a position of Light and harmony. See how quickly those situations change.

Yes, an excellent example, but we would also stress that it is equally important to send out Light into those areas that you cannot see. By all means build up a track record, which will reinforce your recognition of the effect of Light on negative situations, but also send out Light globally, please, daily and know – take our word for it, take God's word for it – that, when you send out Light remotely at a distance, **you are having an effect.**

In conclusion, to go back to the point of this chapter, the radiating soul sends out Light on all levels and to all situations. So, there is Light going into your food …there is Light going into your entertainment …there is Light going into your relationships …there is Light going into your work situations …there is Light going into all corners of the world that need Light …there is Light going into the things that you construct, the things that you write, the things that you make, the things that you wish and the things that you project for the future.

Being a radiating soul allows you to effect change on *so many* levels. You inject change into the present but you are also projecting a future of change. You are bringing a future of change into being because you are radiating Light today, but you are already prepared when you wake up in the morning to bring Light into tomorrow.

What a wonderful thing to do …not to look at the day and say: 'This is another terrible day. I resent my work / relatives / relationship / finances' …but to say: 'This is a day when I am already radiating Light and making a difference.' And the situations of the world that seem so important when seen from the viewpoint of the Field …what to eat …what to wear …what a terrible world it is …how difficult it is to get on with people … how you are feeling less than one hundred per cent in health… **all these things disappear.**

All these things are the way that you once were when you loaded your days, as you woke up, with a potential for negativity. You were already investing in negativity and, prior to being a radiating soul, you were a soul that radiated, yes, because everything radiates (energy radiates and cannot help but do so) but you were radiating a furtherance of the status quo of the Field being set to negative.

You will recognise that, as a radiating soul, you are beginning each day from a different perspective. That is all it takes – a perspective of Light, a perspective that says: 'Today, I will be of use to God. Today I will be of use to and I will repair my angelic brothers and sisters. Today, *this day* is a day of Light – no matter what the Field shows me – I know that that Light is immovable, that Light is eternal, is infinite and that Light is there no matter what my physical eyes show me.'

Does that answer the question?

David: Thank you.

Chapter Eighteen
A Special Meditation

Joseph: I have, for the final chapter of this book, something *special* lined up because, as a reward and a 'thank you' for reading this book and for looking at the other books in the series, I wish today to take you on a journey. I wish, in imagination, to take you away from this world and to take you to *another world*.

So, I wish you to imagine that you are floating in space with me, and that you are looking down at a planet, but this planet is far different from the one you are used to. If you look at its curvature, you will see across that curvature a swirling mass of scintillating, crystal-like colours. You will see areas of the globe that seem to erupt into colour and majesty. The whole surface of the globe is moving and changing as you look at it. And, even from this distance, at this point in space where you can see the whole planet, you are aware of the *pull* of that planet, the excitement of that planet and the invitation that the planet sends out into its surrounding space.

But, before we go down to the planet itself, I want to show you that surrounding area of space. As you perceive space from the Earth, it is areas of 'nothingness' punctuated by heavenly bodies. Look at the space around *this* planet and you will see that it is not areas of nothingness you are looking at. You can see points of light within the darkness of space (which are, of course, the other stars and planets that are at a greater distance from you than this one is) but the areas of space that seem dark *really aren't.* You can see that the areas between the heavenly bodies are alive and are moving. It is as though you are looking at clouds – not dark clouds but clouds that have within them points of colour; clouds that push up against each other and change and twist and turn. What you are looking at are the 'spaces between' – the spaces between the heavenly bodies that have been created by the angelic host.

Those spaces between the heavenly bodies are actually full of *potential*, full of *possibility*, so, when you view space in this particular universe as an angelic being, you do not see dark areas; you do not see empty areas ...except for them being 'empty' in the sense of 'waiting to be filled'. What you see as part of the angelic host is the *potential* between those heavenly bodies to create *new* heavenly bodies, to create new experiences, to bring forth out of the no-thing *everything* ...everything that you can imagine ...everything that you wish to experience.

And, as we hold in this position, looking down at the planet, you can hear – from the heavenly bodies, from the planet itself and from the areas between the heavenly bodies – *their song* ...a symphony ...the music of potential ...the music of actual creation ...the music of possibility as thoughts from the angelic host combine and recombine to bring through new and fresh adventures.

So, you are looking at a total landscape of colour and change and creativity and potential experience and *actual* experience ... and below you is the planet.

Now, we move towards the planet through its atmosphere and, as we move through the atmosphere of the planet, we can feel *the vibrations of intent* from this particular heavenly body impacting on our angelic bodies, drawing us into an experience, drawing us into a journey from which we will benefit and grow.

We touch down and find ourselves in a landscape that is unlike *...and yet in some ways like* a landscape on Earth in that it has, in this case, mountains and trees and streams and valleys and hills, but they are of a *more etheric* nature here. They exhibit a great deal more colour. Here and there are objects that appear to be made out of crystal ...*are* made out of crystal... and trees that reveal, every so often, their crystalline core.

You can see light streaming through and reflecting off the mountains and hills, as though light were hitting a prism ...and yet that is only a small analogy because a prism on Earth splits light into a certain number of light-waves and colours. Here there are *more* colours. Here there are *more intense colours*. Here there is a vitality, strength and purpose to the atmosphere that invigorates you.

And, as we walk slowly through this landscape, you feel more alive than you have ever felt. There is no fear of decay in this sphere. There is no fear of death. There is no fear of anything ending. Things here *do* end, but they end by consensus. They end when they are supposed to end, when they no longer offer prospects and opportunities to grow, but they do not end here in pain or separation.

They end here simply by the angelic children involved in the creation of this sphere determining that, at this point, something needs to come to a conclusion and to be peacefully put away so that other potentials can be brought forth within the matrix of the *intention* of this sphere ...within the parameters of what this sphere has been created for. Each sphere is created to offer a certain set of circumstances to the angelic children visiting it so that they might grow in a particular way and might hone a particular aspect of their being by moving through a particular landscape on a particular sphere.

Now, as we move through the landscape, we come across a 'road'. (It is not a tarmac road but simply a means of traversing this landscape from point 'A' to point 'B', and it does not look like a road – except through the filter of your physical mind, which is used to expecting a road to appear in a certain way.) And we proceed down this road to what appears to be a village.

We move into the centre of the village and look at the houses. The houses are constantly changing ...they are changing in colour ...they are changing in size ...they are, at times, changing in location, and yet there is a harmony to all this change. It is perfectly in line with the rest of the creative area of the village. In other words, one house, in changing colour, shape and location, does not affect another house. It is like an intricate dance ...a dance where everything is in its correct place and everything is evolving. The houses are evolving; they are becoming more refined houses. There is a reason behind the houses changing, which is to investigate *all* aspects of where the houses should be, what colours they should be and how they should connect to each other ...until *perfection* is found.

Having studied that village changing itself into perfection, we then move along the road to another village. Let us examine the people who live in this settlement... The people who live in this village are as harmonious as the houses they live in. The people connect to each other perfectly, and each one is an individual, paying attention to its individual perception of this sphere, paying attention to its individual needs and the things that bring it satisfaction. Yet none of those things that bring it satisfaction are experienced in isolation, and none of those things disturb the other inhabitants of the village. In other words, each individual is in harmony with each of the other individuals, and yet can express itself fully as an individual without violence, without jealousy, without anger, without frustration, without a need to be 'top dog', without any resentment, without any fear. It is a perfect, harmonious connection of life ...**a perfect, harmonious connection of life.**

If you look closely at the inhabitants of this village, you can also see that they are in perfect proportion. There is no lack of sustenance because their sustenance is the Light they absorb from the area they have created. You can see that these people have no physical imperfections because they have not been twisted or upset in the vision of who they are by a negative Field or by karmic circumstances created in the past that pull

273

on them in so many different ways and make them (from a visual point of view at least) less than the perfect angelic children they really are.

These people want for nothing. Their only desire is for the individual and for the group to grow through experiencing what the village has to offer its inhabitants. Then those inhabitants will move on into other areas of the sphere and other challenges ...although 'challenges' is too harsh a word... into other *welcoming adventures* which, when approached and moved through, will add to the richness of each individual angelic child moving through those circumstances.

If we move beyond the village, we see that there are landscapes that are breathtaking to the vision, and those landscapes can be 'called up' instantly. We can find ourselves sitting on top of one of the crystal mountains looking down into rolling valleys where different colours of foliage link harmoniously to be pleasing to the eye. We can find ourselves in wooded areas where we can look with psychic eyes and see other forms of deva-expression around us. Although we appear to be solid (our flesh is of a lighter vibration than it is on Earth) we can see that there are non-corporeal beings here that co-exist with us. There are expressions of deva activity that reveal themselves to us as other people, as lights, as animals, as foliage, but all on the purest deva-level of expression (i.e. non-physical).

There is constant interplay, joy and song between these manifestations of deva activity and ourselves, and we are able to communicate. If, for example, we put our hand on a tree, our hand goes through and into the tree and we feel the tree moving up our arm and into our body so that *we are sharing the same viewpoint* ...the viewpoint of ourselves as an individual angelic child moving through this landscape and the viewpoint of the tree looking back at us and drawing the light and nourishment it needs from the planet. **We *feel* what it is like to be the tree and to exist in that expression of deva activity.** So, we add to our spiritual viewpoint and experience by having touched the tree, and the tree adds to its viewpoint by having connected with us for that moment.

As we move on, we see people in various inhabited areas endeavouring to create art ...endeavouring to sculpt and to paint and to create *with Light* by holding within their open hands an area of space that they then infuse with Light and colour and intent ...to create and mould whatever it is that they wish to bring forth in front of them, and around or through them. We see that these pieces of art are worked on simply by the mind and simply by the hands caressing these emerging forms to change the works of art they are creating into ever more illuminated and harmonious expressions of what they originally had in mind.

And we see artists and artisans joining together because they are creating individual works of art that then appeal to other travellers through this sphere. So two works of art, which can be completely different in original intent, unite to create a piece of art that is a combination of the two and expresses the viewpoints of the two artists involved *in one united piece* ...that is also changing ...and will attract to itself others who are interested in adding to or changing this evolving work of art. So, art is constantly changing. Architecture is constantly changing. Intent is constantly changing. *And it is a wondrous experience.*

We see, as we move along further through various crystalline landscapes, that there is a place where people are (for want of a better word) 'arriving' into this world. They are arriving into this world not by being born as physical babies, but simply by there being a shimmer of the air in front of us in this area that we are observing ...and then they arrive as beings of Light. Initially they are beings of Light that are transparent. Initially they are beings of Light that seem to have a very weak coherence, but, as we watch them over 'time' (as it is measured in this sphere) they become more solid. They still exhibit that amount of Light they originally exhibited as they entered this world but they are now more solid and corporeal. As we have said earlier, this is a perfection of physicality and not the

275

heaviness of physicality that you experience on Earth at this time because of the effects of the Fall.

Similarly, as we move further on we find that we come to an area in this sphere where people, looking no older than they did when they first visited it, suddenly become less corporeal. Suddenly they become more illumined and revert back to their angelic state, having accomplished all that they wished to accomplish by visiting this sphere ...whether they visited for (in your terms) a thousand years or a million years. And we see that they are still able to communicate as a less solidly perceived expression of themselves (from the point of view of the people in physicality inhabiting this sphere) than when they were corporeal in this sphere. They can continue to communicate with those who are still choosing to travel through this sphere in a physical body and there is, therefore, no lack, no loss and no fear of death.

You observe, however, as you continue to experience this sphere in operation, that certain spirits who have made special connections with those who have decided to go back to the angelic host *do feel a pull* and, in wishing to be with those who have moved on from this sphere of experience, then decide to move on *themselves*. There comes a time when they feel that their wish to be with someone is greater than the experience that this sphere has to offer, so, they, too, move back into the point of view of the angelic host, ready to move on into the next area of experience with those they have formed special connections with ...and to pull *potential* out of the 'spaces between' that then forms into another sphere for them to investigate and to move through in order to evolve further.

And so, we move back from this sphere *with regret*, because the place that I have brought you to is inviting ...the place that I have brought you to is not polluted ...the place that I have brought you to knows nothing of war ...the place that I have brought you to knows nothing of power-play ...the place that I have brought you to knows nothing of a lack of *connection*.

There is no loneliness here and no individualism in terms of individualism taken to the point at which it becomes painful.

We have to reluctantly move from this sphere back to our vantage point in space. But, before we come back to your Earth, I wish to point out to you the other heavenly bodies in the sky because each one of those is an area of potential evolution for the angelic child. Each of them has been created by the angelic host in order that the angelic children can move through those spheres ...and progress ...and discover more about themselves ...and investigate aspects of creation ...and bring back the results of their investigations to the Godhead and to the angelic host.

I like to end with a bombshell...

...The bombshell is that:

I HAVE TAKEN YOU TO THE EARTH AS IT *REALLY* IS.

I have taken you to the Earth as it was before the time of the Fall. I have taken you to the Earth as it still can be, and *still is* within the shell of negativity that has been caused by the Fall and has polluted the way that you look at things.

I have taken you to the Earth (as we hope and pray on our knees every day) that *will be again* when you change your minds, when you remember that *this* was the purpose of your planet, *this* was the purpose of your existence here and that you have created a skewed, masked, distorted, greyed and polluted vision of what this planet should be, *and really is at core.*

That 'jewel' that I have attempted *in just a small way* to portray to you today is there waiting to shine again, and you are the only ones who can polish it. You are the only ones that can bring it back to its majesty amongst a field of other majestic planets and stars and spaces in between filled with wondrous potential.

277

I have left this as the last chapter because I wish to elevate you. I wish to say, 'This is the goal.'

When it feels heavy in a morning and you do not wish to send out Light – this is the goal, *remember*!

When it feels as though people will never change and that the Earth is plunging itself into another dark age – this is the goal, *remember*!

When it feels as though the politicians will win …the terrorists will win …the religious fanatics will win – remember that this is the goal and YOU can change things.

In this book I have given you further means to change things. You *have to* change things. This planet cannot forever be the 'blot on the landscape' that it appears to be. It has to change back to its original intention and only you can do it …only you, the reader …only you, the 'ordinary' (as you see yourselves) men, women and children of the Earth. You are not ordinary …you are angelic.

Stop believing in the illusion! Start remembering and bring yourselves back to the start-point. You haven't visited an alien planet, you have visited your *own* Earth. Doesn't it sound better than the Earth you are living in at the moment?

Questions, please!

[*There follows a long period of complete quiet at this point, with Joseph's reveal having shocked the group into a solemn, emotional silence. Eventually Jane asks a question...*]

Jane: Joseph, after that there aren't really any questions, and this one is only slightly related to what you were describing about the sphere where the houses could change without effort and things are created instantly. On the Earth at present we are trying to speed things up through technology so we have instant communication and instant *this and that* but is the difference here that we don't contemplate in between? Things are getting faster and we want things instantly but is that just adding to the speed of the Fall?

Joseph: There are a couple of things to take into consideration here. At the moment you filter everything you create through the matrix of your perception of yourself as a physical and mental being. And, the instant that you filter through your physicality and mentality, you pick up the pollution of the Field. At the moment your instant creation on a spiritual level is slowed down by the dragging and polluting effects of the Field, so the intent becomes polluted. This is why we have advised you in the books to give out Light in your creation because, in encapsulating your creative intent in Light, you push aside the pollution and create a purer image of what it is you intend to create.

You must not confuse instant creation with speed. Instant creation on an angelic level is because that is the way that things are – *you create instantly*. You do not have the volition for speed, but have the volition to create something beautiful and perfect. Speed does not enter into the equation ...it is simply that you visualise and *wish* something and you, therefore, create that something instantly as you would measure it. There is no desire for speed, but there *is* the desire for experience. There is the desire to create something that is of great beauty for all, and there is the desire to express and to *be* and to celebrate being part of God.

Speed on the earthly level at the moment is to do with filling the gaps that are perceived mentally, because the individuals who wish speed have not rediscovered the God-within. There is a great lack perceived on a subconscious level and that lack can never be fulfilled. **That lack on a mental and physical level can never be fulfilled** ...it cannot be fulfilled with food ...it cannot be satisfied with sex ...it cannot be satisfied with the acquisition of material goods because all those things are of the level of the Fall. There can only be less need for speed through the realisation that one has to seek *within* to remember the God-within, express

279

the God-within and appreciate the connection between all people in order to feel satisfied.

So, your speed at the moment is a need to feel satisfied *that can never be satisfied* because it seeks to satisfy itself through mental, physical and material means. The satisfaction has to come through realising that you are a spirit, that you are an angelic being, that you are part of God and that you can create beauty. That beauty is then created instantly – not because you desire speed but because you desire to express. Does that make sense?

Jane: Yes, it does, thank you.

Joseph: I think at this point I will release *you all* ...not just Michael... but will release you all for a period of time from what you have seen with good hearts as 'your duty', and we are thankful for that duty having been performed so admirably.

And I am now showing Michael – who is held in a static position until I have finished speaking – that you are surrounded today, not just by me, but by the *entire* soul group. I am showing him, to pass on to you, an image of hundreds, thousands, millions of souls. And he is impressed by the colours in their robes and by the expressions on their faces and by the fact that there are *so many* linked and harmonious beings united in the task of bringing Light to the Earth.

Until we meet again, *which we will*, I salute you and bless you... from myself, from the heart of the soul group, and from the heart of God.

Revelation

who you are, why you're here

...a book to change your world.

In this first book of the series, Joseph invites you to understand who and what you really are, where you came from, why you are here and the miraculous things you are capable of, revealing the amazing potential of the human spirit and presenting a plan to change the future of this planet before it's too late.

Intelligent, thought-provoking, non-religious. In direct, concise language, **Revelation** will revolutionise your views about life and the nature of reality, empowering you through a new awareness of the active part you play in creation and inspiring you to look at your world in a whole new light.

'I've read every metaphysical book I could get my hands on for years but there is information in this book I've not come across anywhere before. I would wholeheartedly recommend this series to anyone seeking answers and the inspiration to finding wisdom within.' *jmj4 (Amazon).*

'Whatever your religion Revelation will inspire and help you to understand why we are here on this planet and make you think about the way you are living your life.' *Joy (Amazon).*

'The most direct and compelling book on spirituality I have ever read.' *G. R. Munro-Hall (Amazon).*

£13.95 (ISBN: 978-1-906625-07-8)

From good bookshops, Amazon, and direct from

www.thejosephcommunications.co.uk

e-Book also available for Kindle, iPad and other platforms. Listen to the audiobook.

Illumination
change yourself, change the world

...A powerful manual for personal and global transformation.

Time is running out; Earth is heading for cataclysm! **Illumination** reveals how we can literally save this world ...before it's too late.

We need to change and accept personal responsibility now – or Joseph warns there are only three generations left. The Field is so polluted by mankind's negative energy that the planet cannot sustain itself much longer unless radical changes are made to the way we think.

Illumination provides all the 'tools' needed to achieve personal and global enlightenment, empowering readers to direct Light and transmute negativity into harmony, joy, love, peace and spiritual progression.

There is great urgency to Joseph's words – we do not have an infinite number of tomorrows in which to put things right.

'Read the book, adopt its practices, discover a new life of spiritual harmony and lasting fulfilment.' *Jan Quigley.*

'A masterpiece of spiritual work! What is very clever is the way Joseph builds up his case throughout this book with possibilities to test his meditations as you go – this is not dry theory! I will certainly continue the daily Light-work which I now regard as essential.' *Tony Cross.*

'If you wish to bring peace, joy and abundance to yourself and those you love this book gives you the means.' *Mr. C. Fraser-Malcolm (Amazon).*

£12.95 (ISBN: 978-1-906625-09-2)

Available from good bookshops, Amazon, and direct from

www.thejosephcommunications.co.uk

e-Book also available for Kindle, iPad and other platforms. Listen to the audiobook.

Your Life After Death

...your final destination is anything but final!

Countless opportunities and wonders await beyond physical death.

In **Your Life After Death** Joseph delivers arguably the most comprehensive account ever written of what lies ahead when you leave this world behind.

An essential source of comfort and inspiration, **Your Life After Death** is the definitive guide to the afterlife...

... read it and you'll never look at the next life, or, indeed, this one, in quite the same way again.

'Packed with very important information, which should have been made available many, many years ago.' *David Feuerstein.*

'The book is outstanding and one of immense value to humanity, particularly in contrast to the mumbo-jumbo we are exposed to in various religions and philosophies.' *Scott Rabalais.*

'Over the years I have read many books on this subject but none have been more informative and in-depth.' *Peggy Sivyer.*

'I have never sat up nearly all night and read a book from cover to cover in one go before and it has had a major impact on me.' *Valerie Ann Riddell.*

£14.95 (ISBN: 978-1-906625-03-0)

Available from good bookshops, Amazon, and direct from

www.thejosephcommunications.co.uk

e-Book also available for Kindle, iPad and other platforms. Listen to the audiobook.

the Fall

you were there,
it's why you're here

...aeons ago everything changed – AND YOU WERE THERE!

You have forgotten the cataclysm that created today's dysfunctional societies and wounded planet...

In **the Fall**, Joseph reactivates that astonishing inner knowledge of your spiritual origins.

By the last page, many, if not *all*, of those elusive answers regarding existence and the great mysteries will be elusive no longer.

From the Big Bang to your role in creation... if you seek meaning to life in general, and your life in particular, you *absolutely, definitely* should read **the Fall**.

...Your views of spirituality, science, and reality are about to change forever.

'If I had to be on a desert island with only one book, this would be it.' *James D'Angelo.*

'The Fall is the most important spiritual book ever written.' *Jean Whittle.*

'I have been on this journey for more than 40 years and this book just joins all the dots for me. It is astonishing. It is of vital importance, please read it.' *Katydr (Amazon).*

'Here are the answers to life's impossible contradictions, and what we can do for ourselves and others – brilliant!' *Jan (Amazon).*

'One of the most powerful and influential books in my entire life, completely altering my world view.' *Peter De Ruyter.*

£14.95 (ISBN: 978-1-906625-05-4)

Available from good bookshops, Amazon, and direct from:

www.thejosephcommunications.co.uk

e-Book also available for Kindle, iPad and other platforms. Listen to the audiobook.

Trance Mission

enlightening—informing—a record of Joseph in Public

Over three years Joseph was asked more than 150 questions during 12 remarkable trance demonstrations.

His illuminating, eloquent answers are reproduced in this double-sized, 448-page book, in which Joseph focuses on and expands our understanding of a wide range of spiritual topics, including:

pre-destiny and choice • the nature of time • Indigo children • meditation techniques • God • aliens • reincarnation • angels • past-life baggage • sexual energy • healing • the Bible • animals • infant mortality • ascension ...and many more.

Shot through with Joseph's refreshingly no-nonsense approach to spirituality and presenting practical, illuminating, deeply spiritual information throughout, **Trance Mission** also gives insight into Joseph's background and relationship with Michael, immersing readers in the unique atmosphere of his public appearances.

> 'Rarely do you read any "channeled" material that answers questions directly and sensibly. This book does and I highly recommend it to anyone on their spiritual journey.' *Meria Heller.*
>
> 'Wonderful – many of the additional questions I had been asking after reading the other books have been answered.' *Rowen Harris.*
>
> 'Anyone seeking to be uplifted from this negative world view should read Trance Mission – much Love and Light and hope on every page.' *Christine Wood.*
>
> 'Trance Mission is a magnificent read - so many answers to questions that spiritual truth-seekers yearn to know.' *Joanna Eden.*

£16.95 (ISBN: 978-1-906625-06-1)

Available from good bookshops, Amazon, and direct from:

www.thejosephcommunications.co.uk

e-Book also available for Kindle, iPad and other platforms. Listen to the audiobook.

Many Voices, One Mission

Group Soul wisdom from the Joseph perspective

The new Joseph Communications title **Many Voices, One Mission**, giving voice to key members of Joseph's soul group through powerful lectures delivered over many years to medium Michael G. Reccia and life partner Jane, is now available.

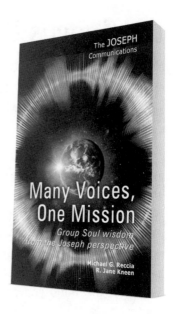

Themed sections Life's Journey, Aspects of the Afterlife, The Sacred Earth, Spiritual Science, Connections, Co-Creation and Health and Healing feature wisdom from Joseph's co-workers, and transcripts of Michael's first two public trance demonstrations are also included, plus fascinating insights into how Michael and Jane's lives have been affected by regular interaction with spirit messengers.

£16.95 (ISBN: 978-1-906625-15-3)
Available from good bookshops, Amazon, and direct from:
www.thejosephcommunications.co.uk
e-Book also available for Kindle, iPad and other platforms.

the Spaces Between

Prepare yourself for an eye-opening odyssey through magical, metaphysical realities

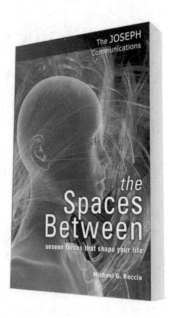

The spaces between...

...Are filled with wonder, spectacle and the unexpected.

So says Joseph, the ancient, discarnate spirit communicator in this, the eighth book of his internationally-acclaimed series, as he draws back the heavy curtain of 'reality' to reveal aspects of the world and of our physical and spiritual lives that have remained unnoticed, unseen and unappreciated for countless aeons.

Within these pages you will meet the many wondrous expressions of spiritual life, both positive and negative, that co-habit and interact with us on Earth – hugely influential beings that at worst have been dismissed entirely and at best confined to the realms of folklore and myth as a result of our current fascination with all things material and the glamour of our express-train society.

You will also come face to face with and discover the nature of some of the deepest facets of yourself, allowing you to gain greater control over your life and to express and project the noblest aspects of 'you' into the world for your personal benefit, the benefit of all humanity and the good of the planet itself.

Prepare yourself for an enlightening, enthralling and sometimes shocking journey through the parallel realms that exist around and within you at this very moment, waiting to once again be recognised and understood.

...By the last page you will be in no doubt that the 'spaces between' – on Earth, in the heavens and deep within yourself – are, in fact, anything but.

£14.95 (ISBN: 978-1-906625-16-0)
Available from good bookshops, Amazon, and direct from:
www.thejosephcommunications.co.uk
e-Book also available for Kindle, iPad and other platforms.